FINDING THE
RIGHT
LAWYER

FINDING THE RIGHT LAWYER

by Jay G. Foonberg

SECTION OF LAW PRACTICE MANAGEMENT

Cover and interior design by Catherine Zaccarine.

List of Bar Association-Sponsored Lawyer Referral Services excerpted from the Directory of Lawyer Referral Services, © 1994 American Bar Association, with permission of The Standing Committee on Lawyer Referral and Information Service.

The views expressed in this book are solely those of the author and do not necessarily represent the views or policy of the American Bar Association or the Section of Law Practice Management.

Nothing contained in this book is to be considered as the rendering of legal advice for specific cases, and readers are responsible for obtaining such advice from their own legal counsel. This book and any forms and agreements herein are intended for educational and informational purposes only.

The Section of Law Practice Management, American Bar Association, offers an educational program for lawyers in practice. Books and other materials are published in furtherance of that program. Authors and editors of publications may express their own legal interpretations and opinions, which are not necessarily those of either the American Bar Association or the Section of Law Practice Management unless adopted pursuant to the bylaws of the Association.

Library of Congress Catalog Card Number 94-76852
ISBN 1-57073-011-3 (paperbound)
ISBN 1-57073-013-X (hardbound)

00 99 98 97 96   5 4 3 2 1

Discounts are available for books ordered in bulk. Special consideration is given to state bars, CLE programs, and other bar-related organizations. Inquire at Publications Planning & Marketing, American Bar Association, 750 North Lake Shore Drive, Chicago, Illinois 60611.

Contents

7 UNDERSTANDING HOW LAWYERS PRACTICE

9 THE ATTORNEY-CLIENT HIRING PROCESS

10 HOW BUSINESSES AND INSURANCE COMPANIES FIND THE RIGHT LAWYER

PART II: Foonberg's Glossary of Legal Specialties

Foreword

The American Bar Association is a voluntary association of more than 400,000 lawyers from every state and territory in the United States. Over the years the ABA has supported numerous initiatives to improve the quality of and access to legal services to all people. The organization itself is comprised of representatives of state bar associations and individuals who participate in a variety of committees and sections related to their areas of practice.

LPM Publishing is the publications arm of the Law Practice Management Section of the ABA. The Law Practice Management Section is dedicated to providing information to practicing lawyers and their staff to help them run their offices professionally and competently. The Section's publishing program has been on the forefront of these efforts.

Finding the Right Lawyer is a book for people who need or who might need lawyers. The author, Jay Foonberg, a founding member of the Law Practice Management Section, has been one of the most popular writers in the legal press, and his other books, *How to Start and Build a Law Practice* and *How to Get and Keep Good Clients,* have been best-sellers in the legal market for years. Mr. Foonberg has written this book for a new audience, the consumers of legal services.

Despite the fact that Americans spend over seventy billion dollars per year on legal services, and that at one time or another almost everyone needs to consult with a lawyer, the average person is surprisingly uninformed about how to find or select the right lawyer to help them when they need legal services. Although most people recognize that there are many different areas of legal practice, they do not understand how lawyers are licensed, or whether they are specialists like doctors, or how lawyers charge for their work.

This book answers the questions that people need to ask before they retain counsel. The purpose of this book is not to tell you how to represent yourself or to avoid using lawyers generally, although Mr. Foonberg acknowledges that not all problems require the assistance of a lawyer. But he states unabashedly that there are many times when legal assistance is necessary to protect and enforce many legal rights, and his constant theme is that you do not just want A lawyer, you want to find THE RIGHT LAWYER.

Gary A. Munneke
Professor, Pace Law School
Chair, LPM Publishing Board

Why This Book Has Been Written

I have written this book because there is a need for it.

The number of lawyers in the United States has skyrocketed. As a result, it's easy to find a lawyer. Finding a lawyer is not difficult. Finding the right lawyer has become extremely difficult. Even lawyers have difficulty finding the right lawyer when they wish to refer their clients to a specialist.

For many centuries, law firms were small, there were relatively few laws and every lawyer handled almost every type of case. Lawyers learned general principles of law in law school or in practice. They also learned the law in a given area when a client had a problem in a particular area of law. Specialty practice was rare or totally unknown.

As cities began to grow in size and law firms began to grow in size, a change began. In some law firms there was an "office lawyer" who did "office work" like wills and contracts and a "trial lawyer" who did trials. Still, most lawyers did some of both. So almost any lawyer would be the right lawyer for any type of legal needs.

In recent years, there has been an explosion of new laws passed by legislatures and of interpretations of these laws and rulings by judges and courts. Businesses and individuals are demanding and receiving huge amounts of legal rights at all levels through increased legislation. Everyday's mail brings new laws, new court decisions, new rights being created, and more government regulation at every level. Simultaneously, there has been an explosion in the number of new lawyers. Today's lawyers have a wide range of experience and of competence. The right lawyer can be of tremendous help, and the wrong lawyer can be of no help or can even be a liability.

Law firms and lawyers can no longer be all things to all clients. Lawyers have been forced to reorganize their individual practices and their firm practices to meet the needs of clients and potential clients.

For centuries, a firm of five to ten lawyers was considered large. Today a firm of less than twenty lawyers is considered small, and firms with hundreds of lawyers are common. The skills of an individual lawyer are obscured by the large variety of client needs and the large numbers of lawyers available in different areas. Lawyers and nonlawyers both qualified and unqualified claim to be able to meet clients' needs. To do the best job for clients in larger cases, lawyers must manage teams of lawyers and nonlawyers with various levels of skills in law and technology.

In the final analysis, a lawyer and client must first find each other and then be sure they are right for each other.

It is the purpose of this book to educate both lawyers and nonlawyers to the many areas of law now being practiced and the many types of lawyers and firms which practice in these areas.

This books brings you up-to-date information on how to find the right lawyer. This book also gives you some alternatives to finding a lawyer. This book represents more than thirty-five years of my helping people to find the right lawyer for their legal needs.

Jay G. Foonberg
Beverly Hills, California

Acknowledgments

This book in its present, accurate, and practical format would not have been possible without my copy editor Delmar L. Roberts of Blythewood, South Carolina.

Del's copy editing and guidance and organizing made this book possible. A writer can write a good book, but it takes a superior copy editor to make a good book excellent.

Writing a book is hard work. Writing an easy-to-use book is even harder. Writing an excellent book that is both easy to use and practical takes everything a writer has. Compiling thirty-five years of experience into this book has taken several years of writing and organizing, rewriting and reorganizing, and re-rewriting and rereorganizing.

Del has guided me through five prior books and revisions and innumerable articles. This book was the most difficult to organize because of its many suggestions. If you like the style, format, and usability, give Del the credit. If you don't like them, blame me.

Thank you, Del.

Jay G. Foonberg
Beverly Hills, California

About the Author

Jay Foonberg is an attorney and a CPA. His client list includes government, corporations, and individuals.

He is internationally known and respected for his teachings in ethics, client relations, and helping American individuals and corporations access the legal system by finding the right lawyer. He has received presidential and papal audiences.

Mr. Foonberg accumulated the information for this book over a period of eight years, interviewing lawyers and clients throughout the world and gathering available information from publications and studies of the gap between what lawyers think clients need and want and what clients really need and want.

He has been honored many times by local, state, national, and international bar associations, and has served on many boards and commissions to help people access the legal system.

A graduate of UCLA and UCLA Law School, he has studied at Harvard Law and at Cambridge University and was the recipient of three very prestigious awards for his accomplishments: (1) The Harrison Tweed Award, for lifetime excellence and achievements in post-law school legal education; (2) The Louis Goldberg Award, for lifetime achievements as the most outstanding attorney–CPA in the United States; (3) The Order of the Southern Cross, the highest award the Government of Brazil can bestow upon a foreigner.

A founder of the American Bar Association Law Practice Management Section, the National Academy of Law Ethics and Management, and the American Association of Attorney–CPAs, Mr. Foonberg is an innovator and a problem solver.

His office is in Los Angeles, California, and he lives with his wife, Lois, in Beverly Hills, California. He credits his writing skills and proliferation to the energies that radiate from the walls of the house, once occupied by film stars Herbert Marshall, Betty Grable, Harry James, and Edgar Rice Burroughs (creator of the Tarzan series).

**OTHER BOOKS BY JAY FOONBERG
AVAILABLE FROM THE AMERICAN BAR ASSOCIATON**

How to Get and Keep Good Clients, 2nd Ed.
How to Start and Build a Law Practice, 3rd Ed.

Introduction

Most people and institutions are unaware of the resources that exist to help them find the right lawyer. Clients don't know where to seek information. People ask for a recommendation, but can't tell whether they are being referred to the right lawyer. Some of them end up with the wrong lawyer for their matter as the result of a well-meaning, but erroneous, recommendation. They sometimes end up with a lawyer who is barely adequate when more qualified lawyers are available.

In the United States, just about every organization, governmental entity, and individual at some time has the problem of needing to find legal help and not knowing where to go. Even the most sophisticated individuals and corporations have this problem. Lawyers themselves often have difficulty finding the right lawyer for the special needs of their clients.

This book is not intended to attack or defend lawyers. Lawyers are a vital part of the system of rights and responsibilities that all Americans enjoy. Lawyers don't create the need for legal services. A need for legal services comes into being after individuals do or don't do something which affects their legal relationship with others. Those who do not seek legal help when they should face the same risks and benefits as those who don't seek medical help when they should. Ignoring legal problems can have the same consequences as ignoring medical problems. One can be lucky or the results can be disastrous.

The definition of legal needs in this book is intended to be broad. Some legal needs can be fulfilled without the services of a lawyer. Some legal needs can be fulfilled by simply getting general legal information from a lawyer. Some legal needs require specific advice from a lawyer and some legal needs require legal action by a lawyer. Legal needs can include solving a problem, avoiding a problem, bringing a claim, defending a claim, starting a dispute, or ending a dispute. The needs can be for future needs, such as tax or estate planning, or immediate needs, such as getting someone out of jail or a deathbed will or protecting a company from a jeopardy tax assessment and closure of the company. The needs for a criminal lawyer can be individual, such as defending an individual charged with a crime of violence, or corporate, such as defending a company in the areas of antitrust, pollution of the environment, or racketeering.

A company or individual may feel it has a right to bring a claim or a need to defend a claim. When the value of a stock crashes in the marketplace, investors consider bringing suits against the broker, lawyers, accountants, and company officials. These professionals, in turn, think about the possibility of being sued.

When debts don't get paid, creditors think about using a lawyer to secure payment, and debtors—whether corporate, municipal, or individual—start thinking about the protection of the bankruptcy court.

When individuals and businesses envision a bright future together, they need help with marital agreements and partnership agreements, incorporations, and with defining their legal relationships to try to avoid inconsistent expectations. When things go sour or don't reach expectations, they need help with ending the relationship by divorce or dissolution of the business entity.

In some instances, a private practice lawyer is not needed because there are governmental or other agencies which can do the job more cheaply or more effectively than the private practice lawyer. Police agencies, social welfare agencies, private legal foundations, or groups with a special interest—such as the National Organization for Women (NOW), the American Civil Liberties Union (ACLU), the Mexican American Legal Defense and Education Fund (MALDEF), and the Sierra Foundation— may save you the expense of hiring a lawyer when their interests and your interests are similar. Small claims and mediation services, where available, are often a suitable alternative to finding and using a lawyer.

Too often, people with a need for legal help are left to their own devices to search for the right lawyer. Forced to make their own way through a multitude of lawyers, nonlawyers, and well-meaning friends, clients find themselves physically and emotionally exhausted by the search for the right lawyer. This is the result of the disjointed, inconsistent, illogical system of legal care existing throughout the United States.

Some groups are at a special disadvantage. The elderly, and people and institutions with unusual problems, are particularly vulnerable to the inability to get the right legal assistance.

The client often goes to a recommended lawyer with a lot of faith because of the source of the recommendation. That doesn't mean they're getting the right lawyer for the problem or the best lawyer for the problem. The panic to find a lawyer often leads them to the wrong lawyer in spite of the best intentions of all involved.

Finding the right lawyer or the best lawyer for the problem may be only half the battle. The other half of the battle can be the ability to pay for the best lawyer or firm. If your case is simple enough, there are many lawyers available who can do a satisfactory, acceptable, or even excellent job for a much lower cost than the "best," or most prestigious, lawyer could. A prestigious lawyer may be saddled with office and marketing costs incidental to having the image of being "best."

This book will tell you everything you need to know to find the right lawyer for your particular legal needs.

PART

Finding a
Lawyer

CHAPTER 1

Finding the Right Lawyer by Getting Recommendations

WHETHER A COMPANY, institution, or individual uses thousands of lawyers every year or just one lawyer in a lifetime, they all prefer to use lawyers recommended to them by people or institutions in which they have trust and confidence. Getting recommendations from trusted sources will cut down on wasted time in finding the right lawyer or firm for the matter. Getting recommendations is what securities and corporate lawyers call "due diligence." By seeking recommendations before selecting a lawyer or firm, an individual can reduce his or her own exposure if things don't turn out well. Getting recommendations will make seekers of a lawyer feel that they are not making a mistake when they interview or select a lawyer or firm. The old saying "If they're good enough for the Joneses, they're probably good enough for us" is very appropriate in selecting any professional.

Recommendations are easy to get if you know where to look and whom to ask and if you have some time and patience to look. Recommendations can be oral, by asking someone you know, or can be written, based on memberships in bar organizations or based on listings in directories such as the Martindale-Hubbell Law Directory. Unfortunately, to get the best recommendations for a lawyer, a small amount of effort may be necessary on the part of the person who needs a lawyer.

CONSIDER WHAT QUESTIONS TO ASK
BEFORE SEEKING RECOMMENDATIONS

It will be very helpful in conserving your time and money and ultimately in ending up with the right lawyer, if you at least know what to consider before asking for recommendations. Consider the following questions:

1. What kind of law is involved? This book will help you define your needs from among nearly 1,000 possible descriptions. (See the glossary in Chapter 12 of this book.)

2. Where, in or out of the United States, are you likely to need help?

3. What type or level of legal help do you think you want or need? The next chapter will help you decide. Do you want general information? Do you need specific advice about your factual situation? Do you want the lawyer or firm to do anything for you, such as draft a document, negotiate a transaction, or handle a court matter? Do you know what type of lawyer or firm will make you happy? Do you want a monster firm (mega-firm) with tremendous worldwide resources? Do you want a smaller or mid-size firm where you will receive personal attention and not be lost in the shuffle of lawyers and departments going into and out of the firm? Do you want a very small firm or solo practitioner where you or your legal matter will be the most important client or case in the office and, as such, get immediate and constant attention?

4. How much time do you have to find the right lawyer? Is there an immediate urgent problem, or are you anticipating possible future needs?

5. Do you have some specific, preconceived concepts you want addressed? For example, you may think you need a "connected" lawyer, a lawyer with a particular ethnic background

or language ability, or of a specific gender, or a lawyer with practical skills in certain industries or types of legal matters (a "specialist").

Common categories of recommenders are listed in the next section of this chapter. This list is not intended to be all inclusive, but rather to stimulate you to contact as many sources as you wish to.

You should be aware of a legal doctrine called "privilege" when you ask others for recommendations. You must be careful about how much you tell other people about the facts of your situation. These people can be located at a later time and questioned as to exactly what you said to them. What you said can sometimes be brought out in court as evidence. In general, lawyers cannot be questioned concerning your conversations relative to seeking legal advice (attorney-client privilege). Likewise, doctors cannot be questioned concerning your conversations relative to medical advice under doctor-patient privilege, and clergy cannot be questioned as to conversations relative to spiritual advice under clergy-penitent privilege. Beyond these three categories, you are at great risk when you tell others about the facts of your case while seeking recommendations.

The law in the area of privilege varies greatly from state to state. For example, in some states, accountants have a limited privilege in limited situations. In other states, they have absolutely no privilege unless they are working under the control of a lawyer. In some states, certain family members, such as legally married spouses, cannot be compelled to testify in certain kinds of matters, but cohabitees, children, parents, and other family members can be compelled to testify. In some states, what you tell a psychiatrist is privileged, while what you tell a psychologist is not privileged because the psychologist is not an M.D. In at least one situation, the tape-recorded conversations between a psychologist and a client were admitted into evidence in a murder case against the patient. When you seek recommendations, your best course of action is to go to a lawyer first. When you go to others, try not to tell them about the facts of the situation until you know what you did right and what you did wrong. It is better to be closemouthed and appear unfriendly than to blab about your case and end up losing it because you said the wrong thing to the wrong person. As my good friend Ken Vercammen of New Jersey says, "Even a fish wouldn't get caught if he kept his mouth shut."

CONSIDER WHO CAN RECOMMEND A LAWYER

Who can recommend a good lawyer? Consider asking the following people:

1. Lawyer friends. Always ask one you know, even if he or she doesn't practice the type of law you think you need.
2. Lawyers you don't know but who were suggested by others listed below.
3. Published listings, in particular the Martindale-Hubbell Law Directory. This is the only directory I know of that attempts to list and carry ratings for every lawyer in America. (See "Finding the Right Lawyer by Using the Martindale-Hubbell Law Directory" in Chapter 4 of this book.)
4. Lawyer referral services of local bar associations. (See the Appendix in this book for a list of bar association-sponsored lawyer referral services.)
5. Legal secretaries, paralegals, and others who work in law offices.
6. Friends.
7. Relatives.
8. Fellow employees.
9. Bankers.
10. Accountants and CPAs.
11. Trade associations.
12. Other businesses in your industry or profession.
13. Clergy.
14. Unions.
15. Bar associations and committees.

16. Yellow Pages of the telephone directory.
17. Direct-mail solicitations (you might receive these after accidents, police accusations, bankruptcy filing, foreclosure notices, etc.).
18. Government agencies and employees (where they are permitted to recommend).
19. Judges.
20. Law professors in the area of law indicated
21. Financial planners.
22. Real estate agents and brokers.
23. Health care professionals.
24. Trainers and coaches in the area of activity involved.
25. Consultants in the business or the area of activity involved.
26. Other consultants listed in various places throughout this book.

Your call will always be given a high priority when you can tell the receptionist, secretary, or lawyer that you were "recommended" or "referred" by someone. The lawyer will always take your call, if possible, to avoid offending the person who recommended you.

I personally give an extremely high priority to people who were referred because this gives me an opportunity to make two people happy, the potential client and the referrer. I have often earned six figures on cases referred to me by people who read one of my books or heard one of my lectures.

The moral of this chapter: "Always get a recommendation whenever possible."

CHAPTER

Deciding What Type or Level of Service Is Needed or Wanted

AFTER IDENTIFYING the area(s) of law involved and before calling a lawyer, the person seeking a lawyer should decide the levels of legal service they think they want or need. For purposes of this book, I have arbitrarily created levels and nomenclature. Other lawyers may have independently created similar classifications.

CONSULTATION ONLY

In a consultation, a person seeks information or advice but does not usually want the lawyer to do anything further.

Information

Asking a lawyer or firm for information is simply asking for general information on a subject without application to your specific facts. For example, a company or person might have heard about a new law and want a copy of it. The company or person may simply be curious or interested in what the general law is on a specific subject. There may be a general question on forms of ownership of a piece of land, or what a living will is, or what the setback requirements are in a certain city. Many of the most common consumer-oriented questions are answered in pamphlets distributed free by bar associations.

Lawyers are often hesitant to provide general information for fear that the person asking won't understand the information given and will erroneously act upon the information given. The lawyer or firm may also be concerned that the person seeking the information may later claim that they came in asking for advice (see next paragraph), and that the lawyer did not do an adequate job of fact getting before giving what the client thought was "advice" rather than information.

Advice

Asking a lawyer for advice is asking the lawyer to recommend a course of action based on specific facts and the applicable law. Based on the lawyer's advice, a client will or won't do something to protect his or her legal rights. If the lawyer is wrong in the advice, there may or may not be a responsibility for malpractice. When you consult a lawyer, you must be clear on whether you want information or advice. Information is general law not applied to your specific facts. Advice is specific law as applied to your specific facts.

ACTION

A person wanting action wants the lawyer to do something ranging from writing a letter or drafting a document to litigating a case.

Advocacy

Advocacy is the next level after advice. The client has been given both general information on a legal subject and specific advice to do or not to do something under the applicable law based on the facts. At the advocacy level, the client wants the lawyer to DO SOMETHING. Either the client wants the lawyer to get the client something the client feels he or she is entitled to, or the client wants the lawyer to do something to help the client keep something which the client feels should not be given up. There will be contact with third parties which may begin with a letter or telephone call. If these efforts at advocacy do not produce the desired result, you may decide you want negotiation or litigation services as well.

Negotiation

A skilled, experienced lawyer will negotiate with the opposing side with a view toward reaching an agreement that maximizes benefits to you. If you have a dispute, a good lawyer will normally try to discuss a reasonable, mutually advantageous negotiated settlement as an alternative to wasting money unnecessarily on litigation expenses. Negotiation, even if unsuccessful, can take place anytime before, during, or after litigation.

Willingness to reasonably negotiate is not a sign of weakness. When a lawyer tries to tell a client that negotiation is a sign of weakness and that bitter "Rambo" litigation is the best way to go, the client should be careful, and possibly seek a second opinion. Some law firms advocate early settlement when on a contingency fee arrangement, but when on an hourly fee arrangement want to do a lot of work before discussing settlement.

There are situations where a client's best interests are served by not being willing to negotiate, but such situations are extremely rare. There are also rare instances where the law firm has lawyers with not enough to do, and is trying to generate fees through unnecessary, overly aggressive litigation. Some trial lawyers see everything as black or white, win or lose. They are unable to understand that the parties' best interests dictate a reasonable settlement where possible, saving the money that would otherwise be used for legal fees, thereby furthering the economic interests of the client rather than the lawyer.

Fortunately, the number of lawyers without negotiation skills or awareness are relatively few. The number of law firms which would deliberately act in their own best economic interests to the detriment of the client's best interest is even fewer, but such firms do exist. Be wary of lawyers who refuse to make even one attempt to negotiate.

Litigation

Litigation is an aggressive form of advocacy. In some rare instances, litigation as a first step is in the best interests of the client. In most instances, litigation should follow only if efforts at negotiating a settlement have broken down. Litigation is interpreted by many clients, especially foreigners, as a sign of bad faith.

Another reason to try to stay out of court is the cost. There is no limit on how much of a client's money a law firm can spend in litigation. It is not unusual for lawyers to suddenly begin recording 13 hours per day and 7-day workweeks in their time records. Innumerable conferences between associates suddenly occur. No matter how much experience the firm claims to have in handling the type of lawsuit involved, there are suddenly tremendous bills for lower-level associates doing research on and off the computer. When the client asks for a copy of the research done, there are suddenly no copies available. Whole warehouses of records are photocopied and reviewed by paralegals because there "might" be something hidden away which the other side doesn't know about. Multiple tons of paper are devoted just to taking, transcribing, and reviewing depositions of people who "possibly" can add to what is already known.

Litigation can be insanely expensive, and no client should ever willingly begin any litigation without having a clear view (or as clear a view as possible) of what the litigation is supposed to accomplish and what it is supposed to cost. There is no point to spending large sums of money to begin litigation and then abandoning it later because you can't afford to continue.

Mediation and Arbitration (Alternative Dispute Resolution)

In my opinion arbitration and mediation can and will replace litigation to resolve most civil (noncriminal) disputes. I have been an arbitrator. I have been a mediator. I have represented clients in both arbitration and mediation for more than a quarter century and I highly recommend consideration of both or either when possible.

Mediation and arbitration are called alternative dispute resolution or ADR because they are alternatives to traditional civil litigation with traditional juries, technical rules of evidence, delays because of the priorities of criminal calendars, and so forth.

In arbitration, a third party acts like a judge, listens to the parties and their witnesses, and makes a decision. In mediation, a third party uses skills and training and experience to get both sides to realistically understand their position and the other persons' position and then to come to their own agreement that they both can live with because it's their agreement. Believe it or not, mediation is successful in 80 percent of all matters. You can have mediation and arbitration without a lawyer. It is not necessary that the mediator or arbitrator be a lawyer. I recommend, however, using a lawyer as the mediator or arbitrator and being represented by a lawyer before the mediator or arbitrator because in the final analysis the result will be affected by what is likely to happen in a court and only a lawyer knows your legal position to give you good advice. Mediation and arbitration is cheaper and faster than litigation, and if it doesn't work, you won't have lost much by trying.

Before authorizing litigation, ask about the possibility of arbitration and mediation.

CRIMINAL DEFENSE

A person accused of a crime needs the legal services of a criminal lawyer. No one but a hardened recidivist (repeat offender) would willingly go to jail as an alternative to defending oneself in a criminal prosecution. Neither corporate executives charged with "white collar" crimes nor those charged with crimes of violence would knowingly trade or give up their freedom to save legal fees.

Unfortunately, even the best legal defense may simply delay the inevitable prison sentence and the result is the same regardless of the amount of legal fees paid. If prosecutors think a client is willing or able to spend unlimited sums in a criminal defense, they may on rare occasions cut a very favorable deal to avoid tying up courts for months with the resultant neglect of many other cases. In most cases, however, the defense could not possibly put up enough resources to influence the state or federal government into making a deal just to avoid tying up a court.

I've seen instances of corporations and people bankrupting themselves and their families spending all their own money and a lot of borrowed money to try to escape the inevitable in a criminal prosecution. I've also seen some defendants who knew they were probably going to be prosecuted and convicted and do jail time, who refused to spend their life savings in an unsuccessful defense. How much of your money to spend in a criminal defense is a very personal and unpleasant decision to make, and you should decide only after consulting with family members and a competent, experienced criminal lawyer with experience before the court and judge involved. Sometimes a public defender with experience before the particular court and judge can get the same result as the most expensive big-name lawyer.

Public defenders are appointed when a person can't afford a lawyer. These lawyers are usually experienced and competent. Unfortunately, their heavy work load often prevents them from offering the personalized attention one would expect from a lawyer in private practice.

Often when a person is arrested or charged with a serious crime there is a sense of crisis or urgency or panic about getting the accused a lawyer and getting the accused out on bail. This sense of panic might result in a hurried choice of the wrong lawyer. Being a prisoner in a jail can be a terrifying experience, but often bail bondsmen can get the accused out of jail and the search for the right lawyer can be made with less panic.

In finding a private practice criminal defense lawyer, one should search long and hard and interview several possible lawyers. The price of not finding the right lawyer can be disastrous.

SET YOUR GOALS AND EXPECTATIONS BEFORE AND AFTER CONSULTING A LAWYER

Consider your possible goals and expectations before you consult with a lawyer and then reconsider them after you have consulted with a lawyer. At your first interview concerning the case, and before you ask for a fee quotation, ask the lawyer if your goals and expectations are reasonable and can be met within a fee you can afford and your circumstances.

Everybody wants to "win" his or her case or "satisfactorily" resolve the situation. Unfortunately, the definition of "win" or "satisfactorily" in your mind and in that of the lawyer may be completely different. For example, the lawyer might have thought he or she was providing what you wanted when A, B, and C results were provided, when, in reality, you wanted X, Y, and Z results. It is normal to have more than one possible goal or expectation on a legal matter, and it is possible to have different expectations on similar matters. Typical possible goals and expectations are as follows:

1. To recover as much money as possible.
2. To pay the other side as little as possible.
3. To get the case over with as rapidly as possible, regardless of the cost.
4. To drag the case out as long as possible.
5. To make the other side suffer financially.
6. To make the other side suffer in some other manner.
7. To go back as much as possible to the way things were before the problem. (Status Quo Ante)
8. To go on to a new life as different as possible from the way things were before the problem.
9. To be able to tell your story in a court or other forum for the whole world to know and for history to record.
10. To avoid going to court or giving any sort of testimony, because you are afraid of court or you fear that information will become public.
11. To spend as little as possible on legal fees.

12. To make the other side spend as much as possible on legal fees.
13. To spend whatever has to be spent on legal fees because the matter is so important to you.
14. To consider legal fees in the same category as amounts paid to the other side, so you are interested only in not spending money, regardless of whether it would have gone to the other side or to your lawyers.
15. To drag the other side through as much aggravation as possible.
16. To force the other side to spend large amounts of time and money in the litigation, regardless of the cost to you.
17. To receive public vindication.
18. To expose in court your side of the story.
19. To bring other people who are connected with the other side into the litigation or the problems.
20. To protect other people who are important to you from involvement in the problem.

I've had clients who didn't care what it costs (within their ability to pay) to avoid paying what they perceived as "blackmail." Other clients care less about paying "blackmail" if it is the cheapest way out.

CHAPTER 3

Alternatives to Finding and Using a Lawyer

SHOULD YOU REPRESENT YOURSELF OR DO YOU NEED A LAWYER?

Can you represent yourself without a lawyer? In some cases, individuals (but not companies) can practice law for themselves without a lawyer. The law in most states allows private persons to represent themselves in legal matters. This is known as "in propria persona." The right to represent oneself usually does not include the right to represents others. For this reason, a corporation normally must have a lawyer represent it in court. Some judges and some courts, however, allow corporations to be represented by corporate officers who are not lawyers.

In most cases it would be foolish—and in some cases stupid or dangerous—to represent yourself in a major legal problem. Chances are, you don't know how to value your claim or your liability. The opposing side may be represented by someone who has handled thousands of cases. Your case may be your only experience. Do you really think the other side is going to pay you the maximum amount of money you are entitled to, or do

17

you think they will pay you as little as possible, trying to convince you not to see the right lawyer, for fear you'll find out the true value of your case? In a family law matter, you don't know what reasonable alimony or visitation rights would be. Your case may have criminal implications that you don't see. You don't know what your chances of winning or losing your antitrust or criminal or traffic case would be. And if you have a losing case, you don't know what a reasonable dollar loss or fine or jail term would be.

You don't know what facts are important and what facts are unimportant to a judge or jury. You don't know what facts are damaging and as such, should not be volunteered or revealed until required to do so. In an attempt to be candid, open, and honest, you may give away your entire case.

If your case goes to some form of trial or hearing, you may be greatly prejudiced by not knowing the rules of court and the rules of evidence. These rules were developed to smooth the flow of cases through the legal system. They were designed to benefit the largest number of people and to ensure that each side gets to tell its story within certain limits.

The judge may be courteous and even helpful to you for a short time. If you have no lawyer, perhaps your matter should have taken only one day to be fully and fairly presented. By the time it gets into the second or third day, and the judge has a backlog of cases and is running behind (causing other people to hang around the courtroom waiting for you to finish your bumbling), you can expect the judge's friendliness and helpfulness to turn into frustration and anger with you and your case. Your independence will be causing innocent people to waste time and money.

If the judge is impatient and angry with you for taking too long, you may find yourself precluded from having enough time to present all your witnesses. You may not have enough time to give your own testimony. It makes as much sense to go into court without the right lawyer as it does to go into an operating room without a doctor.

Sometimes, you can get lucky and handle a major problem by yourself without help, and have everything turn out all right, but what you stand to save in legal fees is very small compared to what your lack of knowledge and experience can cost you in results. You can avoid going to the doctor and get lucky when the medical problem passes, or you can get unlucky and die from lack of medical care. You can guess right and get the proper medicine at the drugstore, or guess wrong and poison yourself.

Some people want to be their own doctor, lawyer, dentist, pharmacist, electrician, or plumber, and end up spending a lot more paying someone to clean up the mess they made. You are foolish if you think you can go to a law library and learn all you need to know in a few hours. A lawyer goes to law school for three years just to be able to begin to analyze your problem. Further research is often necessary, even with three years of training and years of experience. In most cases, trying to save money by not having the right lawyer to help you in an important matter is a major mistake.

There are times when you can effectively function without a lawyer in minor matters. Small-claims court is an excellent example. The important principle is that you can do without legal advice and help only when the other side does not have legal advice or help. Some forms of arbitration and mediation exist to settle disputes without lawyers, but typically the matter involved in not significant in monetary terms or principles.

USING A SMALL-CLAIMS COURT AS AN ALTERNATIVE TO FINDING AND USING A LAWYER

Small-claims courts normally function without lawyers, except where a lawyer is one of the parties and is doing the suing or is being sued. You must be your own lawyer to present your case and/or to defend yourself. You can and should consult with a lawyer before deciding whether to use a small-claims court. The lawyer can advise you what papers you need, what you must prove, and what questions to ask. Sometimes a case is bigger than a small-claims case, but you can't recognize the value or size of the matter and possible alternatives to chose from. I have often advised people and companies on what to say and do in small-claims court. Just because the lawyer can't go into the courtroom does not prevent a lawyer from advising you and preparing you.

Small-claims courts are normally the lowest level of civil court. They are sometimes a division of the city or municipal courts, using the judges and facilities and administration of these courts. Sometimes they are totally independent courts with their own judges, courtrooms, facilities, and administrative systems. Normally the small-claims courts do not involve lawyers or juries or strict rules of evidence. You are likely to get "gut justice" decisions rather than strictly legalistic decisions. The judges are often volunteer lawyers.

The maximum amount of money for which a person can be sued is typically between $500 and $5,000. If you think you are entitled to more than the limits of the court you can still use the small-claims court, but you would have to give up your right to any amount above the court's limits. In legal jargon, this is called "waiving amounts in excess of the jurisdiction of the court." The side which is sued can usually ask the court to award damages to it. Such a request is called a "cross-complaint."

Preparing for Trial

You might have to wait one to five years to get your case heard in other courts, but in small-claims court, you typically are in trial in 90 to 120 days. There normally are no depositions or written interrogatories or other forms of what lawyers call "discovery." Normally you can subpoena witnesses and get evidence from third parties and from the other side for presentation at the trial.

Small-Claims Process, Procedures, and Terminology

If you decide to go to small-claims court you may not have a lawyer represent you in court. I will describe a typical small-claims courtroom and case so that you will know what to expect.

The person or company seeking money is usually called the *plaintiff* and is sometimes called the *complainant* because they are complaining. The person or company sued is usually called the *defendant* because they must defend themselves. Plaintiffs or defendants can be an individual or a company, but sometimes special documents will be required when the plaintiff or the defendant is a corporation, a partnership, or other legal entity.

A small-claims court can normally award a money judgment up to the maximum jurisdictional limit of the small-claims court, typically up to $5,000. A small-claims court normally can't or won't order anyone to do or refrain from doing something. (In technical terms, it can't or won't give an injunction or equitable relief.) Thus, if a painter didn't paint your house after you paid in advance, the court can award you money damages for what you have to pay another painter to finish the job, but the court can't or won't order the first painter to paint the house.

The person seeking money (the plaintiff or complainant) must go to the courthouse where the proper small-claims court is located. Normally the trial must take place in the small-claims court serving the area where the defendant (person being sued) lives or does business or where the events of the case happened. The plaintiff fills out a court form briefly describing what the case is about and how much money the plaintiff is seeking. Filing this usually requires the plaintiff to pay a nominal fee (a few dollars).

After paying the fee (called a filing fee) and filing the form, the plaintiff must take a copy of the form with the court stamp on it to an officer (who might be called a sheriff or marshal or bailiff) located in the same building. The plaintiff gives the form to the officer for service. The plaintiff must pay the officer a fee (called a service fee) and provide directions on where to find and serve the defendant or defendants. The amount of the service fee is typically based on mileage from the courthouse to where the papers will be served on the defendant(s). The serving officer serves the papers (technically called "making service") and files a document with the court called a return-of-service. Without service of the papers the case cannot go on.

The case is normally given a trial date and time at the time of filing. Sometimes there is a later notification of trial date and time.

When you arrive at the courthouse for the trial, you have to find out in which courtroom the case will be heard. This depends on which courtroom happens to be available on that day and time. To learn what courtroom to go to, you may have to read a notice or ask at an information window. Sometimes everyone goes to a courtroom called master calendar from which they are sent out to an available courtroom. Sometimes the plaintiff must carry the court file to the courtroom, and sometimes the court system will get the court file to the courtroom.

When you get to the courtroom usually you will see the following physical layout. There will be rows of seats at the rear for spectators and those waiting their turn. There will be a bar or counter with a swinging door at the front of the spectator seats. On the other side of the swinging door will be the judge's seat (called the bench), which typically is elevated. There will be two tables closer to the spectator section—one for the plaintiff, and the other for the defendant. Two or three chairs are at each table. Normally the plaintiff sits at the right table and the defendant at the left table, although some courts reverse the two and some courts don't care. Look for a sign on the table indicating whether plaintiff sits at the left or right. If there is no sign, ask the clerk or uniformed officer which table to sit at. Some judges get angry if you sit at the wrong table because they keep track of the plaintiff and defendant by where they sit. There may or may not be a lectern or podium or stand in the center of the two tables. If there is a lectern, ask the clerk or officer if you are supposed to speak from the table or from the lectern.

There will be a uniformed officer with a gun in the courtroom. This officer may be called a marshal, sheriff, bailiff, or by another title. This person's job is to be sure everybody stays peaceful and to protect the judge from violence. This officer will not be friendly if you are hostile or appear to be a threat to anyone.

There will be a civilian who will be the court clerk for that courtroom. The clerk normally has a desk in the front of the courtroom below the judge's bench. It is possible, but not likely, that there will be a court reporter present with a machine to make a stenographic record. More often in small-claims court the judge or the clerk normally handwrites the various orders, rulings, decisions, procedures, and so on, rather than depending on a formal transcript. If you are polite and respectful, the clerk and officer can help you with the etiquette of the particular courtroom. If you are rude or demanding they will make things difficult for you.

There will normally be a chair in a box-like structure to the judge's left (your right). This is a witness chair and is not normally used in small-claims procedures unless the witness is someone other than one of the parties suing or being sued. The parties normally talk from their table or from the lectern in the center if there is one.

There may be a box-like structure with 10 to 14 chairs on the left or right side. This is for jurors during jury trials. It is not a good idea for you to sit in those chairs or to go into the box. The role of the jury in our legal system is exalted, and anything relating to the jury will be vigorously protected.

The area between the counsel table and the judge is normally vacant except for the clerk's desk. This area is called the "well" or the "pit." Stay out of this area when the judge is on the bench unless you ask for and receive permission to enter the area, or to approach the bench or to approach a witness. You could find yourself looking at the sheriff's gun pointed at you if you don't get permission to enter the area.

At some point, the clerk will ask you to raise your right hand and swear to tell the truth. This may be done individually or in a group swearing of all people who are going to give testimony.

After you have taken the oath, you are sworn to tell the truth or face the theoretical penalty of going to jail for perjury if you lie.

The trial itself is usually informal. The judge says to the plaintiff, "Present your case" or words to that effect. The judge then allows the defendant to ask questions of the plaintiff and the plaintiff's witnesses, and then the defendant is free to present witnesses and evidence if he or she wants to. The plaintiff can then ask questions of the defendant and the defendant's witnesses. The judge may or may not ask additional questions during or after the two sides put on their case. The judge will then decide. Normally, if the plaintiff loses, that is the end of the case forever. If the plaintiff wins, the defendant is free to appeal the case and get an entirely new trial in another lower court, with judges, juries, and lawyers.

If you win, as the plaintiff or as the cross-complainant, the judge will "enter judgment" for the amount you are entitled to. Typically, this means the judge will give the defendant a certain number of days to pay voluntarily before entering a formal judgment, which might affect the defendant's credit rating.

If there is no appeal and the defendant does not voluntarily pay, you have to collect the judgment. Collection of this judgment may involve liens against bank accounts, examinations of the debtor, taking possession of assets and selling them, liens on real property, and other remedies that are beyond the scope of this book.

Getting Information about Small-Claims Courts

If you want a fast, inexpensive, trial, you should find out about using small-claims court. Getting more information isn't difficult. Almost every major bar association has some sort of free pamphlet or instruction sheet on how to use small-claims courts. Sometimes the courthouse where the small-claims court is located also will have pamphlets or instruction sheets available for you.

Although the scenario described above may vary from place to place, in general this is an accurate description of what happens in small-claims courts. I must caution you not to rely on this chapter without finding out about the local system and asking a lawyer for advice on using this approach for your particular needs. Although I suggest small-claims court as an alternative to using a lawyer, it is also a good idea to consult with a lawyer as to the pros and cons of using small-claims courts as an alternative to using a lawyer. You may inadvertently be starting something bigger than you expected. You might think you are entitled to money when in fact you owe money. Using a small-claims court is often an excellent alternative to using a lawyer to sue, but it is not a smart alternative to getting legal advice before starting the case.

DO YOU NEED A LAWYER TO FILL OUT LEGAL OR OFFICIAL "FORMS"?

Does a person need a lawyer to fill out legal "official" forms? In some states, the state bar or local bar association or legislature prints and even sells some forms such as "simple" wills and trust wills. Often court forms and other forms are designed with check mark blocks to make it easier for a determined person to "Do it yourself." Many forms are printed by printers to comply with legal requirements. You can find these in many bookstores and stationery stores.

After years of practice as a CPA and as a lawyer, I have concluded that the average person could fill out these forms by themselves in simple cases and save the professional fee. In most cases, though, "do-it-yourself" is a false economy because of the risks involved. If nothing else, using a professional will give you the peace of mind that the job was done right.

Furthermore, lawyers have to stand behind their work if a mistake is made by them. Sellers of books and forms and computer disks often have no legal responsibility to compensate you if their forms don't work. The forms are sometimes incomplete or designed for another state. More than one-half of all lawyers have malpractice insurance to protect their clients if they make a mistake. In many states, there are client protection funds to help the client when a lawyer makes a mistake. Bar associations and licensing authorities can sometimes put pressure on a lawyer to pay the client for the damages the lawyer causes through negligence. A client loses all these safeguards and protections when he or she doesn't go to a lawyer.

CAN YOU DO IT YOURSELF BY USING PREPRINTED FORMS AND BOOKS AND COMPUTER DISKS?

Do-it-yourself books and computer disks sell you what the author knows, not necessarily what you need. Determining exactly what you need can almost always be done more effectively by a lawyer than by yourself. You might get lucky in some minor matter which is not seriously contested, but you can make some horrible mistakes when you use the wrong forms because you bought the wrong do-it-yourself handbook or disk. Using forms and form books is like prescribing medicine for yourself. You can imagine the consequences of a mistake.

Many do-it-yourself books have forms in them or on disk. There are also do-it-yourself forms and packages of forms available at some bookstores and at office supply and stationery stores and computer software stores.

In some situations, the forms are good in one state and not in another state. In other cases, simply filling out the forms correctly is not enough. After the forms are filled out they must be processed by some government agency, such as a recorder or clerk or court. Improperly processing a properly filled out form may not help you. Properly processing an improperly prepared form may not help either.

CAN A NONLAWYER DO LEGAL WORK FOR YOU?

There are large areas of law which nonlawyers (anyone who isn't licensed to practice law) try to practice. In some few cases, they can serve as an excellent low-cost alternative to expensive legal services. In other cases they do incompetent jobs at high prices because they may know a little law, but they don't know enough law. They solve one problem and create ten other problems. In such cases, the "client" would have been much better off going to a lawyer.

Unfortunately, (or fortunately, depending on your point of view), lawyers and their firms, although professionals, must have a businesslike approach to economics if they are going to continue to exist. A lawyer or firm that does not continue to exist cannot help anyone. Almost every lawyer I know, and almost every law firm I am familiar with, does some "free legal work" for people and institutions without the ability to pay the fees required by the case. Lawyers and their firms can only accept so much low-pay and no-pay work or they, as indicated, will cease to exist.

In some cases nonlawyers fill a void by serving people whose needs might otherwise be unmet. I have seen examples of nonlawyers preparing living wills and durable powers of appointment for as little as $25, including a visit to the client at home, the hospital, or the retirement home. Some of these nonlawyers do low-priced divorce, bankruptcy, and eviction work for people who otherwise would go without needed legal services. Very few law offices could afford to open a file, do an interview, run a conflicts search, and enter the file into the computer system for what the nonlawyer charges to do the entire job.

Some of these nonlawyers operate in the guise of selling legal forms, or of being some sort of legal clinic, or of being a typing service. Some of them act as feeders for law firms, referring the more complex cases to selected law firms when there appears to be a way of financing the legal fees. I find it difficult to totally condemn these nonlawyers practicing law because they sometimes provide needed services to people whose needs sometimes cannot be economically met by law firms. Sometimes these nonlawyers butcher the case, but certainly the "client" usually gets what he or she pays for.

On the other hand, I've seen CPAs, insurance agents, and bankers draft wills, employment contracts, trusts, promissory notes, leases, and various forms of contracts for people who can afford to pay for legal services, but who don't know they need legal services. These cases are often botched because the nonlawyer didn't know anything about the effect the advice or services would have in other areas of the law. I have no sympathy for either the cheap client or the greedy person who practices law without a license to the detriment of the client's case.

CHAPTER 4

Finding Lawyers through Directories, Referrals, and Other Sources

FINDING THE RIGHT LAWYER BY USING THE YELLOW PAGES

An easy way to locate lawyers is to look in the Yellow Pages. Lawyers as a group are heavy advertisers in Yellow Pages directories. The telephone company's classifications by area of practice and the lawyers' display advertising are simultaneously informative and confusing. The ads can be informative in describing what the lawyer does but confusing in terms of what *you* might need. This chapter and this book can help you more effectively utilize the Yellow Pages as a part of your efforts to find the right lawyer.

There is not necessarily any direct correlation between the size of lawyers' ads and the quality of legal services. Nor is there necessarily any correlation between the quality of their ads and the quality of their services. Some law firms which service primarily corporations and businesses will not even bother to talk to someone who called up saying that they found the law firm's name in the Yellow Pages. Increasingly, however, sophisticated businesses, and even lawyers themselves, use the Yellow Pages when seeking a particular specialty. I don't have a display ad, but I receive many telephone calls from responsible people seeking a lawyer who knows business law, tax law, and international law who found my name in the Yellow Pages. On the other hand, those law firms which practice what is commonly called "people law" (dealing with the problems of individuals as opposed to the problems of corporations) have always welcomed clients who reached them through the Yellow Pages. These firms typically use display ads.

A lawyer indicating in a Yellow Pages listing that he or she wants business in certain areas of law is not necessarily indicating any competence in that area. One would expect that a lawyer would not ask for business in an area where he or she could not produce competent results. There is an exception in those states which have some sort of a "board certification" (see Chapter 6 "Understanding How Lawyers Practice").

Advantages

There are both advantages and disadvantages to using Yellow Pages directories to find a lawyer. Some of the advantages are:

1. The local Yellow Pages directory itself is free and is easily accessible.

2. The local directory can be studied in privacy at your leisure at work or home. You don't have to go to a library or bookstore to find one.

3. Using the directory also is private. You can seek legal help without disclosing to family, friends, or business associates that you need legal help.

4. You can limit your search to your own geographic area or you can expand your search to other areas.

5. Out-of-town Yellow Pages directories can normally be found and used for free in the reference section at a local library or at some local telephone company offices. Directories from

outside your geographic area can sometimes be obtained for free or at a nominal cost.

6. You can assume that lawyers with display ads want new clients or they wouldn't be spending money on the ads.

7. The listings will classify lawyers according to the particular telephone company's classification of practice area. There is no nationwide system. (See the list of areas of Yellow Pages classifications on pages 39–42.)

8. The individual display ads reflect the specific types of legal work the lawyers want.

9. Most Yellow Pages directories I have seen list bar association-sponsored lawyer referral services as the first listing in the Yellow Pages before the individual alphabetical listings.

10. Firms which advertise in display ads understand that people using the Yellow Pages usually have an immediate need for a lawyer. They train their receptionists to welcome Yellow Pages callers.

Disadvantages

Some of the disadvantages to using Yellow Pages directories are:

1. There is similarity but not uniformity in classifications of legal practices. Different directories use different systems reflecting regional practice areas and regional descriptions. For example, in some directories, listings are found under the word "lawyers" and in other directories under the word "attorneys."

2. The description of the areas of practice listed by lawyers in their ads is self-description. There is often an ambiguity and uncertainty in what a word in their ad means or whether the practice area is what you need. It is almost a necessity to have a guide to understand the areas of practice and whether the law firm with the ad might meet your needs.

3. There are often multiple "Yellow Pages" directories in a geographic region. It can be confusing to decide which one(s) to use. The safest thing to do is to use them all.

4. Some older clients and some older lawyers erroneously feel that only lawyers of lesser ability or lesser ethics advertise in

the Yellow Pages. This may or may not have been true at one time but no longer is. Accordingly, many firms with older lawyers may not even want to list their firm by specialty area in the Yellow Pages.

5. Some older clients and some older lawyers erroneously feel that Yellow Pages directories are a last resort for people who don't have a meritorious case or people who can't get a recommendation to a responsible law firm.

6. Except for those states with bar specialization programs or bar certification programs, it is not possible to know whether the lawyers with display ads are competent or experienced in the areas they list (see Chapter 6 "Understanding How Lawyers Practice"). States which have some sort of board certification include Arizona, California, Florida, Iowa, Louisiana, Minnesota, New Jersey, New Mexico, North Carolina, South Carolina, and Texas.

7. Large firms often practice in many—sometimes hundreds—of areas of law. If every lawyer in such a firm had one to five listings or areas of self-interest, it could result in a single law firm's having many pages of listings. Many Yellow Pages directories limit law firms to a single full page of advertising. One page wouldn't begin to be sufficient for a large firm. Accordingly, larger law firms often are underrepresented or completely absent.

8. Large firms often do not want smaller clients and deliberately exclude themselves from Yellow Pages advertising. They believe that those clients who seek services offered by the firm will find law firms through other directories such as Martindale-Hubbell Law Directory.

Using the Yellow Pages More Effectively

Here are some steps you can take to get the most our of the Yellow Pages listing:

1. Spend some time studying all the listings and all the ads in the directory before you call anyone.

2. When you find a word or phrase in an ad or listing which you think might describe what you are looking for, but you

aren't sure about the practical meaning of a word or phrase you see, look it up in Chapter 12 "Foonberg's Glossary of Legal Specialties" to see if it might be what you need.

3. Make a list of all the lawyers whom you intend to call based upon their geographic location or based upon the contents of their listings.

4. Have a pen and a pad of paper with you when you begin calling lawyers. Don't depend on the margins of the Yellow Pages or a matchbook or a scrap of paper. You won't have enough space. You will need to jot down such information as the names of the people you speak with, directions for getting to the office, and documents or information you will need to bring with you. Also, write down important phone numbers such as direct-dial, fax, or other automated-dialing numbers for particular lawyers, as well as any times you are supposed to call back. If the people you talk to give you names and telephone numbers of other lawyers or agencies, you will need to record those as well.

5. Use a separate sheet of paper for each lawyer or firm you call. Otherwise, you will become confused as to whom you called or spoke with or what they said.

6. Start calling when you have a list of lawyers and firms which seem to be possibilities for help.

7. Call from a quiet place so that you can both hear and be heard on the telephone. Use a desk or table so that you can take legible notes. You will need to be able to read them accurately at a later time.

8. If the person who needs a lawyer doesn't speak English, try to get someone who does speak English to make the calls. The people who speak the foreign language may not be in the office when you call. There may be an English language automated system that might not be understood by the person calling.

9. When you call, tell the person who answers the telephone "I saw your listing in the Yellow Pages. It says you do [whatever listing or description you saw in the listing]. I think I have a

problem that is in your area of law. May I please speak with a lawyer?"

10. A well-organized law office will be ready to handle that call. You will be put on hold and someone will be located to take your call. Be patient. It may take a few minutes for a very busy receptionist to process your call. When you are on the telephone, a few minutes can seem like an eternity. Give them at least two or three minutes to connect you with somebody. If after several minutes you remain on hold and no one comes back on the line, your call is being mishandled. Hang up and redial. Tell the receptionist you were on hold for a long time and were concerned that you had been accidentally cut off. Your second call will usually get priority treatment.

11. If the person answering the call doesn't know what to do with your call, be careful. You may have reached an incompetent law firm. If personnel can't handle a simple telephone call, how will they handle a complex legal problem? If the firm uses underpaid, poorly trained people to answer telephones, you can reasonably assume it will use underpaid, poorly trained people to handle your legal work.

12. Your call may or may not be screened by a legal assistant or a secretary before you can speak with a lawyer. You will probably be asked your name, address, and telephone number, and possibly where you saw the ad. You may be asked to identify the ad by some coding in the ad such as department number. This is normal and should not upset you. Lawyers pay for directory advertising and listings. They may want to determine the cost effectiveness of the money that has been spent. They want to know the geographic area from which the listing draws calls. They need your name in order to pronounce it correctly. They need your address in order to give you directions, to send you a letter, or to put you on the mailing list to receive more information about the firm. They need your phone number to call you back if there is an interruption in the call.

13. If you have a reason for not giving your name, address, and telephone number, be sure to explain it to the person who

takes your call. Without a good reason for withholding the information, there is a good chance your call will be terminated and you will have wasted your time.

14. If someone starts asking questions about your legal problem, be sure you get his or her name. You should also get the person's direct-dial number or extension number so that you can get back to him or her, if necessary, without starting from the beginning with a new person if you have to call back.

15. You may be asked for a few preliminary facts or the names of the other parties. This is for your protection. The firm may want to determine if it is the right firm for you, and it wants to be sure there is no conflict of interest. It would be embarrassing for you, and possibly harmful to your case, for you to tell all and then find out that the firm you are speaking to is representing the other side and is going to use your inside information against you. (See the section in Chapter 9 on "Conflicts of Interest.") If the firm can't do your type of work or if there is a possible conflict, the person with whom you are speaking will terminate the call. Ask if the person can recommend other lawyers or firms that might be interested in your representation. You may or may not get a recommendation to another firm. If you do get one, use it immediately. Call the recommended firm and give them the name of the firm that recommended you. Your call to the next firm will get a high priority and high attention level if you are recommended by a law firm. The likelihood of finding the right lawyer will be much higher if you follow up on a recommendation from a lawyer rather than simply use the Yellow Pages.

16. If you get turned down for any reason by the firm you are calling, or indeed by any firm, ask for another recommendation for a lawyer or a firm which might be able to assist you. As indicated above, there will be a higher probability of finding the right firm and you will get immediate attention when you are recommended by a law firm.

17. Don't be disappointed or surprised if there is no lawyer available to talk with you at the exact moment you call. Good

lawyers are busy. They are constantly in court, in depositions out of the office, at meetings, on the telephone, or in conference with other clients.

18. If no lawyer is available to speak with you, ask what will be a good time for you to call back. Some lawyers have specific time blocks open to return telephone calls (3 P.M. to 4 P.M., for example) and plan specific times to receive appointments or telephone calls (4 P.M. to 5 P.M., for example). If there is no one to take your call, try to indicate when a good time would be for a lawyer to call you. If you designate a specific time, stay off the telephone during that time slot. If you are on the phone and the lawyer receives a busy signal or an answering machine, the lawyer might not try to call again.

19. When you do get to talk with a lawyer or legal assistant, tell him or her that you think you have a problem in the area of law that the firm practices. Explain that you don't want to waste your time or theirs if your needs are not within the areas of their practice. Describe what area of law you think is involved (based on Chapter 12 "Foonberg's Glossary of Legal Specialties"), and give them a brief sketch of what happened and what your damages are.

20. Don't act desperate or urgent unless for unforseen reasons you truly have a desperate or urgent problem. When you try to push or squeeze a lawyer for an immediate appointment, you make the lawyer nervous. People who procrastinate with their legal problems until they become urgent often procrastinate about cooperating with their lawyer and procrastinate about paying their legal bills. It is reasonable to expect an appointment in two or three days. It is not reasonable to expect an appointment on the same day as the first call.

21. If the firm or lawyer is interested in your problem, ask if there will be a fee for the initial consultation (see "Is It Reasonable to Expect a Free First Consultation" in Chapter 5 of this book). Indicate that you are willing to pay for a consultation, if necessary (this will make the lawyer happy), and ask what the

amount of the consultation fee will be. In many cases there will be no fee, but your willingness to pay a fee will elevate your status in the eyes of the lawyer.

22. If the initial consultation fee policy is agreeable, then set up an appointment.

23. Except for asking about the fee for the initial consultation, do not try to discuss fees by telephone. Most competent lawyers will not discuss fees until after they have met with the client and gotten the facts. Do not be pushy about asking for fee information. Lawyers regard clients who are only interested in fees as potentially problem clients. You will be sending out negative vibrations if you keep asking the fees when the lawyer has already told you that he or she doesn't want to quote fees by telephone or until after a consultation.

24. When you call by telephone remember there are certain types of cases and clients that lawyers traditionally do not like to get involved with. You should be prepared for a cold reception (see "Anticipating Cases and Clients Lawyers Don't Want" in Chapter 7 of this book). Typical of these types of cases are landlord-tenant disputes, barroom brawls, assault and battery cases, and hurt feelings cases where the conduct is wrongful but where there are no monetary damages.

By going through the above steps, you should be able ultimately to make an appointment with one or more lawyers for a consultation. You will have narrowed the field down to lawyers and firms that appear to be able to serve your legal needs and who want to meet with you. However, you still have to satisfy yourself as to competency, and you will still have to make satisfactory fee arrangements. These areas are covered in later chapters.

If after going through the Yellow Pages listings you can't find a lawyer or firm you want, you can still use the Yellow Pages to find the local bar association lawyer referral services (LRS). The local LRS is normally the first listing in the Yellow Pages before the individual attorneys and firms. (See "Finding the Right Lawyer or Other Legal Assistance by Using Bar Association Lawyer Referral Services" later in this chapter.)

Yellow Pages Classification

In using Yellow Pages ads as a source, keep in mind there are two classifications which have to be dealt with. The first classification is the listing classification of law practice areas created by and used by the telephone company in a particular geographic area where the Yellow Pages are distributed. There is no uniformity in listing classifications from telephone company to telephone company nor from directory to directory. Unfortunately, in some communities, the Yellow Pages do not classify lawyers by practice areas. In addition to reflecting the local terminology used by the various telephone companies, the Yellow Pages often reflect the type of law practiced in each community. Nonetheless, while there is no uniform system, there may be at least a similar system of listings.

The second source of classification is the classification system used by lawyers themselves in describing their own individual practices. There are as many variations and discrepancies among types of practices listed as there are law practices. The particular descriptions used by a particular lawyer in the lawyer's Yellow Pages ad may be a great help or of little help to you.

Hopefully, the following list of practice areas as utilized by many of those telephone companies which do list practice areas will help you classify your legal question and find the right lawyer. Each classification comes from a Yellow Pages directory. Each of the classifications listed is explained in Chapter 12 "Foonberg's Glossary of Legal Specialties." There may appear to be duplication in the listings, especially with use of the singular and the plural and the inclusion or the omission of the word "law" in the description. This is due to the fact that the telephone companies themselves are not uniform. I have listed various areas exemplary of how the telephone companies list.

List of Practice Areas

Accidents—Personal Injury and
  Property Damage
Administrative Agencies and
  Governmental Law
Administrative Agency Law
Administrative and
  Governmental
Administrative and
  Governmental Law
Administrative Law and
  Government Agencies
Administrative Law—Board
  Certified
Administrative Law
  (Government Agencies)
Admiralty
Admiralty Law
Adoption
Adoption Law
Adoptions
Agricultural—Livestock
Antitrust and Trade Regulation
Antitrust and Trade Regulation
  Appeals
Antitrust and Trade
  Regulations
Antitrust and Unfair
  Competition
Appellate Practice
Auto Pac Claims
Aviation
Aviation Law
Banking
Banking Law
Bankruptcy
Bankruptcy and Debtor Relief
Bankruptcy
  (Creditor's/Debtor's Rights)
Bankruptcy Law
Business Bankruptcy Law—
  Board Certified

Business, Corporation, and
  Partnership
Business Law
Civil Appellate Law—Board
  Certified
Civil Litigation
Civil Rights
Civil Rights Law
Civil Trial Law—Board
  Certified
Collections
Collections Law
Commercial and Corporate Law
Commercial Law
Commercial Leases
Commercial Real Estate Law
Communications Law
Computer
Computer Law
Condemnation
Condemnation Law
Constitutional Law
Construction
Construction Claims
Construction Law
Consumer Bankruptcy Law—
  Board Certified
Consumer Claims and
  Protection
Consumer Law
Consumer Protection
Consumer Protection Law
Contract Law
Copyright Law
Corporate Finance and
  Securities Law
Corporation and Business Law
Corporation and Partnership
  Law
Corporation, Banking, and
  Business Law

Corporations and Business Law
Creditor's Rights and Commercial Law
Criminal
Criminal Law
Criminal Law and Traffic Offenses
Criminal Law—Bar Certified
Criminal Law—Board Certified
Criminal Law General Practice
Discrimination Matters
Divorce, Adoption, and Family Law
Divorce and Family
Divorce and Family Law
Driving Under the Influence
Driving While Intoxicated (DWI)
Drunk Driving Defense
Education Law
Elder Law
Elderlaw
Eminent Domain
Employee—Employer Rights
Employer—Employee Relations
Employment Law—Wrongful Termination
Entertainment and Sports Law
Entrepreneurship Law
Environmental
Environmental Law
Environmental Law and Natural Resources
Estate Planning
Estate Planning and Probate— Board Certified
Eviction
Expropriation Law
Family Law
Family Law—Board Certified
Farm and Ranch Real Estate Law—Board Certified
Franchise

Franchise Law
General Practice
Government Contracts
Hazardous Waste Law
Health Care and Hospital Law
Health Law
Housing and Development
Immigration and Deportation Law
Immigration and Nationality Law—Board Certified
Immigration and Naturalization
Immigration, Naturalization, and Customs Law
Indian Affairs
Insurance
Insurance Law
Intellectual Property
International
International and Foreign Law
International Law
Juvenile
Juvenile and Children's Law
Juvenile Law
Labor
Labor Law
Labor Law—Board Certified
Landlord and Tenant
Landlord and Tenant Law
Landlord—Tenant
Land Use and Zoning
Legal Research
Malpractice Law
Malpractice—Professional
Marital and Family Law
Marital and Family Law—Bar Certified
Maritime Law
Medical
Medical Malpractice
Military
Military Law
Military Veteran's Rights

Mortgage Law
Motion Picture and Television
    Law
Municipal and Planning Law
Municipal Law
Oil, Gas, and Mineral Law—
    Board Certified
Patent
Patent Attorneys
Patent, Trademark, and
    Copyrights
Patent, Trademark, and
    Copyright Law
Patents, Trademark, and
    Copyright Law
Patents, Trademarks, and
    Copyrights
Patents, Trademarks, and
    Copyrights Law
Pension and Profit Sharing
Pension and Profit-Sharing Law
Pension, Profit Sharing, and
    Employee Benefits
Personal Injury and Property
    Damage
Personal Injury and Wrongful
    Death
Personal Injury Property
    Damage
Personal Injury Trial Law—
    Board Certified
Personal Property Security
Probate Law
Product Liability
Real Estate
Real Estate Law
Real Property Law
Real Property Law—Bar
    Certified
Residential Real Estate Law—
    Board Certified
Securities Law
Securities Litigation
Social Security

Social Security and Disability
    Law
Social Security Law
Social Security Law,
    Unemployment,
    Compensation, and Welfare
Social Security, Unemployment
    Compensation, and Welfare
Sports Law
Taxation
Taxation—Bar Certified
Taxation Law
Tax Law
Tax Law—Board Certified
Taxes
Toxic Waste Law
Trade Mark and Copyright
Trademark Matters
Traffic Offenses
Traffic Violations
Transportation Law
Trial Practice
Trial Practice—Bar Certified
Trial Practice—Business
    Commercial
Trial Practice—Civil
Trial Practice Commercial
Trial Practice General
Trial Practice General—Bar
    Certified
Trial Practice—Personal Injury
    and Wrongful Death
Trial Practice Personal Injury
    and Wrongful Death—Bar
    Certified
Trials and Appeals
Water
Wills, Estate Planning, and
    Probate
Wills, Estates, and Estate
    Planning
Wills, Estates, and Trusts
Wills, Estates, Estate Planning,
    and Probate

Wills, Estates, Estate Planning, and Probate—Bar Certified	Workers' Compensation
	Workers' Compensation—Bar Certified
Wills, Trusts, and Estate Planning	Workers' Compensation Law
Wills, Trusts, Estates, and Estate Planning	Wrongful Termination
	Wrongful Termination Law

FINDING THE RIGHT LAWYER BY USING THE MARTINDALE-HUBBELL LAW DIRECTORY

The Martindale-Hubbell Law Directory is probably the largest, most comprehensive, directory of lawyers in the world which currently exists. The ABA Internet listing of lawyers may soon eclipse Martindale-Hubbell. About 800,000 lawyers and firms are in the directory. It can be of great help to you in finding the right lawyer for your legal needs anywhere in the world. It is the only directory of which I am aware in which lawyers are rated by other lawyers in their community. You may wish to think of the rating system as a way of finding a "recommended" lawyer.

The law firms taking up the most space in the directory tend to be the larger firms, and tend to be business, corporate, and insurance defense oriented. On the other hand, many of the firms and lawyers listed in Martindale-Hubbell will help you find the right lawyer, even if they themselves can't or won't help with your legal problem. Although the directory gives the impression of being dominated by the larger corporate firms, a great many are smaller firms and many are individual law and claimant oriented.

The most likely place to find Martindale-Hubbell is in a law library. Most law school law libraries have it. Many public library business or reference sections also have it. Some law firms (including mine) have it. Most courthouse law libraries have it and almost every U.S. Embassy and Consulate in the world have it. About 40,000 customers buy it every year. Many large corporations have it at their corporate headquarters or in the offices of their in-house law department. It exists in a CD–ROM disk version which requires special equipment to read it, and it can be accessed through LEXIS, a computer electronic research service used by many lawyers.

Because 800,000 lawyers and firms are in the directory, the directory is big and bulky. It runs about twenty volumes, each of which is the size and weight of a telephone directory for a good-sized city. It is relatively expensive, so some buyers use a directory for two or three years before buying a current one.

It is worth a few minutes to learn how to read and use the Martindale-Hubbell Law Directory. Even many sophisticated corporate counsel and private practice lawyers who have had the directory for many years don't realize how much useful, valuable information is in it. The directory is organized geographically by county, state, and city.

The best way to use the directory is to look for a listed firm near to where you live or near to where the work is to be done. Within that geographic area, look for firms that identify themselves in their listings as practicing the kind of legal skill(s) you need. A firm near you which practices the kind of law you need can probably do a better job via "networking," or using Martindale-Hubbell, than you can in finding the right lawyer. It is worthwhile for you to remind any law firm helping you find the right lawyer about the directory's rating system, a most unique feature.

The Martindale-Hubbell directory allows lawyers to self-describe their areas of practice. More than 600 areas of practice are currently recognized. Many if not all of these 600 areas are included in the nearly 1,000 areas listed in Chapter 12 "Foonberg's Glossary of Legal Specialties." After you have reviewed the section in this book on describing a legal matter, these 600-plus descriptions will be much more meaningful to you.

Every lawyer who wants a free listing can have it. The publisher periodically sends out a request for information to every lawyer in America and to many foreign lawyers. Obviously, some lawyers will not get a request for a variety of reasons, including an incorrect address. All the lawyer has to do to be included is to simply return the request for information. Unfortunately, the free listings won't be of much help to you in knowing if the lawyer whose name appears can be of help with your particular needs.

The free listing will, however, give you the name and city of lawyers near the geographic region where you need a lawyer. The free listings, all of which are geographical, will simply show the lawyer's name, date of birth, year of admission to practice, undergraduate university or college, undergraduate degree, law school, law degree, and Martindale-Hubbell rating, if the lawyer has one. The firm name also may be included. Unfortunately, there is no address, telephone number, or indication of type of practice in the individual listings of lawyers.

Firms and individuals can buy ads called biographical listings in Martindale-Hubbell. About 80,000 firms do so. These ads can be helpful in finding the right lawyer for your legal needs, because the firms' areas of practice are listed. The ads are in the white pages while the individual lawyers are in the blue pages. Even if none of the firms where you are located or where you need a lawyer seem to have the kind of lawyer you think you need, another firm may be willing to help you find the right lawyer. Most law firms "network" with other firms who do the kinds of work they don't do.

What makes Martindale-Hubbell very different from other directories is its rating system. It might be more correct to say that Martindale-Hubbell prints the ratings, but that the ratings are actually based on the recommendations of other lawyers in the lawyer's community. You may wish to think of Martindale-Hubbell as a place where you can find "recommended" lawyers.

In Martindale-Hubbell, lawyers are rated by other lawyers according to their legal ability and their general recommendation. The ratings are A, B, or C. A-V means Very High to Preeminent for legal ability and V for Very High for recommendation (the highest in each category). About 30 percent of American lawyers carry this highest designation of A-V. The rating of a lawyer's firm may be different from the rating of the lawyer in the firm. (The individual lawyer may have a higher or lower rating than his or her firm.) The firm's rating, if it has one, will be found in the biographical ads. The individual lawyer's rating, if the lawyer has one, will be found in the individual listing. There is unhappiness among some lawyers over the rating system, especially those lawyers and firms who are not listed or not highly rated.

Martindale-Hubbell also contains a corporate law section. This section contains listings of the in-house legal sections of lawyers who are employed by corporations rather than by traditional "outside" law firms. This section can be very useful to corporate lawyers seeking a recommendation from other corporate counsel in the same industry or geographic area. (See also "Finding the Right Lawyer through the American Corporate Counsel Association" in Chapter 10 of this book.)

Not all highly rated lawyers or firms are necessarily the best and not all lesser-rated, nonrated or nonlisted lawyers or firms are necessarily lesser in ability. Not all included lawyers and firms are good, and you should not jump to any conclusions or reach any judgments as to lawyers or firms not listed or rated or without ads. Remember that the ads are bought and paid for and the information came from the lawyer or firm without verification. Some law firms spend a great deal of time and money putting together their Martindale-Hubbell ad and then simply photocopy it for people who want a description of the firm and its lawyers. (There is a confirmation or verification system used for the ratings, however.)

It is my personal experience and opinion that, on balance, the firms listed in Martindale-Hubbell are generally better firms and are generally responsible firms. You should not, however, exclude a firm or lawyer from consideration just because they are not in, or not rated by, Martindale-Hubbell. I have been told by large corporations and large law firms that they would never even consider contacting a lawyer that wasn't listed in Martindale-Hubbell. By limiting their efforts in finding the right lawyer to firms which are listed in the directory, they are simply conserving time.

Although there are many good lawyers and firms that are not in Martindale-Hubbell, it will be a more effective use of your time to consider that directory as one of your starting points.

FINDING THE RIGHT LAWYER BY USING VARIOUS OTHER ATTORNEY DIRECTORIES

Go to the local public library and locate the business reference section. They often have one or more directories of lawyers in addition to Martindale-Hubbell. Familiarize yourself with what is locally available. Many public libraries will also have Yellow Pages from other cities.

There are many directories of attorneys. Some directories claim to have criteria for the listings they accept. You can reasonably assume that any attorney directory contains lawyers who want business (or they wouldn't be listed); are willing to pay money to be listed (depending on the directory or size of the listing, they may be willing to spend very large amounts of money on advertising in the directory); and claim to have expertise or experience or interest of some sort in the area of law covered by the directory.

The directories are numerous and can be of great help or no help at all. You simply have to find what is available in your local library's reference department. Then you can decide whether any of the directories can help you.

FINDING THE RIGHT LAWYER BY USING THE ADVERTISEMENTS OF EXPERTS AND CONSULTANTS

Some cases are so rare or unusual that it is difficult or impossible to find the right lawyer using normal methods. The area of law or factual knowledge required may not exist in your community. Although it may be time consuming, you or your lawyer may have to go to advertising in specialized listings of experts to find the right lawyer.

You or your lawyer may feel that a case requires technical or practical or nonlegal expertise. Or you may feel that you would prefer to work with a lawyer or consultant who already has the technical experience or expertise the case may require. You may be able to find the expertise and/or find the lawyer with that expertise by contacting consultants and experts available to lawyers. Many lawyers and nonlawyer firms earn their living by providing expert services and consulting services to lawyers in a wide variety of specialized areas.

The difference between an expert and a consultant is sometimes blurred. In general, an expert can, and does, testify in court. In addition to being knowledgeable in the subject area, the expert is supposed to be skilled in communicating the expertise to the jury and the judge. The expert knows how to use body language, voice, eye contact, dress, and demeanor to present what is needed from your side of the case. The expert will normally have a long list of credits of cases in which he or she has been a witness. Many lawyers think of experts as being highly trained actors with technical expertise who can tell a technical story to a judge and jury the way the lawyer wants it told. Because of their long list of cases, the experts may be able to recommend one or more lawyers who are skilled in the area(s) of law that the expert knows.

A consultant normally does not testify in court. The consultant analyzes your situation from a technical or scientific point of view to help you determine the underlying merits of the matter. A consultant may deal in litigation avoidance procedures. The consultant can typically educate the client and the lawyer in the technical areas involved. The consultant can help develop a case for trial or develop procedures for avoiding litigation in the future. In either case, the consultant will point out factual information needed and help plan the budget for the matter. Many consultants have previously worked closely with law firms and lawyers and may be able to recommend the right lawyer for the matter.

Some of the areas of expertise are fairly routine while others are exotic. These experts and consultants typically are not lawyers, but in some cases the consultant is, or was, a practicing lawyer. Many of the experts are, or were, engineers, accountants, scientists, professors, etc. They often have expertise in the narrow areas indicated.

These nonlawyer consultants can often direct your lawyer or you to a lawyer with whom they have worked in the past on the same problems as those involved in your case. The lawyer you need may not be available in your community. These consultants and experts may have good contacts outside your area who can work with you or your lawyer.

One way to find experts and consultants is to look at their advertising. They usually advertise in national and local publications intended for lawyers, such as the *American Bar Association Journal,* the journals of state and local bar associations, and in the Martindale-Hubbell Law Directory. They also buy listings in various directories put out at irregular intervals by bar associations. The Los Angeles County Bar Association Directory of Experts and Consultants lists about 300 areas of expertise claimed by those who advertise their skills. Also, consultants often advertise in CPA journals, because they know that CPAs can be good referral sources.

Finding the right lawyer or finding the right help for your present firm by going through the various experts and consultants directories can be time-consuming. You may have to go through back issues of the indicated publications. There is no guarantee that experts or consultants exist in the field of law where you may need help. On the other hand, the long search may eventually lead to the perfect lawyer or the perfect assistance for your needs.

If you already have a lawyer but can't seem to find the right one for your particular need, you should ask your lawyer to contact a consultant or expert for you. The listings on pages 48–50 give some examples of experts and consultants chosen at random from advertising placed in recent issues of *Trial* magazine, the *ABA Journal, The National Law Journal,* and *California Lawyer.*

Experts and Consultants

Accident, depression, and suicide

Adverse drug reactions

AIDS litigation

Airport safety, compliance, grants

Arson defense in insurance cases

Asbestos and lead consulting

Bakery machinery accidents

Bank lending practices

Battery explosions and fires

Bicycle accident reconstruction

Boating litigation, design, construction, and operation of boats

Boilers, furnaces, chillers, electrical piping, refrigeration, steam, ventilation, canals, coal mining, dams, hydraulics, hydrology, lakes, and storm drainage

Campus safety and security

Casino, disco, bar, hotel, and restaurant liability

Ceramics, glass, and plastics materials problems

College campus security, including rapes, assaults, concerts, and athletic events

Computer-related cases

Construction accidents, including cranes, hoists, rigging, forklifts

Convenience store security, robbery deterrence, and crisis management

Courtroom design and safety

Crowd control in public places

Diet fraud

Document examination

Elevators, escalators

English language, syntax, grammar, vocabulary

Environmental, air pollution, groundwater pollution, soil contamination, hazardous wastes

ERISA and fiduciary responsibility

Escrows

Evaluation of professional practices

Evaluations of closely held business

Firearms and explosives accidents

Government contract claims

Hotel and motel food service

Injury of the elderly

Jail malpractice, including excessive force, deadly force, handcuffing, suicides

Lawn mower accidents

Leaking underground storage tanks (LUST)

Libel, slander, bias, innuendo

Linguistic analysis

Manufacturing quality control for airplanes, helicopters

Marine engineering

Medical device failure analysis

Nuclear and fossil power

Metallurgy and fracture analysis

Military law and veterans administration

Motorcycle helmet injuries

Offshore corporations and trusts

Oil and natural gas

Personnel practices, selection, promotion, wrongful termination

Police malpractice and law enforcement, including vehicle pursuits, excessive force, deaths, overcrowding, standards, policies, hiring, promotion, selection, negligent use of firearms, false arrest, roadblocks, lock-up management, domestic violence

Powerline distribution and transmission

Railway, highway, bridge, and station crossings expert
Recreation accidents
Rollover analysis for tractor-trailers, lift trucks, mobile equipment
Roofing and waterproofing
Seat belt claims
Securities fraud
Sexuality and sexual behavior
Ski injuries
Snow and ice control
Sports accidents
State-of-mind testimony for will contests, competency, wrongful death
Swimming pool construction and safety
Tires, rims, and wheels—failures and explosions
Toxic chemicals
Trademark searches
Tree expert—limb break and powerline contact
Truck loading and packaging
Utility hazards and safety, electrocutions, cars hitting poles
Warning-label readability and effectiveness
Waterskiing and scuba accidents
Weather experts—records and testimony effectiveness
Windows, doors, glass, and water leakage
Wood products and preservatives

FINDING THE RIGHT LAWYER BY USING LAWYER'S ALERT PRESS AND *LAWYERS WEEKLY U.S.A.*

First, let me disclose that I have a financial relationship with Lawyer's Alert Press and *Lawyers Weekly U.S.A.* It is the company that prints my book *How to Get and Keep Good Clients.* I do not have any other financial interest in the company and will not achieve any financial gain if you subscribe to it or buy current or back issues of their publications.

Lawyer's Alert and its successor *Lawyers Weekly U.S.A.* is a national publication for lawyers. It is published in Boston, Massachusetts. Its telephone number is 1-800-444-LAWS. Each issue contains information about new and expanding areas of law. The publication often contains the name and city of a lawyer advancing a new theory or application of law. Each issue also contains advertisements from lawyers looking for help from other lawyers in specific types of cases. They also publish an index every six months.

In an unusual or novel situation you may be able to find a lawyer who has already done work in the area you are interested in. If your case is so unusual or novel that you can't seem to find a local lawyer familiar with your particular area of law, you might find such a lawyer with the experience you need in the *Lawyer's Alert* advertising or articles. That lawyer may be able to help you or to find another lawyer in your community who can help you. Looking in *Lawyer's Alert* or *Lawyers Weekly U.S.A.* is no guarantee of finding the lawyer you need, but in special situations it is often worth the try.

FINDING THE RIGHT LAWYER OR OTHER LEGAL ASSISTANCE BY USING BAR ASSOCIATION LAWYER REFERRAL SERVICES

A lawyer referral service (LRS) is an excellent source for a person or company to locate the right lawyer. I highly recommend that lawyer referral services be used anytime you cannot get a satisfactory recommendation from a trusted, competent source, and anytime you are new to a community. A lawyer referral service is also worthwhile in finding a second or back-up lawyer, and often worthwhile even if you don't need a lawyer or can't afford one.

It is worth a few minutes of your time to read this section now rather than leave it to later. A bar association LRS is typically sponsored and staffed by a bar association. If the LRS makes a profit, the profit goes to support some other bar association activity, such as legal aid.

Non-bar-sponsored lawyer referral services are businesses run at a profit for the benefit of the owners, the sponsors, or others. Medical groups often are involved in lawyer referral services where there are likely to be medical services paid for. Workers' compensation and personal injury lawyer referral services in some communities are reputed to be backed by medical groups looking for patients. I have been told this by many lawyers, but have never independently verified the information.

All comments in this section are directed toward bar-sponsored lawyer referral services. I express no approval or disapproval of non-bar-sponsored lawyer referral service programs, however.

It's easy to find a bar association LRS. You can look in the Yellow Pages. In most of the advertising I have seen, lawyer referral services are listed before the listings of individual lawyers. You may find the bar-sponsored and the non-bar-sponsored services together, requiring you to distinguish between the two.

I've received referrals through bar association LRS's of people and companies who had no present or anticipated needs for a lawyer. They simply wanted to meet a lawyer for the purpose of establishing a lawyer contact who could be their entry point into the local legal situation, when and if a lawyer would be needed.

The LRS gets lawyers to serve on panels in certain designated areas of law. One of my local bar associations has ten non-lawyer full-time "counselors" on duty and maintains more than thirty different legal practice panels. Another local bar association LRS uses a part-time person to handle live calls, and does not try to define the specialties needed by callers. Most LRS counselors are skilled in drawing from the often-hysterical client enough relevant facts to determine what kind of lawyer, if any, the caller should contact. One LRS survey has determined that as many as 60 percent of the people calling do not need a lawyer. The callers sometimes need legal aid because they can't afford lawyer fees. They are sometimes directed toward public assistance programs and appropriate government and law enforcement agencies.

If you do need a lawyer, and if your case is of a type that matches their available panel member listings, the LRS will direct you toward a private practice lawyer. You will have to pay a nominal sum, normally about $25, for this referral process. The lawyer will see you and interview you to determine what your legal needs are. The lawyer will then describe to you what you need and what the fees are likely to be.

You have no further obligation to use or pay the lawyer, and the lawyer has no obligation to accept your case. If you do decide to use the lawyer, you will pay the fees you agree to. Often the lawyer will remit 10 percent or 15 percent of the fees collected from you to the LRS for its advertising, salaries, etc.

Even if you do not want to use that lawyer, you will have a better understanding of your legal situation. You can then go to any lawyer you wish. You will have benefited from getting a more accurate picture of your legal situation and by having heard it from a lawyer at a very low price. Although the lawyer is usually obligated to give you twenty or thirty minutes under the rules of the LRS, in almost every case the lawyer will take all the time necessary to make an evaluation of your problem. When necessary, I have spent as long as two or three hours with an LRS referral, to give the client a preliminary opinion of his or her situation. Very few lawyers on LRS panels are desperately short of clients. They typically are very busy, very successful lawyers who are simply trying to provide help through the bar association to clients who have been determined by LRS counselors to need a lawyer. A $25 consultation with a bar association LRS lawyer is a great bargain and even if the LRS lawyer cannot help you with the particular problem that brought you to him or her, you will have met a lawyer who may be able to help you in the future.

The lawyers permitted to be on lawyer referral panels have varying minimum legal qualifications and minimum malpractice insurance to be eligible for the panels. Some LRS's have no minimum level of experience requirements; others have varying levels of requirements. A level required may depend upon the area of law involved and the number of lawyers in the community willing to serve on the LRS panels. You should ask a specific bar association LRS for its minimum requirements in the legal area involved. Each LRS may be slightly different from the others.

Telephone numbers of lawyer referral services frequently change. For a local bar association, call local directory assistance (typically 411). To reach telephone information for at distant city, dial 1-(area code)-555-1212. Ask the operator for both the city bar association lawyer referral service and the county bar association lawyer referral service.

Some local lawyer referral services will recommend other lawyer referral services in other geographic areas. Some will not. There's no harm in asking the local LRS for a recommendation to another LRS. If you don't mind spending the time in interviews, you can get two or three more consultations for very nominal fees by asking for referrals from different bar association lawyer referral services.

A list of bar association-sponsored lawyer referral services in the United States and Canada is located in the Appendix to this book. It is possible that I have omitted some LRSs. In the event I have, I encourage you to call your local county or city bar association to determine if they do or do not sponsor an LRS.

As indicated, it is estimated that between 40 and 60 percent of all the callers to lawyer referral services either do not need a lawyer or cannot afford a lawyer. These callers are directed by trained counselors toward alternative sources of help such as legal aid or public defenders or various governmental and private agencies which exist to help people without the individual having to select or pay for a lawyer.

Even if you can't afford a lawyer or don't need a lawyer, calling a bar association lawyer referral service can be time and effort well spent.

FINDING THE RIGHT LAWYER THROUGH BAR ASSOCIATION COMMITTEES

Finding a lawyer through bar association activities can be rather laborious and time-consuming but it can be done. The lawyers involved in bar association activities are usually caring lawyers, otherwise they wouldn't belong to the voluntary bar associations. Those who are dedicated to maintaining and improving their competence in their area of legal practice often belong to the committees of the bar association which have members involved and interested in the particular area of law. If a bar association has a lawyer referral service (LRS), you should access the lawyers through the LRS. The LRS is staffed and equipped to help individuals, companies, and other organizations find lawyers.

Some bar associations maintain "lawyer to lawyer" referral panel listings wherein lawyers offer their specialized skills to other lawyers. This list may or may not be available to a lawyer if he or she is not a member of that bar association. If the bar association does not maintain an LRS with a panel member in the area of law you need, you might still be able to find the right lawyer through the committee structure of the association. You may waste a lot of time, because you may have no way of distinguishing private practice lawyers who might be interested in helping you with your problem from government lawyers, corporate counsel, professors, retired lawyers, and many other lawyers who don't accept all private practice clients. Ask the bar association's executive director for a list of the committee members and begin calling them. If the executive director won't give you, or sell you, a copy of the members of the committees which might have lawyers who can properly handle your legal needs, then ask your general practitioner or other lawyer acquaintance to help you get the list.

Purely as a starting point, the listings below provide the various groupings of lawyers used by the American Bar Association. You'll have to determine which areas of law among these are pertinent to your need. Each of these areas has hundreds of subareas. Additionally, every bar association reflects the practices of its members. Other bar associations may be organized into different committees.

ABA Committees

Administrative Law
Administrative & Regulatory Law
Admiralty & Maritime Law
Affordable Housing & Community Development Law
Agricultural Law
Air & Space Law
Antitrust Law
Appellate Judges
Appellate Practice
Arbitration/Mediation
Aviation & Space Technology

Bankruptcy/Insolvency/ Reorganization
Business Law
Civil Rights
Communications Law
Constitutional Law
Construction Law
Corporation Law—Banking & Savings
Corporation Law—General Corporate Practice
Corporation Law—Finance & Securities

Corporation Law—In-House Counsel
Criminal Law—Prosecution
Employee Benefits
Entertainment & Sports Law
Environmental Law
Family Law
Federal Trial Judges
Franchise Law
General Practice
Government—Federal Level
Government—State/Local/Urban
Individual Rights And Responsibilities
Insurance Law
Intellectual Property Law
International Law
Labor & Employment
Law Practice Management
Legal Education
Libel
Litigation—Commercial
Litigation—General Civil
Military Law
Natural Resources Law
Patent Law
Private Defense
Product Liability Law
Prosecution (State & Local)
Public Contract Law
Public Utility/Regulated Industry
Real Estate Law
Science, Engineering & Technology
Special Court Judges
State Trial Judges
Taxation—Corporate & Business
Taxation—Personal
Tort And Personal Injury Law
Trade And Professional Associations
Transportation Law
Trust Probate & Estate Plan

FINDING THE RIGHT LAWYER THROUGH ETHNIC BAR GROUPS

If you want a lawyer of a specific ethnic, cultural, or religious background, then say so. There are many such bar groups in existence. These groups are often called the ethnic or hyphenated bar because there is sometimes a hyphenated name identifying them. A typical example might be the Italian-American Lawyers Club. These bar groups typically concern themselves with problems and opportunities for members of their ethnic or cultural group or for their own social and economic interests or both. You may want a lawyer of a certain ethnic extraction for a number of reasons, including language ability or cultural empathy or your belief that a person of a certain ethnic or cultural background will be more sensitive to the type of problem or persons involved. There are a great many of these ethnic bar organizations, but they are not always easy to find. You may or may not find them in the phone book or by a telephone call to the local county bar association or the state bar group. These hyphenated bar groups frequently have some sort of special liaison status with the rest of the organized bar, and may sometimes be found by contacting the bar group with which they have this special status. Consulates of appropriate foreign countries can often refer you to these groups.

FINDING THE RIGHT LAWYER THROUGH PRESTIGIOUS LEGAL ORGANIZATIONS

Many lawyers belong to various prestigious legal organizations, and most of these organizations have membership lists. Unfortunately, it is not easy to determine just how prestigious an organization really is. In some cases, the only requirement for membership is to send in a check and an application form and membership is automatic. In other organizations, membership is only granted by invitation or after screening for various degrees of experience and ability. In some organizations, membership at the regular member level requires only an application blank and a check, while membership at a higher level requires legal skills. Additionally, membership in some organizations may be representative of the person's interests and not of their legal ability. On balance, you should be careful about choosing a lawyer from the membership list of an organization unless you really know something about the organization and what legal skills, if any, are required for membership.

FINDING THE RIGHT LAWYER THROUGH NEWS STORIES

1. Should you pick a lawyer who is in the news? In most cases, I personally would not pick a lawyer merely because I saw his or her name in the news. There are a few exceptions, which I'll cover later.

Many "famous" lawyers simply pay a lot of money to get favorable publicity. Instead of buying ads that are clearly ads, they pay large sums of money to press agents or public relations firms to get their name before the public in print or in other news media. The lawyers or their firms often "plant" news which is not really news to anybody, but just an excuse to get their name in print as "experts."

A public relations expert once told me that less than 20 percent of what people think is "news" in a newspaper is actually news in the sense of a reporter getting the information. More than 80 percent is information given to a newspaper by someone seeking publicity. Only about 20 percent of "news" is actually news, such as weather, sports results, wars, revolutions, etc.

The press releases that law firms, lawyers, and clients of law firms continually give out are just advertising. The articles are printed as news because it saves the newspaper the cost of hiring reporters to go out and get news. The articles are often well written from a journalistic point of view. This is to be expected because they are written by professional writers who are paid by the people who want the publicity. Additionally, the articles may in fact be interesting reading. Accordingly, the newspapers are happy to print the materials.

In some cases, newspapers will print "news" which is simply additional information an advertiser wants printed. For example, a law firm or client of a law firm may buy a lot of advertising space in the classifieds and demand the "news" article as additional free space in recognition of the advertising dollars spent.

2. If you see a lawyer in a newspaper or on television being quoted or asked for an opinion, does that mean the lawyer or firm is good? Unfortunately, you have no way of knowing. In some cases a reporter interviews a particular lawyer because the lawyer is really an expert on the subject and is willing to be quoted by name. But in most cases, that lawyer is being interviewed because a press agent or public relations firm is being paid to get the reporter to call that lawyer.

In some big cases, a firm pays to get press coverage of a case in court because it is trying to influence the judge or jury, hoping that the judge or jurors will read the articles or see the TV broadcast outside the courtroom before the case is decided. In a big case, a party may spend millions of dollars to set up TV cameras, press rooms, and studios, or provide hotel rooms, meals, and other benefits for the reporters to get "news" coverage during the trial.

3. If you see a lawyer being quoted or interviewed in the newspapers or on TV as an "expert," does that mean the lawyer is really an expert in the legal area involved? Not necessarily. You have no way of knowing whether the lawyer really is an expert or whether the lawyer simply paid a lot of money to get press coverage to influence people to believe he or she or the firm is an expert. The lawyer depends on the fact that you saw his or her name in the media as a validation of his or her expertise. That's why lawyers and law firms spend money for publicity. Some lawyers even "stage" news interviews, using actors for news staff and then send the videotape to clients and prospective clients.

4. How can you distinguish between the lawyers who really are experts in the area of law and those who simply pay money to appear to be an expert? In most cases you can't tell the difference, and you should assume you are reading or viewing paid advertising rather than news. However, if the lawyer you see on TV or read about is actually the lawyer handling the case while it is going on, you are more likely to be seeing news than advertising.

5. Are lawyers who write articles in newspapers and magazines really experts? Unfortunately, many of the articles and article reprints you see printed in newspapers and magazines were not written by the author. They typically are written by some junior person in the firm as a research assignment, then signed off as though the person whose name you see really was the author. In most cases, the "author" will have read the article before he or she signed as the author. In most cases, the person who signed as the author will actually know a little or a lot about the contents of the article. But the "author" often is not the author. If you are able to meet the "author," you should ask the person if he or she wrote the article alone or with help. The way that question is answered (assuming you get an honest answer) may give you a clue as to whether the author really is a knowledgeable author.

6. Are lawyers really politically well-connected if I see their names and pictures in the newspapers with politicians? The answer to this question, surprisingly, is "yes." No politician can get elected to any office unless there is money to pay for the advertising and campaign to get elected. It has been said that money is the mother's milk of politics. Politicians are usually happy to pose with the people who give them this money. You can use your own judgment as to whether that lawyer is close to the politician. If you pay enough money to the political party, you can usually get a breakfast and a personal photo of yourself with any politician in the United States, up to and including the President of the United States.

If you need a lawyer with political connections for such things as real estate usage, a special law to benefit you or your company or industry, or some sort of permit or license, then calling a lawyer who is well-connected to the politician involved is usually a smart move on your part. That lawyer may not be able to get you what you want or need, but that lawyer will usually get you fast, accurate answers to your questions.

7. Do society page photos of lawyers wearing tuxedos or party dresses and holding drinks at a charity event really indicate powerful lawyers with access to the social and power structure of the city? Many of these lawyers are from firms that give a lot of money to the charity. As a result, their lawyers can appear in the society pages to create the impression the firm are established and well-connected. I often suspect that the only qualification for being in the charity publicity is that the lawyer photographs well. It is possible that the lawyer is all the things he or she wants you to believe, but you can't rely on society page photos alone to get the right lawyer.

FINDING THE RIGHT LAWYER THROUGH PREPAID LEGAL PLANS

Prepaid legal plans can assure you that you will get access to a lawyer. Whether that access will be on a Monday through Friday from 9:00 A.M. to 5:00 P.M. basis (32 percent of the week) or at any time of the day or night depends upon the particular plan.

I have been solicited to participate in many different prepaid legal plans as one of the lawyers. The promoters of the plans were sometimes trying to make money from the lawyers by getting them to pay for inclusion. The promoters were sometimes trying to get the lawyers to charge unreasonably low prices as a "come on" to ultimately get bigger cases and clients from the plans. The promoters of the plans were looking in some cases to make money from the subscribers by hoping that the subscribers would never call after paying a premium or a membership fee. I have seen membership plans with premiums ranging from $100 per year to $500 per year.

In fact, for the $100 to $500 annual fee, these plans give very limited service. Generally, about all you will get is advice over the phone, plus the writing of a letter.

I have not seen any definitive studies done by independent bar associations or organizations that determine whether the users of a prepaid legal plan on balance are truly happy and whether they feel they have gotten value for the money spent. I personally would see a benefit to belonging to a plan which would guarantee me access day or night to being in contact with a competent lawyer (not a paralegal or a law clerk or a student or a telephone operator). The lawyer provided by the plan would then be available to me as an option to other lawyers and as a backup for emergencies.

As I have indicated elsewhere in this book, with prepaid legal plans as with most other things in life, you get what you pay for.

FINDING THE RIGHT LAWYER THROUGH 1-(800) MARKETING SERVICES

I have conflicting reports from lawyers participating in 1-(800) marketing plans. Typically, a TV or direct-mail ad provides a toll-free number to call for a referral to a lawyer. Some lawyers who have participated in this type of marketing service tell me they receive a large number of referrals from the service, which has properly interviewed clients by telephone before directing them to the particular lawyer. Other lawyers report that the telephone operators receiving the calls have no training or poor training and are putting the clients in contact with the wrong lawyers for their needs.

Unless, as a client, you know the criteria for a lawyer being included in a 1-(800) marketing group, you have no assurance of the lawyer's competence or experience. You also don't know whether the lawyer has adequate malpractice insurance to pay you if the lawyer doesn't handle your problem adequately. If a marketing service used only lawyers who are board certified or who have a minimum of perhaps ten years experience or who met some other objective criteria, you could have some degree of comfort that you will end up with a competent experienced lawyer for your needs. However, I am not aware of any 1-(800) marketing service that publicly announces its criteria for inclusion of lawyers.

Marketing of legal services through toll-free 800 numbers is a relatively new service. In spite of these drawbacks, it would be unfair to make any recommendations or condemnations of these services until more experience is gained. Certainly, it would be great of you found an 800-number service that publicly announces its criteria for including lawyers in the group (assuming that the criteria included more than the ability of the lawyer to write a check payable to the promoter).

FINDING THE RIGHT LAWYER THROUGH PIETY

Are pious lawyers generally good lawyers? Many pious lawyers are excellent. It is my opinion that piety and service to one's religious organization are generally qualities to be admired and respected, but they should not be relied on exclusively in selecting a lawyer. Recommendations of religious leaders often are of great value in finding the right lawyer.

Unfortunately, skill in the laws of the Lord does not equate to skill in the laws of society. I personally have seen many instances of clients who received exceptionally poor representation from pious lawyers. The lawyers (or their firms) milked the clients for fees, began protracted litigation that never should have begun, and recommended against settlements or deals that were clearly in the client's best interest, all to keep the matter alive and fee-producing. The clients apparently had blind, un-wavering faith in the lawyers because of their piety or position in the religion (many were ministers, congregation presidents, etc.).

FINDING THE RIGHT LAWYER ELECTRONICALLY WITH A COMPUTER

As this book is being finished in 1995, there are major changes occurring in the ability of people to seek information electroni-cally via computer.

Many of the sources listed in this book are available online via a computer either through a legal provider such as LEXIS/NEXIS or West Publishing or through general providers such as Prodigy or Compuserve. Martindale-Hubbell, West Publishing, and other lawyer directories are now available to electronic com-puter access. This book itself is available via computer through the LEXIS/NEXIS system.

It now is possible to find a lawyer or a recommendation to a lawyer via message boards and user groups.

The American Bar Association is currently (in 1995) putting together a project to become part of the world-wide Internet, with every member of the American Bar Association (about half the lawyers in America) being able to have an Internet address and e-mail sending and receiving ability. The ABA members will be able to list themselves in a database accessible from anywhere in the world via the Internet. People seeking a lawyer will be able to define what they are seeking in terms of lawyer location, areas of practice, expertise in the problems of specific busi-nesses, and so forth.

Commercial Internet providers such as Prodigy, Compu-serve, America Online, AT&T, MET, and Microsoft and Inter-net service providers such as NetGM, PSI Com, and UU Net will be able to connect you from anywhere in the world to the ABA to access the lawyer listing databanks.

The American Bar Association project to make all ABA members available via the Internet and the common commercial providers may make many now existing sources obsolete or unnecessary.

If you do not have the technical ability to use a computer for electronic communications and searching, you should seek help from someone who does have the ability.

You should do the background work necessary to finding the right lawyer (classifying the legal problem, etc.) and then let the technical person help you with the electronic communication part.

CHAPTER

Legal Fees

THE PROCESS OF FINDING the right lawyer or firm includes having a proper financial arrangement. No client, regardless of size or financial ability, wants to pay more than they should for legal services. The amount of legal fees and the times and methods of payment of legal fees can impact any client from an individual to a multinational corporation.

This chapter describes the most typical customs related to legal fees. Three areas that every client and lawyer must consider are:

1. Payment of the legal fees.
2. How legal fees are calculated.
3. The Fee Agreement.

GENERAL QUESTIONS

Is It Reasonable to Expect a Free First Consultation?

Some lawyers offer a free initial consultation and others do not. This is a matter of local practice.

In many smaller communities, a large part of a legal practice consists of providing short answers to short questions and other general information or general advice without any further legal action. In that situation, a lawyer simply has to charge for this type of consultation or go broke.

If a potential client has a potential case where the fee comes out of the recovery (plaintiff's personal injury or claimants workers' compensation for example), the initial consultation is normally free.

Some lawyers charge an initial consultation fee to weed out people who really don't want to pay any lawyers and who are trying to get free legal advice by going from lawyer to lawyer to learn all they can for free. (This is apparently a serious problem in immigration work, for example.)

Large corporations often expect even more than a "consultation." They will often ask competing law firms to submit strategies and budgets for handling a particular matter. The law firms involved will often put in large amounts of time and money on a speculative risk that they may or may not get the work. Obviously, when one law firm gets the work the other law firms will not get the work. Often the large corporations are just as guilty as individuals of "picking the brains" of lawyers in order to get free legal advice. The corporation may end up using concepts taken in part from each firm which has made a presentation to them. They will then utilize the information and concepts gotten from these firms while never having paid for them.

I personally encourage people and companies to come in for a free consultation. I want people and companies to feel that they have access to the legal system. After getting the facts, I'll tell them whether or not they need a lawyer, what kind of lawyer they need, whether or not I can help them, and how I charge. If they need another lawyer I'll try to help them find the right lawyer for their legal needs. I don't necessarily expect that other lawyers will or will not do what I do. It is an individual decision that depends on the types of clients and cases and the community involved.

Does a Lawyer Have to Take a Meritorious Case If the Client Can't Pay?

Absolutely not. Most lawyers do a certain amount of free (pro bono) legal work because they want to help people (see the section on "Pro Bono Publico" later in this chapter)—not because they have any obligation to do so. A few lawyers are very selfish and won't help anybody unless they are paid. This is their legal right. Lawyers must strictly control the amount of free legal work they do or there won't be money to pay rent and payroll, and for the books, secretaries, and telephones a lawyer needs to practice law. A lawyer simply has to say "No" at some point or the lawyer and the client may go under together.

Can a Lawyer Refuse a Potential Client Who Can Afford the Fee?

Yes. A lawyer can properly turn down a case or a client for any number of reasons. A common ground for turning down a case is that the lawyer doesn't feel he or she or their firm can do a good job in the area of law involved. Lawyers tend to specialize in some areas and turn down work in other areas where they don't feel they'll do a good job. The lawyer can turn down a case if the lawyer believes that what the client wants is illegal or unethical. In general, a lawyer is supposed to represent a client with both zeal (or at least enthusiasm) and competence, and if either or both quality is likely to be absent, the lawyer can and should turn down the case.

Can a Lawyer Stop Working If Not Paid as Agreed?

In general, a lawyer cannot prejudice a client's case based on the fact that the client is not paying as agreed. The lawyer or firm cannot use the unfinished work as a ransom to coerce a fee from a client if it would prejudice the client's case to stop working or to slow down the work.

A lawyer can, however, normally discharge the client for not paying as agreed, if the discharge would not prejudice the case. In absence of prejudice, the lawyer must either make new financial arrangements with the client or discharge the client.

67

Can a Lawyer Stop Working If the Client Can't Pay Because of Financial Problems?

With a few exceptions, such as serious criminal matters and divorce matters, a lawyer can be relieved of professional responsibility when the client doesn't pay as agreed. Even though there is no element of "fault" in the client's inability to pay, the lawyer doesn't have to continue working on the case.

The economic reversal or financial downfall of the client does not require the lawyer to continue work if the lawyer is not being paid as agreed. The lawyer will work with the client where possible, but no lawyer or firm wants to commit economic suicide because a client has unexpected financial problems.

Can a Client Barter Goods and Services in Order to Pay a Legal Fee?

Surprisingly, many lawyers, especially in rural areas and small communities, are willing to barter legal services for goods and services. I personally don't approve of barter because I think it leads to arguments over the relative value of what is being traded, but I know that many lawyers accept goods and services as payment. If barter is the only way a client can pay a legal fee or if the client simply prefers to barter, there certainly is nothing harmful or insulting about asking the lawyer for such an arrangement.

Can a Client Pay with a Credit Card?

Some lawyers accept credit cards for payment and some won't. Until recently, many lawyers felt that accepting credit cards was too commercial. Additionally, until recently, credit card companies were nervous about allowing legal fees to be charged on a credit card. Perhaps they were afraid of not getting paid if the case were lost.

The world is changing. Lawyers themselves have become used to using credit cards for convenience and safety, as opposed to paying cash or facing the difficulty of getting checks approved. The world is also changing as credit card companies aggressively seek new business.

Some law firms that accept credit cards don't advertise it. In my opinion, a lawyer should be happy to receive payment by credit card. A bank is much better equipped to handle monthly payments and collect delinquencies than most lawyers. If the fee in a given case is substantial enough, the lawyer should be happy to become a "merchant" for credit card purposes for the given case just to have assurance of getting paid.

As of the writing of this book (Summer 1995) the American Bar Association was finalizing an agreement for every member of the ABA to be able to accept credit cards from clients for legal fees and costs.

Should a Law Firm be Willing to Accept Monthly Payments on Account?

Most law firms will accept monthly or other periodic payment plans if the client and the firm really have no option. Most firms, however, will try to pace the work being done with the payment schedule, so long as pacing the work doesn't prejudice the case. Frankly, most firms are afraid of doing a tremendous amount of work at the front end of the case with a resultant bill far beyond the periodic payment schedule. Sometimes clients change their mind about proceeding with the legal matter or decide to change lawyers and stop using the firm. Perhaps when additional facts come to light, the lawyer advises a client it would be wasting money to continue pursuing the matter. In these cases, the client may feel that continuing to pay a bill for something he or she no longer wants is wasting money. Accordingly, a law firm is more willing to accept a large initial payment followed by monthly or periodic payments if the client can assure the firm that the fee will be paid in full, even if the client has a change of mind about proceeding.

There is no question of bad faith or bad intentions. Often a client's legal matter looks favorable based on the facts known at the beginning of the case. As the case progresses, additional opposing witnesses may become known, or favorable witnesses may become unavailable. New facts may become known, or the damages or costs become lesser or greater than reasonably anticipated at the beginning of the matter. The lawyer may have to advise the client that it would be wasting money to proceed further. Any or all of these surprises, unknown at the beginning of the case, may cause the client not to proceed further. It is for these many reasons that the firm may be reluctant to accept monthly payments.

Will a Law Firm Accept Monthly Payments If the Client Can Provide Some Sort of Security?

In most cases a firm will be happy to accept periodic payments with some sort of security, such as a mortgage on property or a guarantee from a third party (for example, a relative). Local rules may require consulting with another lawyer before agreeing to the arrangement. In some jurisdictions, the lawyer may be prohibited from accepting certain kinds of security.

Can a Law Firm Accept Payment from a Third Party?

A lawyer can accept payment from third parties. Payment of fees by employers or insurance companies' lawyers is common. However, the lawyer must make it clear that the client must get all the loyalty in the event of a future conflict of interest. An employer may not be happy to pay a lawyer to advise an employee who has a claim against the employer. A third party may expect the lawyer to violate the attorney-client relationship to get information to help the third party. Where a corporation pays the bill, the lawyer may have to make certain disclosures to a board of directors. In certain cases (criminal cases for example), accepting payment of legal fees from a third party may create the impression that the client is "taking the blame" to protect the third person, or to keep the third party informed of what is happening. A prosecutor may suspect obstruction of justice or conspiracy. The government or opponent may try to subpoena the lawyer's books and records as to the source of the fee, and then use the information found to hurt the client's case. All of this should be spelled out in writing to both the third party and the client. In most cases, it would be best for the client to obtain the funds from the third party, and then pay the lawyer directly.

Will an Insurance Company Pay All or Part of the Legal Fees?

You may already have legal insurance and not know it. Anytime you are sued you should immediately try to determine whether you are insured for the legal fees and costs of defending yourself. If you are insured for some form of liability, your insurance contract (technically an insurance policy is a contract) normally includes a duty on the part of the insurance company to defend you from claims. The insurance company must provide a legal defense including lawyers and investigation costs if a claim or potential claim against you falls within the scope of liability for which you are insured. For example, if you are sued for ten different reasons in a single lawsuit based upon multiple theories, the insurance company may have to defend you on all ten even though they might have responsibility in only one of the ten areas. The insurer must defend you even if the possibility of winning against you in only one area is very small.

There is no point in paying for legal services you have already bought with your insurance premiums. So before you spend a significant amount of money on legal fees when you have been sued, ask the lawyer or your insurance agent if you might have the type of insurance policy or policies where an insurance company has to pay the legal fees. It is almost always worthwhile to pay a lawyer out of your pocket to determine whether your insurance company or some other insurance company has to defend you or represent you. Don't accept your agent's "no" answer without getting a lawyer's opinion to be sure. A good general practitioner will know how to read your policies to help you. If your general practitioner can't help, or if you don't know a lawyer, you should try to find a lawyer who specializes in—or knows a lot about—"insurance coverage" problems. Lawyers who do "bad faith" or "insurance claims" might or might not know how to read your policies and apply the law. It never ceases to amaze me that clients willy-nilly hire and pay other lawyers to do work the insurance company lawyers would do for free.

You should not only try to get your own insurance company to protect you but also determine whether someone else has a policy to protect you. You might be surprised to learn that you are insured under a policy of your employer. People are often pleasantly surprised to learn how much legal protection they have under their standard homeowner's or apartment dweller's policy. There may even be protection from the insurance policies of the owner or of a tenant other than yourself. An automobile insurance policy may have some feature you are unaware of. A driver or passenger in your vehicle, or the owner or financing agency of the vehicle, may have some coverage.

Whether or not one or more of your insurance companies has to defend you depends, of course, on the facts of the case and on your local law. Whether or not you have insurance defense protection may be a question of what someone claims you did, rather than what you actually did. It is sometimes the rule that if, under any theory, there is any possibility that your insurance carrier might have to pay a claim under the policy, then the carrier has to defend you. Sometimes your enemies are doing you a favor by making wild accusations in their demand letter or lawsuit. By making wild, unfounded claims, they may be bringing in an insurance company to pay your legal fees.

Unfortunately, when an insurance company pays your legal fees, you rarely have a choice as to the lawyer or firm that will represent you. Your case may be handled by a series of lawyers in the firm, none of whom seems to know anything about you or care about you or seems to know anything about the case. Although you are legally and ethically the client of the lawyer or firm, you will often be ignored and often mistreated. Your own lawyers in the firm may treat you as though you were the enemy. These poor client relations are occasioned by the fact that the law firm often regards the insurance company, not you, as the true client. The only interest of the insurance company is to get the cheapest result the cheapest way. Your emotional concerns and fears and hopes are of no interest whatsoever to the insurance company or to its lawyers. If you are treated badly enough, and ignored enough, you may have to remind the law firm or the lawyer handling the case that under the law and under the rules of ethics of most bar organizations you are the client and entitled to be kept informed through proper communications. Insurance companies often refuse to pay for the investigators, experts, or skilled experienced lawyers you need. A mention of a possible ethics complaint to the bar association may get you the attention you should have had from the beginning.

Prepaid Legal Plans

Prepaid legal plans might be of some help. The prepaid legal plans often have nominal premiums and very small protection. In most of the plans which I have seen you only get protection for small matters, such as writing a lawyer's letter or getting a quick informal opinion from a lawyer of unknown qualifications. You may find that your "insurance" disappears as soon as the need for insurance becomes big.

Some of these prepaid plans are simply cooperative advertising marketing systems paid for by lawyers looking for clients. Some are marketed through credit card companies and through associations as "member benefits."

On the other hand, in some plans, you might get very personalized and attentive services because the lawyer is looking for the big-fee case that often begins as a small-fee case. In some plans the lawyer does not render additional services beyond the insured services.

I cannot express a general or specific opinion on the value of prepaid legal plans to a client. I have seen and heard some favorable publicity and I have seen and heard some unfavorable comments. I have not seen the results of any definitive surveys of the insureds conducted by bar associations or by unbiased third parties. My preliminary feeling is that these legal plans are of limited value but, on the other hand, you get what you pay for.

"Pure Insurance"

"Pure insurance" is from time to time available from commercial sources. Some commercial insurance companies will offer "pure" insurance against legal fees. As with some forms of medical insurance, you can pick the professional firm or lawyer you want to represent you and then the insurance carrier will pay the legal fees in whole or in part. When available, this insurance is normally a rider to other policies. I have had excellent reports of this type of insurance from clients who have had it. You will have to check with your insurance agent or insurance broker to see what, if anything, is currently available for clients in your area.

Limitations

You should note that any form of insurance protection will have limitations, and that the most common limitation is that you are protected only when you are sued, not when you want to bring a lawsuit. Except for the minor services available under prepaid plans, no insurance policy will help you to initiate a lawsuit.

When Should You Tell a Lawyer You May Have a Problem Paying Legal Fees?

If you know there is going to be a fee problem, it is better to tell the lawyer as soon as possible to prevent wasting your time and theirs. The lawyer may still try to help you. Many times clients or potential clients have told me during an initial phone conversation that they have some sort of fee problem. I usually tell them to come in anyway. I try to find a way to help them or to refer the matter to a lawyer who is willing and able to work within the problem. The problem may entail getting paid in cash or barter or from a third-party source, or may require a delay in payment until some event takes place. If both sides have limited ability to pay fees, I often recommend arbitration or mediation as an alternative to traditional litigation.

If the lawyer has been highly recommended, you should ask the lawyer if he or she would meet with you to listen to the facts and then possibly recommend another lawyer to help. The lawyer may respond yes or no or interview you over the phone to gain more information. It is generally a mistake for you as a client or potential client not to disclose a financial problem as soon as possible. Eventually the lawyer will find out, and he or she may become angry or feel cheated that you knew about the problem in advance and said nothing. I and many other lawyers will normally give any potential client a free telephone or office interview just to determine if we can be of help. This can conserve both the client's time and our own. We normally don't discuss fees until the very end of the office interview. First, we must conduct a thorough interview and get as many facts as possible to determine whether to accept or reject a case. Only then are we in a position to quote any fee arrangement. We do not wish our concern over getting paid to interfere with our trying to help the client find the right lawyer. Sometimes, after learning all the facts, an imaginative, creative lawyer will help the client arrive at a fee plan or course of action that is fair and reasonable for both the lawyer and the client. Thus, disclosing the existence of a fee problem helps the lawyer to help you.

Keeping in mind the lawyer's expectations for payment of legal fees, you are ready to evaluate the fee quoted by the lawyer you interview. Most often, the lawyer will be able to discuss fee calculation at the end of the interview. By then, the lawyer has a general idea of your needs and can propose a fee arrangement.

How Are Legal Fees Calculated?

In the final analysis, every fee arrangement is a combination of the efforts and skills of the particular lawyer or firm and the amount involved. The specific calculation of a legal fee depends on the kind of case, the client's economic situation, and prevailing community practices. Most lawyers sincerely try to charge a fair fee. There is no national standard or national system. There are as many different ways for lawyers and clients to agree on fees as there are lawyers and clients. In this section I'll identify some of the most common methods, and some of the more common situations where these methods apply. Naturally, the fees in a given case reflect that particular case, the going rate in the community, and the difficulty of the case. I was one of the authors of *Beyond the Billable Hour,* published by the Law Practice Management Section of the American Bar Association. That book contains all sorts of formulas and methods for calculating a "fair" fee. If there is enough money involved, or if you are a company which hires many lawyers, then I recommend the book to you.

The numbers and methods given in this book may not be anywhere close to what prevails in your community. Incidentally, the charges of lawyers are determined by where the lawyer practices, not where the client is located. There can be great differences in the cost of legal fees from community to community.

The following are common fee arrangements.

Flat Fees

Flat-fee, or fixed-fee, cases are those where a single fee is charged, regardless of the amount of work involved or the results. In most flat-fee cases, the legal problem is routine for the lawyer or the firm. The lawyer can therefore estimate the time and difficulty involved and, thus, come up with a flat fee to charge. Some common examples include defending a criminal case, sending a lawyer's letter, forming a corporation, a noncontested divorce, preparing a living trust or will, getting a patent or copyright, bankruptcy, and certain types of litigation.

It never hurts to ask a lawyer if he or she can set a flat fee for your case. The lawyer may quote a fee a bit on the high side to anticipate problems, but you will know going in what your maximum obligation will be.

Contingent Fees

A contingent fee is a fee which only gets paid out of the proceeds of a settlement or judgment—if there is no recovery from the other side, there is no fee. Contingent fees are common in cases such as personal injury and collections. Contingent fees are most common for serving clients who can't pay an hourly lawyer's fee on a monthly basis. These clients are often unable to bear the financial burdens of a lawsuit. They want the lawyer to advance all funds and take all economic risks in the event the case is lost.

Contingent fees in personal-injury cases typically run between 25 percent and 50 percent of damages awarded depending on the type and difficulty of the case. It is my experience that clients with contingent-fee agreements typically pay two to three times what the fee would have been had they simply paid the lawyer on an hourly basis. Nonetheless, many people feel better with a contingency representation. Realistically, many clients do not have the ability to pay the lawyer on a pay-as-you-go basis.

Straight Hourly Fees

This fee arrangement involves a mechanical application of the lawyer's hourly rate to the number of hours worked on the matter. This method of charging legal fees is normally done in connection with clients and individuals who are defendants being sued and for business matters. This method assumes that the lawyer's hourly rate matches his or her abilities with respect to the needs of the legal matter involved. Lawyers can and do have different hourly rates for different clients or for doing different kinds of work. This method also assumes that the right lawyers are working on the case so that you don't have high-priced lawyers doing low-priced work or low-priced lawyers who are wheel spinning. Hourly rates are common in corporate, business, and insurance defense work, and in most litigation. This method of calculating fees is sometimes referred to as the "Lodestar" method.

The fee examples which appear in this chapter reflect the current situation in the United States. The numbers reflect my own personal observations and do not reflect any scientific survey or poll. They are given only as examples of how some hourly rates compare to others. In 1995, my hourly rate was $295. Lawyers of my experience (I started practicing in 1964) commonly charge between $250 and $350 per hour. Most nonspecialty lawyers of comparable experience charge about $200 to $250 per hour. New lawyers with up to five years' experience may charge about half of what experienced lawyers charge. Lawyers of five to fifteen years' experience charge about two-thirds of what the most experienced lawyers charge.

What Are the Elements of a Fair Fee?

Most lawyers sincerely try to charge a fair fee. Lawyers are no different from other people. They want to live reasonably well in reasonably crime-free neighborhoods, and send their children to reasonably good schools. Very few lawyers look at the practice of law as a way to get rich quick.

For legal reasons bar associations do not publish "fee schedules," but many bar associations and others conduct "surveys" of their members and publish the results as general guidelines for legal fees. Unfortunately, it is almost impossible to determine a fair fee from those guidelines alone. Some factors commonly considered by lawyers in charging a fair fee include the following criteria:

1. The customary fee in the community where the lawyer practices. This fee reflects local conditions of supply and demand.

2. The amount involved. Lawyers tend to charge slightly more when they have a greater professional liability if the matter goes bad. They also tend to be more precise on larger matters than smaller matters, and this requires more time.

3. The time required to handle the case. Even when they set a flat or contingent fee, lawyers generally charge an amount that reflects how many hours a matter is expected to take. Lawyers normally keep time records.

4. The effect of the case on the rest of the practice. A case that requires huge amounts of time will cause a lawyer to give other clients less attention. This can easily result in losing clients who go to other lawyers or firms to get their work done when needed. I have turned down very high-fee cases which would have monopolized all my time to the damage of the rest of my practice.

5. The experience of the lawyer in the field of law. The most expensive lawyer in terms of hourly rates is often the cheapest in terms of total fees, and the cheapest lawyer can ultimately charge the most. An expensive lawyer who has a high hourly or daily rate often knows exactly what has to be done, and does it with no lost or wasted time. The result: a lower total price.

The cheaper lawyer with a lower hourly rate may take a long time to get the job done well, with a resultant higher total fee.

Deciding a fair fee is sometimes as difficult for the lawyer as it is for the client.

Are There "Quantity Discounts" for Legal Fees?

Absolutely, yes. Insurance companies and large corporations that use tremendous amounts of lawyer time commonly pay only 60 percent to 75 percent of the lawyer's normal rates. They often get the big discount because they pay as soon as they receive a bill. Also, they provide enough routine work that the firm can forecast its needs for lawyers and other personnel. However, the bankruptcy of one of these firms could destroy a law firm which provided large amounts of low-profit work for which the law firm never was paid. To add to their clout in negotiating fees, large users also have the option of using in-house lawyers when outside counsel is not available at a price the client is willing or able to pay. To get a quantity discount, you may have to guarantee a minimum amount of hours or fees.

Are Legal Fees Negotiable?

Most lawyers do not like to negotiate price or payment after they have quoted a fee. For a variety of reasons, good lawyers are generally not comfortable backing down or lowering a fee once they have given a fee quotation. However, some clients (especially those from cultures where bargaining is the norm) want to negotiate fees. A sophisticated lawyer will not be angered or insulted by an attempt to negotiate legal fees. Some lawyers are willing and possibly even eager to negotiate fees after they have been quoted, but most of the better ones don't like to.

Can You Reduce Legal Fees by Selecting a Lawyer in a Different Geographic Area?

Very definitely yes. Remember that legal fees are generally determined by the geographic area of community where the lawyer practices rather than the geographic area or community where the client is located or where the work is to be performed.

Hourly rates are higher in large cities and in downtown areas. In any law firm in the world, the biggest expense is salaries. People who work in major cities and in downtown areas demand and get higher salaries for a number of reasons, including longer commuting time, the high cost of dressing more fashionably, and the costs of parking and commuting. In addition, it costs more to eat in downtown restaurants, which typically are both crowded and expensive. Rent is also a major item for law firms. Downtown rents in major buildings are typically much more expensive than elsewhere.

You can save money by avoiding downtown and large urban areas. Many major corporations place as much of their legal business as possible in small towns, if the work can be done from a remote location. Electronic mail, faxes, delivery services, etc., often can eliminate the need for the client and the lawyer to meet each other face to face, especially where much of the work is document preparation or legal research. Sophisticated clients often place legal work in rural areas and even outside the U.S. in India where the lawyers speak English and earn very little. There is no loss of legal skills involved in using lawyers from small towns and outside of downtown areas. In fact, in such areas there is often a better pool of legal talent and support staff at lower prices, because many lawyers and nonlawyers have become more concerned with the quality of their professional life than how many hours they can grind out into a timesheet. Often you can also find good legal talent at relatively low prices from firms located in college towns near a law school. Here, the firm can augment the professional staff as needed with part-time law professors and law students.

It may, however, be a false economy to rely on lawyers who are not part of the local scene, especially when your case involves adversarial or administrative proceedings. It is most important for the lawyer to know the personnel and rules of the local forum. Relying on an out-of-area firm can easily be penny-wise and pound foolish. Other factors that may dictate a need for an urban lawyer include the need to be near major airports, a need for large (and expensive) hotels, and an anticipated large number of meetings where you would be paying for travel or commuting time for the lawyer to attend meetings or proceedings. Paying a lawyer $200 per hour or more to drive a car or sit in a plane can be a big waste of good money.

Finally, in any legal matter, your lawyer and your legal matter are often at an extreme disadvantage if the lawyer doesn't have an excellent working relationship with the local court or administrative agency involved, as well as a good knowledge of its procedural rules. Your particular legal needs may leave you no alternative to using the more expensive local lawyer in the center area of a big city.

Is It More Economical to Spread Legal Work among Multiple Firms to Get Fee Competition?

If your legal needs are modest, you generally want to limit the number of firms you have to deal with. Assuming you have a choice, you should have one firm that is your primary or "general counsel" firm, and use other firms if and when you need them. The advantage of using a single firm is that you and the firm will come to understand each other. No two firms are the same and no two clients are the same. There is an investment of time and money in learning to work together efficiently and in minimizing the waste of time and money devoted to legal affairs. Accordingly, it is generally cheaper to use a smaller number of law firms. On the other hand, you may want or need specialty advice that your general firm can't provide. Your primary firm may try to help you for fear of losing you if they allow another firm in the door or if they have a shortage of work for associates. They will try to learn the law at your expense. They may or may not be efficient in the area, and may or may not be able to get you the results you need.

However, you don't want all your eggs in one basket if you have a large number of eggs. When you use more than one firm, each will pay closer attention to you. You won't be taken for granted or relegated to the bottom of the priority pile. Law firms do go bankrupt or dissolve, and law firms do divide and multiply like amoeba. The lawyer or department you like to work with can suddenly become part of another, bigger firm. Suddenly you are being charged 25 percent more for the same people to do the same work. Spreading some of your work around is simply prudent long-range financial management in the event your primary firm goes under or undergoes some form of major upheaval.

Can a Case Qualify for Free Legal Work (Pro Bono Publico)?

Law firms handle some cases for free as part of the work they call pro bono publico or "pro bono" for short. Is there a difference between free legal work and pro bono?

Pro bono publico is a Latin phrase that means "for the good of the people." It is loosely referred to as "pro bono." As used today, it has a different meaning to different people and to different law firms. At one time a pro bono case was one that involved some great public principle, but where the person affected did not have the economic ability to fight a war in the courts. These cases were sometimes called "test cases." A law firm or individual lawyer would take on the case to help a great number of people even though the lawyer had no hope of being adequately compensated. The lawyer or firm would represent the individual client merely to establish a legal right or principle. Often the lawyer would be at battle with major corporations.

As law firms grew in size, those dependent on fees from large institutional clients were reluctant to go against these powerful clients for fear of creating law which would be detrimental to their own clients' interests. Simultaneously, the advent of class-action lawsuits and consumer protection laws enforced by state attorneys general reduced the need for private law firms to take on pro bono cases to establish legal principles. Bar associations have created foundations to litigate these cases, and law firms contribute money to the foundations, rather than handling the cases themselves. The emphasis then switched to those who needed legal help but could not afford to pay for it. Thus, even where no great principle affecting the public is involved, most law firms simply gave money and manpower to support legal aid and similar clinics that provide legal service to the poor at little or no cost. The system of financial support of the foundations for the cases with legal principles involved and the financial support of legal aid clinics for cases with no great principles involved became known as pro bono. In reality, pro bono became simply a form of charitable donation to help meet the legal needs of the poor.

In recent years, law firms have grown rapidly. Law firms became immense and charged high fees to their clients for inexperienced young lawyers. An easy way to give them experience has been to allow new lawyers to take in a limited number of cases for free. In doing so, the new associate got experience and the client got free legal help. In some cases, the client and the case got the full supervision and resources of intermediate-level lawyers, who watched and guided the new lawyer. In other cases, the new lawyer was left to flounder with the case as best as he or she could. The new lawyer also got help from law students. The cases accepted were carefully screened to make sure that no paying client's interests could be hurt by the results of the cases. To avoid the possibility of a conflict of interest with existing clients, the new lawyer often would take on a case in an area of law where the firm did not practice. The help given to the nonpaying client by new lawyers in a large firm is now called pro bono.

Accordingly, pro bono publico stands for any or all of the following:

1. Taking a case for no fee where an important legal principle is involved.
2. Providing financial support to a bar-supported foundation or other organization that litigates cases involving important legal issues of public concern.
3. Providing financial support to legal aid clinics or similar organizations to help meet the legal needs of the poor, even though there are no important legal issues of public concern.
4. Allowing new lawyers to work for free on individual cases where no important legal issues are involved, but where the lawyers can get practical experience on non-paying clients.
5. Some combination of the above.

It is possible for you to get free legal representation from a large firm by asking to be included in its pro bono publico program. While beggars can't be choosers, you can even request that the lawyer handling your pro bono case receive some guidance and control from an experienced lawyer in the firm. But keep in mind that even the lawyer's experience may not be in the field of law of your case. The new lawyer might get some guidance from a lower-level junior partner or an intermediate-level nonpartner.

What a Fee Agreement Should Include

A FEE AGREEMENT SHOULD BE IN WRITING

Should you have a written agreement with the law firm? The answer to this question is an unqualified "yes." In some states, lawyers are required to have written fee agreements with their clients. In a very few situations, the law prohibits a written agreement. Even in those situations where a written agreement is prohibited, you should at least have a letter from the law firm stating that written agreements are not permitted.

The written fee agreement should be signed by both the client and the law firm to eliminate future disputes.

A good fee agreement will be tailor-made to the facts of the case. Obviously, the agreement will differ from situation to situation, but normally a fee agreement should cover the items described in this chapter.

You might want to photocopy this part of the book and hand the photocopy to the lawyer or firm. Request that they cover all relevant points in the agreement. No ethically responsible lawyer will be afraid to cover fully all the points raised, if they are applicable. In the event of a subsequent dispute or misunderstanding, the burden will be on the lawyer to show that you understood your obligations and that the firm met its obligations.

IDENTIFY THE CLIENT

First, the agreement should spell out who the lawyer is representing: Identify the client. This is important where there is more than one possible client. Often there is a potential conflict of interest, and you must know if the firm considers you or someone else to be the client. If there are other people involved the agreement should spell out if they are or are not clients in the case. This is discussed more thoroughly in the section on conflicts of interest in Chapter 9 of this book. This problem commonly arises when someone else is paying the bill or part of the bill. Common examples include a corporation and an individual, an employer-employee situation, a husband and wife, two family members, an estate and a beneficiary, or two injured people in the same vehicle.

RESPONSIBILITY FOR PAYMENT

Determine who is going to be responsible for paying the legal fees. Will they be paid by you? Will they be paid by your insurance company? Will they be paid from the subject of the legal matter? (For example, out of the settlement or by the court judgment?)

LEGAL MATTERS TO BE INCLUDED

Identify the specific case or legal matter where the firm will be representing you. You may have more than one pending legal matter, or a legal matter may have component parts. You don't want to find you have hired a lawyer when you don't want a lawyer.

LEGAL MATTERS NOT TO BE INCLUDED

Spell out any legal matters you discussed orally but in which the firm will not be representing you. It is best to be specific.

You should reasonably expect that a firm will represent you thoroughly in all aspects of your legal problem. If the lawyer has casually said that the firm doesn't want to handle some part of your problem, that should be spelled out in writing. You may need a second opinion as to whether limited scope or less than full representation will be in your best interests. For example, one of the potential adversaries may be a client of the firm, or the firm may have a policy against going against, or with, certain types of clients or cases.

INSURANCE FOR LEGAL FEES

Ask the lawyers to state in the fee agreement whether or not they have investigated, or will investigate, whether these fees are of a type that could be paid by one of your insurance policies or some third party. This provision will help protect you if it turns out that the lawyers didn't do their job thoroughly. It will also force the law firm to be careful before taking your money for a matter someone else would have paid for if asked.

MINIMUM AND MAXIMUM FEES

Establish either a maximum fee amount or an estimated maximum fee. If a firm wants you to sign a blank check, be sure you have unlimited overdraw privileges with your banker. There is no point in spending a lot of money on a case and then abandoning it without finishing it because you didn't have the resources to finish the case. If a firm can't at least give you a range of estimated maximum fees, then it doesn't have enough experience in the type of case. You should keep looking until you find a firm with enough experience to give you at least an approximation, if not an actual maximum fee. If you can't get a maximum fee quoted to you, consider asking about arbitration or mediation in a litigation matter.

SCHEDULE FOR PAYMENT (CASH FLOW)

The agreement should provide a schedule for payment. That is, it should say when fees are to be paid. At the end of the case?

All in advance? Some at the beginning, some in the middle, and the balance at the end? Be sure there is a clear understanding of the cash flow so that you know you can keep your end of the agreement, or alternatively, don't enter the agreement. You don't want to see the case abandoned after it has begun with the result that the money you spent was wasted.

OUT-OF-POCKET COSTS

Out-of-pocket costs may include the costs of investigators, court filing fees, and deposition reporters. Who will pay for this? Who will lay out the money for experts such as accountants, engineers, appraisers, and doctors? Will the law firm lay out the money as the costs are incurred, with you paying for the costs at the end of the matter? Is the firm expecting you to lay out the money, and if you don't pay, the firm stops working? How much are these costs expected to be? If the firm can't give you an estimate of the costs, it may not have the necessary experience to handle your legal problem. Again, you don't want to start something you can't finish, with the result that you've wasted the money you've spent.

RATES FOR DETERMINING FEES

Find out the rates of the firm personnel. When fees are calculated on an hourly basis, be sure the fee agreement identifies services for which you are expected to pay and the rate applicable to each person or service. No two law firms are the same. Some firms charge an hourly rate for the lawyer and also charge for myriad services that other firms include in the hourly rate. (See the section in Chapter 5 of this book on "How Are Fees Calculated?") The fee agreement should identify the rates or fees for the following people (if they exist in the firm): senior partners, junior partners, senior associates, junior associates, law clerks admitted to practice, law clerks not admitted to practice, certified paralegals, noncertified paralegals, secretaries, word-processing operators (or charges per page), electronic research (research done using a computer), librarians, file clerks, and messengers on the firm's payroll.

Some firms will try to charge you overtime for night and weekend work. You should not pay these charges unless your case actually required work to be done out of normal hours. There's no reason you should pay a premium when the firm is understaffed, or when it chooses to do one client's work during the regular working day and another client's work at night or on a weekend. It could have switched the two clients and charged the other client for the premium.

Keep in mind that a firm wants to make a profit (or at least not lose money) on each and every thing done by each and every person in the firm. Clients who require certain services should expect to pay for them and not expect other clients to absorb their costs. I have no problem with this approach and neither should you. It's just that you have a right to know in your fee agreement what you are expected to pay for and what it is likely to cost.

The fee agreement should also identify whether you will be charged for such items as photocopying, printing letters, sending faxes, receiving faxes, phone charges, and the like. If so, the agreement should give the rate for each category of expense.

PROVISIONS IF THE CASE IS LOST

Ask the law firm to specify what fees and what costs you will have to pay if the case is lost. No one anticipates losing a case, but it happens. In fact about 50 percent of all cases that go to judgment have a losing side. Be sure to ask what costs of the other side you will have to pay if the case is lost.

PROBABLE AND POSSIBLE RESULTS

If the firm gave you an estimate of the probable or possible result, ask that this information be repeated in a letter. If a firm won't repeat in a letter what they told you orally, you should be concerned that the firm might have engaged in overselling to get you and your case. If the firm did or did not make any predictions as to outcome, this should be specified in the letter for your mutual protection.

89

NONBINDING ARBITRATION

Ask the firm to agree to use nonbinding bar association-sponsored arbitration before any litigation in the event of a fee dispute. Nonbinding arbitration is usually the cheapest and fastest way to find out what is likely to happen in the event of a litigated dispute between you and the firm. There may be times when this approach would not be the best way to go. Ask the lawyer to discuss with you, and include in the fee agreement, what the two of you should do if you have a difference of opinion in the future.

DEFINITION OF RETAINER

Define the word "retainer." Identify whether the "retainer," if there is one, is a minimum nonrefundable fee or just a deposit to be refunded if not used. Lawyers are often very sloppy in clearly identifying what the word "retainer" means.

IDENTIFICATION OF WHO WILL WORK ON THE CASE

Identify in the fee agreement which lawyers and nonlawyers will work on your case. Be careful of a firm that wants to hand you over to whomever has nothing more important to do on the day your case requires attention. You may find yourself with a changing string of lawyers in a firm who know nothing about the case or about you, but are expected somehow to represent you adequately. You may pay again and again to educate lawyers to the facts of the case when you've already paid money to other lawyers in the firm to learn the case. Demand an identification of those lawyers and nonlawyers who will be working on the case. Don't pay for service by people not listed in the agreement, unless you are willing to go along with a system where lawyers learn on your case, possibly at the expense of the outcome. If the firm won't identify by name the two, three, or four lawyers who will work on your legal matter, you should seek another firm.

PROVISIONS FOR HANDLING FUTURE PROBLEMS

What happens if you can't pay as agreed? Will the firm stop working and abandon you if you can't pay costs or fees as agreed?

PROVISIONS FOR CHANGING LAW FIRMS

What happens if you fire the law firm? Do you have a right to fire the law firm after it has begun work? If so, how will its fee be calculated? Does it simply get paid for work done to the moment of discharge (and the necessary work to legally disengage)? Will the fee be calculated at an hourly rate, or by an award or division of fees to be calculated at an hourly rate, or by an award or division of fees as determined by a court, or will you face litigation with the firm over the fees to which it is entitled? This is a serious problem where a firm represents a client on a contingency basis and then the client wants to change lawyers. The client may end up owing two full legal fees. Be sure the agreement answers these questions. It would be reasonable for the law firm to put a clause in the fee agreement making its claim for fees into a lien on the money involved. In that way, the firm would have a priority on getting paid before the recovery was dissipated.

The fee agreement should cover whether the client may change lawyers after the work is started. Generally, a client may change lawyers rather easily at the beginning of a case. However, the client may have to pay the first lawyer for what he or she did or spent.

Some cases require a minimum fee for the lawyer to accept the case. The client may or may not be stuck paying the first lawyer's minimum fee and the second lawyer's entire fee. In some cases, the lawyer may have to prove why it is reasonable to keep the minimum fee. In other cases, the client will be obligated to honor the agreement with the first lawyer.

If a client wants to change lawyers, the client should do so as early as possible, before the lawyer is too deeply involved in the case. Occasionally, even when a client is happy with the first lawyer, something happens to make the client want to change lawyers. As the case goes further and further along, it becomes not only more difficult to change lawyers but also more expensive. It is often necessary to pay a second lawyer to learn what the first lawyer already knows about the facts and the law of the case. You will be paying both lawyers for the same work.

Will a second lawyer be willing to take the case of a client who already has a lawyer? In general, lawyers don't like to take on cases or clients where they are the second or third lawyer the client has come to. (See "Anticipating Cases and Clients Lawyers Don't Want" in Chapter 7 of this book.) Having multiple lawyers often is a sign of a difficult client or a problem case. For example, by some estimates more than half of all divorce clients want to change lawyers. Often in a divorce case, or in a serious criminal case, the client—not being in his or her normal setting—simply never can be satisfied or happy with what has happened to his or her life.

Clients sometimes blame a lawyer or the legal system for their poor state of affairs. Sometimes, a client can't change lawyers because a lawyer willing to be the second or third lawyer can't be found. Even if another lawyer can be found, the additional legal fees may not be affordable. If a client is truly unhappy with the choice of lawyer, eventually he or she may find a second lawyer who is willing, perhaps even eager, to take the case. It is imperative because of possible double fees, that any decision to change lawyers be made as soon as possible at the beginning of the matter.

Paraphrasing the late Sam Walton, creator of Wal-Mart Stores, "Go down to the office. Check them out. See what they've got to offer, see how they treat you, and decide for yourself if you want to go back."

CHAPTER 7

Understanding How Lawyers Practice

SPECIALIZATION

Do lawyers and law firms "specialize"? In a word, yes. All lawyers and law firms "specialize," even though they don't necessarily use that word. No lawyer or law firm can possibly keep current or practice in all areas of law. Even lawyers who claim they are in general practice specialize. Depending on who is doing the counting, there are between 1,000 and 1,500 different descriptions of legal practice areas. This book alone contains nearly 1,000 possible descriptions of law practices.

Unfortunately, unlike medicine, not all lawyers in America have clear definitions of what "specialization" means. In some states, no lawyer can call himself or herself a specialist in any area of law. In other states, any lawyer may call himself or herself a "specialist" with no testing, qualification, or screening. Yet in some states only board-certified specialists can call themselves specialists after testing and experience. To identify a specialty, lawyers in some states can say they "specialize in" some area of law without saying they are a specialist. In other states, lawyers can say "practice limited to," "practice devoted to," "practice emphasis on," "practicing in," "areas of practice," or "engaged in the following fields of practice." Some lawyers can also use the adjective "professional," as in "professional bankruptcy lawyer." Guidelines are being developed by various states, but there is confusion and inconsistency as to when and where a lawyer may properly call himself or herself a "specialist." Unfortunately, you simply have to ask an individual lawyer whether or not he or she is a specialist. If the lawyer answers yes, you need to ask if he or she is board certified. It is an unfortunate fact of life that when a lawyer says he or she specializes in an area of law, it could mean anything from their having many years of education and training—with review by a board—down to their having absolutely no experience in the area of law. Perhaps the lawyer is only interested in the specialty, or once took a course in that area of law while in law school.

In this book, I use the word *specialist* broadly to include any lawyer who has handled enough cases in a given area to feel competent to handle that specific area of law. I've made no attempt to comply with the definitions of any particular state. Some lawyers say that if you've never handled an area of law but want to take the case, call yourself a general practitioner. Or, that if you've handled the area of law one time, you can call yourself an expert. Or, if you've handled the area of law more than once, you can call yourself a specialist. You must leave it to the individual lawyer's definition and integrity in answering your question, "Are you a specialist in this type of case?" or "Do you specialize in this kind of law?" You may feel more comfortable asking the lawyer, "Are you experienced in handling this kind of case?" rather than asking if the lawyer is a specialist.

Should you pick your own specialist? In almost every case, you're better off to allow a lawyer to pick a specialist for you than to try to find one on your own. A lawyer is better qualified to determine whether or not you need a specialist, in which areas of law you need a specialist, and which lawyer or firm is the best one available for you.

Most law firms will recommend two or three possible firms. They give you more than one name for several reasons, including the possibility the right chemistry will not exist between you and the first specialist you meet with. If the referring firm only gives you one name, ask for a second or third name immediately.

Loyalties of Specialists

Have a frank discussion with the specialist as soon as possible in the case. Tell the specialist you are expecting that he or she will always act in your best interests regardless of the best interests of the firm that recommended you.

Specialists depend on other lawyers to refer them business. They do not want to say or do anything that might reflect negatively on the referring firm for fear of losing future referrals. Accordingly, a specialist might remain silent if he or she sees the referring firm has done something or is doing something that is not in your best interests. The lawyer might even affirmatively try to protect the referring firm or cover up for it. It will not be a pleasant conversation, and you can say something to this effect: "I have a good, secure relationship with the referring firm. You don't have to worry about damaging the relationship. If you see something you think might be wrong, I want to know about it, even if it might reflect badly on the referring firm. Does this cause you a problem?" The answer should be an immediate, unhesitating, unquestioning "no." If there is hesitation, or if the lawyer says "What do you mean?" or says "Give me an example of what you're concerned about," then the lawyer may be giving you a subconscious message that the referring law firm will be protected even if it is against your best interests. At this point, simply go on to the second or third referral which you received. (If you didn't get more than one name the first time, then you may wish to ask the referring firm for another recommendation or you may wish to find your own specialist.)

If you have to go back later to ask the referring firm for another recommendation, simply say you didn't feel comfortable with the first referred firm. Say that the chemistry just wasn't there for a good long-term relationship. The referring lawyer should have no hesitation in recommending another lawyer. If you can't get a second recommendation, then you may have to start the process over again or find your own specialist.

There is no reason for you to act paranoid and suspect that all lawyers are in some sort of conspiracy to protect one another at the expense of our clients. It is simply human nature to send clients to those professionals who think enough of you to send you clients. Unfortunately, the question is not whether the referred firm is competent, but whether the referred firm will protect you or protect the referring firm if a problem exists or arises. Your referral out may be treated by some lawyers as a commodity to be traded for future or past referrals in. If you feel the referring firm is "hammering" you to use only one firm, you'll have to make your own decision as to whether the referring firm is simply acting in your best interests because they've already chosen the firm they feel is the best firm for you, or if they really don't know a second firm to recommend, or if they only recommend firms which protect their best interests. In most cases, if time and circumstances permit, I would recommend that you keep looking for a different specialist.

I've personally lost some referrals over the years because I frankly told clients that their problem was caused by, or worsened by, the lawyer, accountant, or other person who handled or ignored the problem before referring the client to me.

BASIC QUESTIONS ABOUT LAWYERS AND LAW FIRMS

What Is the Range in Size of American Law Firms?

The organization of U.S. law firms has been transformed since the mid-1970s. New relationships are being tested with varying degrees of success. Although this chapter deals with "average" or "typical" law firm sizes, there may not be any such typical firms. The descriptions here are simply composites of many different firms and communities. For purposes of simplicity, I will start with the smallest of firms and work upward.

Solo Practitioner (or Sole Practitioner)

A solo practitioner is a lawyer with no partners. Such a lawyer may hire any number of lawyers and paralegals as employees, however. It may seem astonishing, but about half of all private-practice lawyers in the United States are solo practitioners.

Small Firms

What would be considered a small firm in one city would be considered a large firm elsewhere. Firms with fewer than ten lawyers are usually considered small. Typically, one-third to one-half of the lawyers are partners and the rest are salaried employees, commonly called associates. Associates normally have little or no voice in firm policy, management, or priorities. Associates have jobs which they are free to quit if they are not happy. In some firms, senior associates (typically with five to seven years' experience) are viewed as potential partners and are given a small voice in management. In small firms, the lawyers all know one another reasonably well and tend to be aware of what the firm's partners and clients are doing.

Medium-Sized Firms

The definition of a medium-sized firm again depends on the locality. My definition of a medium-sized firm is one that has twenty to fifty lawyers. Again, about one-third of the lawyers are partners and can make major decisions about what cases to accept or not to accept. In the medium-sized firm, the lawyers know one another and the clients fairly well, but they tend to practice in departments or practice areas, often unaware of what the firm as a whole is doing with or for a client. Decisions to accept or reject cases and clients typically are made at the departmental level, since the responsibility for making profits is often at that level.

Large Firms

Most lawyers and most clients would consider a firm with 50 to 100 lawyers as being a large firm. Lawyers in 300-lawyer firms look upon 50- to 75-lawyer firms as small. In firms of more

97

than 100 lawyers, the lawyers often don't know one another well, and they don't know the clients of other lawyers in the firm unless the client is a major one or the lawyer works on that client's cases. In a large firm, there are often subdepartments within departments where lawyers practice super-narrow specialties. The narrow specialist you may need may be hidden within some department or subdepartment.

Megafirms

Megafirms usually have multiple branch offices and multiple departments and subdepartments. Lawyers in these firms often don't know all the lawyers in the other departments or other branches. Again, a firm may have just the lawyer you need, but no one in the firm knows it.

A recent trend among law firms of all sizes is for many lawyers to share office facilities with firms of which they are neither partners nor associates. The largest of firms may have lawyers "of counsel" in their office facilities. Small firms and solo practitioners may share facilities and work together without being regular partners or employees of the others.

Are Some Lawyers Incorporated?

Many law firms and individual lawyers are incorporated. Many became incorporated during the 1970s and 1980s when incorporation brought significant tax advantages. In the 1990s, these tax advantages are in many cases marginal or nonexistent, so fewer and fewer lawyers incorporate. Many, like myself, are now unincorporated. Lawyers who are incorporated usually call themselves a "law corporation," "professional corporation," or a "P.C.," standing for "professional corporation," or "P.A.," standing for "professional association." They may have "Ltd." or "Inc." after their name. The owners are called shareholders instead of partners. Such firms have officers and boards of directors. In most if not all states, a lawyer has the same unlimited personal liability for professional competence, regardless of whether he or she is incorporated.

What Is the Difference Between an "Attorney" and a "Lawyer"?

In the United States, there is absolutely no difference between an "attorney" and a "lawyer." The words *attorney, counselor, counselor-at-law, lawyer, attorney-at-law, attorney* and *counselor* all mean essentially the same thing. All of these titles refer to someone who has a license to practice law in the place where he or she uses that title. In the past, lawyers in the English legal system used to be clearly divided between barristers, who argued cases in court, and solicitors, who did not. The distinction between barristers and solicitors has disappeared, or is rapidly disappearing, in England as it already has in those countries such as the United States and Canada that basically copied the English system.

You should be aware that an attorney-at-law or an attorney is a lawyer. A person acting under a "power of attorney" or an "attorney in fact" may not be a lawyer, however.

In some places outside the United States, the word *attorney* is considered an unfavorable word to identify a lawyer. The term has a connotation that the lawyer who insists on being called an attorney is a shyster or someone hustling for clients. I personally tend toward calling myself a lawyer who has a law office, but I could also call myself an attorney who has a law office. But in choosing or seeking a lawyer, don't be concerned about the label used to identify the lawyer.

How Should a Lawyer Be Addressed in a Letter?

You have several choices of how to address a lawyer in written correspondence. A male lawyer properly can be addressed as "Mr. John Doe, Attorney-at-Law," or as "John Doe, Esq." (Note that you omit Mr. if you use Esq.). "Esq." is an abbreviation for "Esquire," an English term originally used for men with land or education. A female lawyer can be addressed as "Ms.," "Miss" or "Mrs." Mary Doe, Attorney-at-Law. Whether you wish to use "Ms.," "Miss," or "Mrs." depends on your own local custom and preference.

Some female lawyers also prefer to be addressed as "Esq." Other female lawyers object to this formerly masculine-only form. This is an area in a state of flux, and, accordingly, I personally offer no advice other than to use good taste and common sense to do what you feel is appropriate. If the lawyer involved, male or female, has a strong personal preference as to how he or she is addressed, the lawyer should let you know so that you'll have a better professional relationship. There's no harm or insult in calling the lawyer's office and asking the receptionist or secretary what is appropriate in that office.

If you don't know whether the lawyer is male or female, simply omit any reference other than "Attorney-at-Law" after the name (for example, "J. T. Smith, Attorney-at-Law"). The letter's salutation could say "Dear J. T. Smith."

If the lawyer is or was a judge, it is acceptable to call the lawyer "The Honorable John Doe, Attorney-at-Law." In some parts of the United States, all lawyers are called "Honorable," whether or not they were ever a judge. This is purely a local custom. In some parts of the United States, all attorneys are addressed simply as "Attorney" Smith or "Attorney" Jones.

Don't be overly concerned or worried about using the wrong title. If the lawyer is intelligent and experienced, the lawyer will realize that people in different areas of the United States have different customs. The lawyer won't be offended, think less of you, or be overly concerned if you use a form of address other than that which the lawyer might prefer.

How Should a Lawyer Be Addressed in Conversation?

It is always appropriate to call a male lawyer "Mister." Female lawyers should be addressed according to the local professional standards of business and courtesy where the lawyer practices, if you know. If you're uncertain, address the lawyer as you would where you live or do business.

In some communities, lawyers are called "Attorney" Smith, regardless of gender. In some communities all lawyers are called "Judge." As indicated previously, there's no harm in asking the receptionist or secretary what is appropriate in a particular law office before speaking to the lawyer.

As with other professional relationships, you should not call a lawyer or member of the firm's staff by their first name unless invited to do so.

As with written communications, if the lawyer involved has strong preference concerning the form of address in conversation, that lawyer should let you know rather than make you guess.

Is a Law Degree Enough to Practice Law or Say One Is a Lawyer?

In most states, a law degree does not carry with it the right to practice law. In some states, graduates of some law schools in that state can automatically get licensed to practice upon application, but a law degree does not give the person holding it the right to practice law or to say he or she is a lawyer. When someone says they "have a law degree" rather than that they "practice law," the probability is that they are not licensed lawyers.

What Does "Admitted to Practice" Mean?

"Admitted to practice" means that the person has a legal right to practice law in the state or states where admitted. "Admitted to practice" means a person has a license to practice law in a particular state or before a particular court.

If a Lawyer Is Admitted to Practice Before a Federal Court in One State, Does That Mean They Can Practice Before Federal Courts in Other States?

Absolutely not. Permission or admission to practice in the federal courts of one state does not carry with it the right to practice in the federal courts of any other state. In general, a lawyer who can practice in one state would have to get admitted to the state courts of the second state before getting admitted to the federal court of that state. Sometimes, an out-of-state lawyer will be allowed to participate in a single case if a local lawyer accepts responsibility for the case. This is done on a case-by-case, judge-by-judge basis.

Can a Lawyer from One State Give Advice and Practice Law in Other States?

Generally, no. Every state requires people to apply for the right to practice in that state court, and that permission is good only for those courts. It is not permission to practice before any other state or federal court. Similarly, a license to practice before one federal court in a state is not valid for practicing before any other federal court in the same state. Every federal court requires a separate admission. My license to practice before the Supreme Court of the United States is good only in the Supreme Court of the United States. It is not permission to practice in any other state or federal court. Generally, once a lawyer is admitted to practice before a federal court in a state, the other federal courts in that one state make it easy to get licenses. On the other hand, a license to practice before a federal court in one state normally is of no value outside that state.

Can My Spouse Be My Lawyer in Court?

If your spouse is a lawyer admitted to practice before that court, he or she may represent you before that court.

Can I Be My Own Lawyer?

Theoretically, the law allows you to represent yourself. In various courts, this is sometimes called "pro se," "pro per" or "in propria persona." Quite frankly, most judges do not like people representing themselves—for a number of reasons. Not knowing the law or the legal system will cause a huge waste of the court's time, including the judge's, the clerk's, the bailiff's, the court reporter's, and that of everybody else involved in the case. Some judges will feel sorry for people without a lawyer and may try to help them out, especially when they are against a large corporation and it is obvious that they can't afford a lawyer. Other judges will just get angry over the time being wasted and tend to rule against the person without a lawyer. Naturally, a client can normally represent himself or herself in small-claims court.

In criminal cases, where substantial fines or jail time are possible, the judge may force the defendant to have a lawyer, whether or not the defendant wants one. If the defendant appears to be of at least average intelligence and experience, a judge in a criminal case, especially smaller cases such as traffic violations, may allow a person to proceed without a lawyer.

In my opinion, a person with a legal problem should always get legal advice. Not having legal advice is like playing cards for money in a game where you don't know the rules and the other players do. Lawyers often say of themselves, "The lawyer who represents himself has a fool for a client." Lawyers get legal advice when they have a legal problem; so should nonlawyers.

What Is the Difference Between "the Judge" and "the Court"?

Sometimes lawyers say "the judge" did something; at other times they say "the court" did something. Which is correct? Both are correct. Lawyers sometimes use the two terms interchangeably. Obviously a judge is a person and does things. The court is the governmental agency within the judicial system. The place where the court does its business is called the courtroom. A lawyer might say that the judge came to a decision, that the court came to a decision, that the judge held (decided), or that the court held a certain way. Lawyers sometimes loosely refer to the judge as "the court."

Lawyers sometimes say that the court is located in a city or at an address.

Is court always held at the same location? The lawyers are referring to where the permanent offices of the court are located. When lawyers say that the court "sits" at a city or place, they are referring to where the court is holding hearings, taking evidence, or listening to argument. Some have their headquarters or permanent offices in one city but sit at different cities for the convenience of witnesses, the parties, lawyers, and others. Lawyers say that the court is "riding circuit" when it holds hearings outside of the city where it is headquartered.

What Does "Of Counsel" Mean?

A lawyer may tell you he or she is "of counsel" to a firm, or you may see this designation on a firm's letterhead or a listing of its lawyers. The term "of counsel" has many different meanings, depending on the arrangement between the firm and the lawyer. Because of the many different meanings, the American Bar Association has tried, without universal success, to issue some rules, but these may not apply in every state and therefore should not be relied upon.

In general, "of counsel" is more negative than positive. It means that the lawyer is not a partner, associate, or employee of the law firm. It normally means there is some sort of "arrangement" between the lawyer and the firm whereby the lawyer works only on specific cases with the firm. The lawyer may handle cases that have nothing to do with the firm and the firm may handle cases that have nothing to do with the lawyer. The lawyer normally brings in the firm when the case is too big or complex for the lawyer to handle without help. The firm brings in the lawyer when it needs the lawyer's expertise, reputation, or connections. From your point of view, you want to know whether you are engaging the "of counsel" lawyer, the firm, or both. If you are dealing with an "of counsel," or if an "of counsel" is going to be brought into the case, ask the lawyers to state in writing who is handling your case and who is responsible for getting the job done.

ANTICIPATING CASES AND CLIENTS LAWYERS DON'T WANT

My reason for including this section is to prepare you for a possible cold shoulder or bad reception when you contact a law firm with certain types of cases or positions. Even though your case or legal inquiry is bona fide and the law firm can earn a good fee, you may have difficulty finding a good law firm even willing to talk to you or meet with you. If you have one of the cases described in this section, your best bet is to tell the law firm you are calling that you are seeking a specialist in the type of case. With more than a million lawyers in America, someone will want the case. In fact, some lawyers actually love to handle the cases and clients described below. Some lawyers specialize or concentrate in these cases and welcome them. You will save yourself a lot of aggravation and wasted time if you seek law firms who want these cases.

Landlord-Tenant Cases

Lawyers don't like landlord-tenant cases because the clients usually hate to pay the law firm for the work it is doing. Landlords have to follow a legal process designed to protect tenants. The legal fees can be significant. Landlords hate to pay good money to evict a tenant who often is delinquent in paying rent, is damaging the premises, or is causing other tenants to leave. The landlord considers all money spent as throwing good money after bad. A landlord is never happy over the bill. This type of work often engenders ill will between the client and the lawyer. If you are a landlord, you should consider using eviction lawyers recommended by or hired by apartment owners' associations, or else learn how to do it yourself, using the manager.

For their part, tenants often have no money to pay either rent or legal fees. They blame the landlord for insisting on money when they just don't have the funds to pay the rent. Certainly rent is often a higher priority with them than legal fees, and someone who can't pay rent is a bad candidate to pay legal fees. If you are a tenant, find out whether your community has a consumer agency that will use its services to get a tenant more free rent by dragging the case out in the courts for awhile. These agencies are also trained to recognize the times when a tenant has a meritorious defense. They may even find that the tenant is entitled to money for some mistake or misdeed on the part of the manager or the owner. If you are the tenant and think you might have a meritorious claim, be sure you tell the lawyer or

105

the person screening the lawyer's calls. Unless the law firm does a lot of tenant work, it may not recognize a valid tenant claim or want to represent a tenant in a dispute against a landlord.

Hurt Feelings Cases

Lawyers generally don't like to accept or handle hurt feelings cases, such as libel, slander, barroom brawls, and assault and battery cases. In hurt feelings cases the wrongdoer was wrongful but there is difficulty in obtaining monetary compensation for the injured party because the defendant has no insurance or ability to pay. In many hurt feelings cases the injured party recovered quickly from any physical harm leaving only hurt feelings and no monetary damages.

To get a lawyer to accept hurt feelings cases or even to talk to you, you must show that your injuries were substantial, provable, and monetary and that the other side can pay if it loses. Alternatively, if you have serious injuries and are willing to pay money out of your pocket to prove that you were right, let the lawyer know as soon as possible and you'll have a better chance of finding a lawyer to represent you. A lawyer will almost always meet for a consultation with someone who is seriously injured to review the facts and advise the client.

Vengeance Cases and Cases without Legal Merit

Lawyers value their reputation with judges and other lawyers as well as their reputation with clients. A law firm with a good reputation can often get a client a better result than a law firm with a bad reputation. Lawyers and clients can be sanctioned (penalized with monetary awards against them) for starting or maintaining cases without merit. In addition to the risks of sanctions, the lawyers and their firms risk loss of reputation when they accept or prosecute cases with no legal merit. After the initial flurry of legal action, clients in these cases often lose interest in their own cases and refuse to cooperate with the lawyer or to pay their bills. Thus, you shouldn't be surprised that lawyers typically don't want these cases.

If your case appears to be without merit or only for vengeance, be sure to explain to the potential firm that you honestly feel the case has merit and that you are so serious about the case that you are willing to pay the lawyer in advance into a trust account for work to be done. This will increase the likelihood of the lawyer or firm consulting with you and accepting your case. If you have difficulty finding a lawyer because the case is simply too small to prosecute economically, consider small-claims court. (See the section in Chapter 3 on "Using a Small-Claims Court as an Alternative to Finding and Using a Lawyer.")

Cases Where There Have Been Prior Lawyers

When a case has had prior lawyers, a new lawyer will be concerned about the case being without merit or that the client was noncooperative or that the client was not paying for the services rendered. Be ready to anticipate this concern and be ready to explain why you want to change lawyers.

Clients Who Badmouth Prior Lawyers, the Legal System, or the Legal Profession Generally

If you are considering suing a lawyer or firm, you should be consulting with a firm that specializes in legal malpractice. If you are not considering suing a law firm or lawyer, you should be careful about badmouthing lawyers because you'll simply scare off the next lawyer.

Most lawyers are rightfully concerned that people who are unhappy with lawyers and the legal system will eventually be unhappy with them. No lawyer wants to start a relationship that is likely to end badly. Unless you are consulting with a lawyer who specializes in legal malpractice, you'll be better off not ranting and raving about your dislike of the legal system. You certainly have a right to express your dissatisfaction and you should do so, but you should do so in a calm, intelligent manner. Don't allow your unhappiness to mask any underlying meritorious legal position.

107

Cases Where Clients Can't or Won't Pay in Full for What They Want or Need

Criminal cases, bankruptcy cases, family law and representation of defendants in debt collection cases are common examples of cases where clients often don't pay their lawyer in full. It is foolish for you to spend time and money starting something you can't afford to finish. Neither you nor the law firm wants to abandon a case which is unfinished. Ethical law firms will not abandon a client or case for nonpayment of fees if the abandonment would prejudice the client or case. The firm won't be happy or enthusiastic about doing work for free and will try to get out of the representation if they can.

To prevent being stuck on a nonpaying case, the firm may refuse to begin work or to accept a client unless the client can assure the firm of payment in full. An offer to pay the fee or most of it in advance into the firm's trust account will alleviate the firm's concerns and will get you a much better reception. If you can't do this, consider turning to the public defender system, the legal aid system, or other agencies. Bar associations' lawyer referral services can often direct you to the proper agency as an alternative to using a lawyer.

Clients Who Are Religious Fanatics

If you honestly believe God or fate sent you to the lawyer, keep your thoughts to yourself until the case is over and you wish to express your thanks in addition to paying the final bill. Religious fanatics sometime have track records of not paying their bills and not cooperating with their lawyers. It is not realistic to expect your lawyer or firm to have the same fervor as you do about your religion as applied to your case. If you have strong convictions about combining your religious beliefs and your legal affairs, try getting a recommendation from your church leader, or choose a lawyer from your congregation. (See the section in Chapter 4 on "Finding the Right Lawyer through Piety.")

Clients Who Are Unwilling to Come into the Office

Potential clients who won't come into the office for a face-to-face meeting are not likely to be well received. Lawyers don't want to start or maintain a professional relationship with someone they've never met. Your appearances may be a factor in whether or to what degree your case will be deemed meritorious. Lawyers equate refusal to meet them with having a non-meritorious case or being an uncooperative client. Naturally, lawyers make exceptions for injured, disabled, or elderly clients when appropriate. In those cases a lawyer may be willing to make a "house call" or to send out a nonlawyer to get the necessary information.

Clients Who "Don't Care about the Money"

Don't tell a lawyer: "Its the principle, not the money. You can have all the money." Lawyers are concerned when they hear these words, as they suggest the client is so angered or so emotional that they have lost the ability to be practical concerning the problem. This type of client often becomes uncooperative with their own case, believing that all economic incentive should be with the lawyer and the lawyer should do everything without help from the client.

If you don't care about the money, that's your privilege. But, to avoid making the lawyer concerned, be quiet about your lack of concern—at least until the case is over. You can always give any money you are awarded to charity.

CHAPTER

Evaluating Lawyers' Qualifications

EDUCATION

How Are American Lawyers Educated?

The United States of America is a country of fifty "nations." Every one of the fifty states has its own set of rules. In this chapter, I will present a generalized description.

In almost every state, a lawyer must go to law school before being eligible to take the bar examination. Almost every law school insists on a four-year bachelor's degree from a college or university before allowing a student to enter law school. In practice, however, many law schools, including the so-called prestige law schools, may allow a student to enter law school after only two years of college. Generally, however, they will select applicants with a four-year bachelor's degree before accepting students with only two years of college. Other law schools award the four-year bachelor's degree to the student while the student is in law school, and some law schools allow students to enter and graduate from law school without ever having received a four-year bachelor's degree.

There is no prescribed curriculum of courses required of a person before being admitted to law school. While a student is in college or university, the student is called a pre-law student. Pre-law students major (concentrate their studies) in everything from philosophy to engineering to accounting. Students do not begin to study any law courses until after they enter law school. There are no required undergraduate courses to enter law school. In my opinion, English and writing courses should be required, but this is my opinion and not the system. I personally am appalled by the inability of some young adults to read or write or speak English after four years of high school, four years of college, and three years of law school.

The four years of undergraduate studies ultimately provide lawyers with a varied educational background which they can sometimes use to help their clients. Lawyers who majored in accounting, for example, are usually better able to help clients with business matters. Similarly, engineering or mathematics helps in patent and computer law. Languages, of course, are of value in international law and immigration law. Courses or a major in English are especially valuable because they can help lawyers write and understand documents and correspondence.

Pre-law students normally prepare for an exam called the LSAT (Law School Admissions Test). They normally take the examination during or following their last year of college. The law school admissions committee then considers the applicants' LSAT test score, along with their undergraduate grades, to determine whom to accept. Nonacademic factors, such as the applicant's race, cultural background, amount of contributions to the university, family members who attended the university, etc., also can be significant factors in admissions. There are far more applicants than openings in the nation's law schools. Most law schools receive at least two to three times more applicants than they can accept.

While in law school, students' courses are fairly standardized during the first two years, even though the exact titles of the course may vary somewhat. Commonly taught subjects are contracts, torts, criminal law, constitutional law, real property, personal property, history of the English and American legal systems, common law and code pleading, partnerships, agency, corporations, wills, estates, trusts, family law, future interests, legal research (how to use a law library), and legal writing. Ethics is usually added at the third-year level. There is relatively little choice of courses because these standard courses are usually included in the bar exams given by the various states. Schools want their students to do well on the bar examination because the results are public information and reflect on the school.

During the third year, the student is usually given some freedom to select a few courses of special interest to the student. The variety of optional subjects available usually depends on the availability of a law professor to teach the subject. In addition, students may participate in clinical programs, participate in pro bono public activities, and attend advanced seminars.

Upon graduation, the law student is awarded a law degree. The traditional degree granted to lawyers was the Bachelor's of Law or LL.B. For various reasons, the degree awarded has been changed to Juris Doctor (J.D.). Contrary to public opinion, the law degree and the medical degree of M.D. (Doctor of Medicine) are not graduate degrees, but professional degrees. One does not normally study law or medicine for four years to receive a bachelor's degree, followed by two to four years' study to receive a master's degree, followed by three to five years of study to receive a doctoral degree. However, some law schools do have a program to allow a student to attend an additional year or two and receive a Master's Degree in Law.

The major difference between American legal education and the legal education in other countries seems to me to be the amount of nonlaw study. In other countries, a student leaves high school or its equivalent to enter a university with a faculty of law, or an equivalent teaching staff. The university does not have a separate college or school of law. The foreign student attends the university three or four years and devotes 60 to 80

113

percent of study to law courses taught by professors from the faculty of law. Graduation from the three-year undergraduate institution signals the end of the person's legal education. In contrast, the American student puts in a total of five to seven years, including three years of law courses exclusively.

After more than thirty years of practicing law, I'm not sure whether American lawyers are overeducated in legal and non-legal subjects or whether others are undereducated. The differences in educational preparation show up in the degree to which American lawyers are comfortable participating in the managerial and financial decisions of the client's business affairs. The American lawyer, for better or worse, has a more prominent role in the conduct of people's lives and businesses than his or her counterparts in other countries. Foreign lawyers often function as clerks to type up the papers and don't participate in the negotiations.

How Important Is the Lawyer's Law School?

The lawyer's law school should be almost a nonfactor in choosing a lawyer unless the lawyer received some very specialized training in a very specialized field of law taught only at that law school. Many large firms try to hire graduates of "prestigious" schools in an attempt to impress clients and potential clients with their "stable" of thoroughbreds. I personally attended and studied at UCLA Law, Harvard Law, and The University of Cambridge. I have taught and lectured at more than thirty private and public law schools. I was honored by the American Bar Association and the American Law Institute as the most outstanding post-law school legal educator in the United States. I have found good and bad at every type of institution.

With enough money behind the applicant, or if the applicant is the right (or wrong) color or background, the applicant can go to almost any law school in the world. Very few law schools flunk out students, so no matter how stupid the student is, or how little the student learns in law school, chances are the student will graduate with a law degree. In some states, anyone with a law degree from a local school gets a license to practice, with no testing. Many years ago, when law schools and universities were under less pressure to make profits, classes were smaller and there were fewer schools. Attendance and graduation from some law schools was meaningful in predicting a lawyer's being good because he or she attended a particular law school. Today, attendance at a particular law school doesn't tell you much about a lawyer except that the lawyer somehow got in with money or connections and paid tuition until the degree was mailed.

How Important Is a Lawyer's Class Standing?

Although academic achievement does not equate to common sense or practical life experience, I have found a very high correlation between academic achievement in law school and being a good lawyer. Good class standing is, in my opinion, indicative of excellence. High standing indicates that the lawyer learned well, and the knowledge gained in school can presumably benefit the client. The better students tend to be more creative and better able to quickly identify and isolate important legal factors. This ability seems to last their entire professional life, not just at the beginning of their career. Although there are academic achievers who are simply good test takers, and nothing more, I find in general that students who were high in their class standings are good lawyers. All other things being equal, I would recommend a lawyer who graduated in the top 10 percent from a nonprestigious law school over a lawyer who graduated in the middle or bottom of the class from a prestigious law school. (Understandably, those in the bottom 90 percent and those from the prestigious schools might not agree with me.)

However, in gauging academic achievement, do not rely upon titles such as "Honors," "Provost's List," or "Distinguished Graduate." In some schools, titles are given to just about any graduate who can pay the tuition. If you really care about academic preparation, insist on knowing the size of the class and the lawyer's standing in the class. I personally think you make

115

better use of your time looking for experience in the field of law where you need help rather than wasting time checking out universities, law schools, and class standings.

Are Three Years of Law School Always Required?

Every state has its own requirements for completing law school. In some states, a person can even take the bar examination without a law school degree or education. This is commonly called the "Abraham Lincoln method," after President Abraham Lincoln, who never attended law school. He received on-the-job training as a clerk in a law office before taking and passing the bar examination in Illinois. By my own estimate, 95 percent of all lawyers now practicing in the United States attended and graduated from some law school. In contrast, most foreign lawyers never went to any law school. Only a few of the states allow foreign lawyers to take the bar examination and practice. California is one of the states which allows people to study for the bar exam and pass the bar exam and practice law without having attended a law school, which is one of the reasons California has so many lawyers (165,000 in 1995).

LICENSING

How Are American Lawyers Licensed to Practice?

Each state has its own system of admitting lawyers to practice. Most states require a written examination. In some states, graduates of some local law schools are admitted to practice without their taking a written bar examination. The bar examination normally covers the materials taught during the first two years of law school. Due to the time lag between the second year of law school and the bar exam, most students take some sort of a review course before taking the exam. The bar exam is entirely written, often with multiple-choice questions, and typically lasts two to three days, depending on the state. No demonstration of practice skills is required, and no practical experience is required. In some states, almost everyone passes the bar—as high as 90 percent. In other states, only 50 percent may pass.

Once a candidate has received a passing grade on the bar examination, the state may check into the individual's moral character. The successful applicant typically takes the oath of office as a lawyer before the supreme court of the state. The process of taking the oath is often referred to as being "sworn in." After taking the oath, the person can call themselves an "attorney-at-law" or a "lawyer," or words of similar impact.

Is a License to Practice in One State Valid in Another State?

In general, a license to practice in one state is only good in that state. A few states have reciprocity with one another; that is, they will admit lawyers from selected other states to practice without their taking the local written examination. Again, this is a state-by-state situation.

Is a License to Practice in State Court Valid in Federal Court?

A license to practice in the courts of a state normally makes a lawyer automatically eligible to apply for, and receive, a license to practice in the federal courts of that state only. Some federal courts and agencies, such as tax court, do not require a state license in the state or district where the court holds its hearings.

Do Law Students or Law Graduates Receive Any Practical Experience While in Law School?

In general, there is no requirement that a law student receive any practical experience before graduating. Some law schools may offer a clinical course of some sort to give a law student the opportunity to spend a few hours training in areas such as interviewing or arguing hypothetical appellate cases. But this normally would be optional for the student who has sufficient free time and credits available to take the course. A very few law schools, one being Campbell University Law School in North Carolina, extensively train their students with practical experience in client relations and office management as a prerequisite to graduation. In some other countries, students must serve an apprenticeship (called articling) before they are eligible to take the bar examination.

Which States Have "Specialty Practice"?

The word "specialty" has different meaning to different people in different places. To be technical, the words "specialty practice" usually—but not always—indicate a certification procedure by some sort of certification board. States that recognize "specialty practices" include Arizona, California, Florida, Iowa, Louisiana, Minnesota, New Jersey, New Mexico, North Carolina, South Carolina, and Texas.

In other states, lawyers use different words to indicate the narrowing of practice areas. These words used by lawyers may have absolutely no legal significance as far as education or ability or experience. (See the section on "Specialization" in Chapter 7 of this book.)

Is the Lawyer Admitted to Practice Before the Court, Agency, or Department Where You Need Representation?

Most courts and most agencies have their own rules as to who may practice before them. They also have their own rules as to the manner of presenting information or asking for something.

Many courts and agencies are not very liberal in allowing lawyers or others to waste their time and their resources. A lawyer unfamiliar with their rules can prejudice the client's case by angering the judges or board members because the paperwork was not done the way they wanted it done, or because the lawyer didn't properly anticipate the facts, information, or argument required. Accordingly, you should always ask if the lawyer you are considering is licensed or admitted to practice before the particular court or place where you will need help. A lawyer who is already licensed or admitted to practice before the particular court or agency where you need help is more likely to know the rules of the body, the procedures of the body, and what the people are like than one who is not. Being admitted to that body is a plus, and not being admitted can in some situations be a minus. If the lawyer you are dealing with is not so admitted, ask if he or she has an arrangement with a lawyer who is.

The American Laws and Courts

Most foreigners and many Americans are surprised to learn that the United States is a nation of more than fifty little nations called states and that every one of these little nations has its own set of laws. What is legal in one state often is not legal in other states. An act or an agreement may be legal and enforceable in one state and be a crime in another. An act may be punishable by a small fine in one state and by a heavy prison term in another.

Because the laws of every state are different, each state normally has its own bar examination. In most circumstances, a lawyer may only practice in the state where he or she has been admitted to practice. Some lawyers are admitted to practice in more than one state, but you could reasonably question how that lawyer could possibly stay current on the law in more than one state.

Federal Courts

A license to practice in a state court is not simultaneously a license to practice in a federal court. Most people are surprised to learn that a license to practice in one federal court does not allow a lawyer to practice in other federal courts. Accordingly, a New York lawyer who is licensed to practice before the federal district court in New York City is not automatically licensed to practice in any other federal court. That admission to practice in New York City means nothing in Pennsylvania, New Jersey, California, or any other state. Indeed, a license to practice before the federal district court in one city in a state does not carry with it the right to practice before other federal district courts or appeals courts in other cities in the same state.

Every state has at least one federal district court in the state. The more populous states have more than one federal district court in the state. Each one of these federal courts often requires its own system of admission.

Administrative Agencies

There are hundreds, if not thousands of administrative agencies at the state, federal, county, city, district, and other levels. Each of these bodies has its own set of rules as to who can act to represent others before them. Some bodies allow accountants, engineers, corporate officers, employees, spouses, or other family members, in addition to lawyers, to represent people before them.

CHAPTER

The Attorney-Client Hiring Process

CALLING FOR AN APPOINTMENT

The way your first phone call is handled may give you insight into the kind of lawyer or law firm you would be dealing with. When the phone is answered, say something like this:

> My name is [your name]. You don't know me. I have a new case. I was recommended by [person who gave you the name]. I understand that your firm does work in the areas of [name the two or three primary areas of law your inquiry seems to cover]. I would like to talk with [lawyer's name] or with another lawyer about my situation.

You should get immediate attention. The receptionist, if properly trained, will be alert to words like "new case" and "I was recommended." These should be trigger words to get your call to a lawyer immediately. You should be concerned about the competence of that firm to take care of your or your company's legal matter if the staff can't take proper care of a simple telephone call.

If the particular lawyer you want to speak to is not immediately available, don't be upset. Good lawyers are busy. Trial lawyers are frequently in court or in deposition. Business lawyers spend from early morning to late night in endless meetings.

If you are told that the lawyer you called is not in or not available, ask to speak to the lawyer's secretary or assistant. Ask the secretary or assistant when the lawyer will be available to take your call or call you back. If the secretary or assistant doesn't know when the lawyer will be available (a true rarity), then you should be concerned. Ask the secretary or assistant if he or she can help by telling you whether or not the firm accepts or handles certain types of work.

If the secretary or assistant is not helpful, ask for any lawyer. If the most service a firm will give to a prospective new client is to take a message for a "maybe" return call by some underling, then you may be disappointed later; things are apt to get worse. The firm called may have some technical expertise, but you'll always feel like an extra piece of baggage. They will end up treating you with lack of concern over the result of your legal matter.

Insist on talking to the lawyer before making an appointment to go in. Describe your problem as best as you can using the legalese found in Chapter 12 "Foonberg's Glossary of Legal Specialties." There's no point going in and enduring an emotionally grueling interview, only to find out you've reached the wrong lawyer or firm.

Further, if you feel that no one wants to listen to you when you initially call, you probably will always have that feeling.

If you are told that someone will call you back, ask when to expect the call so you can make it a point to be near the phone. If you can't get a straight answer, perhaps you should move to the next law firm on your list.

Unless there is some very special situation, you should be able to get an appointment with a lawyer within forty-eight business hours of your call. The law firm can call you with the appointment date and time. You should be prepared to do your part, which is to be there on time.

If it will help you feel more confident, take a family member or friend along to help you decide upon the lawyer for the case. A person who needs a lawyer for himself, herself, or another is often in an abnormal state or mind: nervous, apprehensive, angry, and unable to make a rational decision or to make a conscious choice in selecting assistance. It may help to bring along a close family member or friend to help you decide. If someone does make calls for you or goes with you, be sure you tell the lawyer that the third person is there to help you present information to the lawyer, and that you have no intention to waive attorney-client privilege by virtue of the third person's presence.

YOUR FIRST VISIT TO THE LAW OFFICE

Your first impression of the law firm will be formed upon entering its reception area and from speaking with the receptionist. The reception room and the receptionist often indicate a caring or an uncaring firm. An attentive receptionist and a proper reception area can be symptoms of a truly professional firm.

A law firm that doesn't properly train and supervise receptionists may also fail to properly train and supervise lawyers, legal assistants, paralegals, word processors, and other staff. A law firm that is unaware of what is or is not happening in the reception area may also be unaware of what is happening on clients' cases or problems.

A caring, professional law firm knows that the receptionist and the reception area are often the client's first impression of a firm. Was the reception area clean and well lit? Were the ashtrays empty or overflowing? Were the periodicals current and neatly arranged?

Was the receptionist friendly? Did the receptionist at least smile at you? Did the receptionist ignore you while you stood there?

If the receptionist was answering telephones in the reception area, was the receptionist telling the lawyers the names of the calling clients so that you also could hear their names? Would you like your name announced as a caller in front of people you didn't know? Mentioning client names in front of non-clients can be a serious breach of ethics. You should be concerned about the firm's level of proficiency in ethics and keeping your confidences.

Did the receptionist tell you that you were expected? (A good firm will notify the receptionist whom to expect). Did the receptionist offer you a drink or was there at least candy on the counter? Clients are often nervous in a lawyer's office, and a dry throat is common.

Was there a conference room near the reception area? If there was such a room and it was occupied, were the drapes or blinds left open so that you could stare at the people inside the room? If so, you can expect people to gawk at you while you're in that room.

Was the receptionist oblivious to your existence while you were waiting? Did you have the feeling that you were an unwelcome intrusion into the steady stream of messengers and telephone calls?

Did the firm personnel smile at you as they passed you in the reception area or did they ignore you as if you were part of the wallpaper?

If you feel welcome in the reception area, you will probably always feel welcomed by the firm. If you feel unwelcome in the reception area, there's a good chance you'll always feel unwelcome in the firm.

YOUR FIRST MEETING WITH THE LAWYER

At your first meeting try to determine whether you and the lawyer or firm you are considering using are really compatible within the area of the service you need. Your relationship with the lawyer may be a brief one lasting for only one meeting, or it could last for several months during a period of negotiation or deal making. A matter that goes to court could last several years. The relationship can last indefinitely if your needs for legal services are ongoing. You may have to trust the lawyer with secrets or information that you wouldn't share with a spouse or parent. You may seek advice or information that will impact how you live the rest of your life.

A comfortable feeling with the lawyer is as important as his or her professional competence. If you are unhappy with a lawyer or firm, you may be afraid to follow the professional advice given, no matter how accurate it is. If you are not comfortable with the lawyer, you may put off contacting the lawyer when it is important for you to do so. The result could be damaging to your legal needs. In sum, if you dislike the lawyer, you will never be happy with the result, the fees, or the service, no matter how good a job the lawyer does.

It probably is an oversimplification to say that you have to like the lawyer or firm and have confidence in them if you are going to get maximum benefit for your investment of time and money. At best, you should like the lawyer. At worst you should not hire or work with a lawyer or firm you really don't like, if you have any choice.

The remainder of this section provides guidelines for deciding whether you've found the right lawyer for your needs. Try to get the answers during your first meeting. Of course, no lawyer or firm is perfect. Additionally, it may help if you put your needs in writing to give to the lawyer when you have no choice as to the lawyer you'll be using. (Examples of situations when you have no choice include: when you must use the company's firm, the insurance company's lawyer, or the in-house counsel.) When you don't have the choice of using a different firm, ask whether you can use a different lawyer in the firm. Be frank. Give the lawyer a photocopy of this section of the chapter. Explain that you want to be able to write a letter of praise when the matter is concluded, not a letter of complaint. Say that if you're happy, you'll recommend others to the lawyer, and if you're not happy, you won't. Any reasonably intelligent lawyer interested in your type of case will want to keep you happy and will try to accommodate you.

Courtesy

Did the lawyer smile and offer to shake hands when meeting you for the first time? A smile and a handshake usually indicate a happy person who is looking forward to meeting you and working with you. In contrast, you don't want a grouch just doing a job with as little effort as possible. Lawyers who hate their job often hate their clients.

Did the lawyer come out to the reception area to meet you? A lawyer who would abandon you to find your own way in a new surrounding, or who will tell someone else to guide you, may do exactly the same thing when you need legal services.

Was the lawyer punctual or late? If late, did the lawyer offer a reasonable excuse for being late, or merely ignore the fact he or she was late? Did the receptionist, secretary, or anyone else apologize for the delay? A lawyer or firm that treats your time as being unimportant, or less important than theirs, at the first meeting is giving you an indication of how it will respect your needs later.

Work Habits

Are you and the lawyer in the same time zone as to work habits? Some lawyers, especially young lawyers, can sleep until 11:00 A.M. and show up at the office at 11:45, still sleepy but ready to go to lunch. They are at their mental best in the late afternoon and early evening. Other people are up with the birds and by 7:00 A.M. have run three miles, showered, and dressed. They are on the phone talking to clients before the office routine and its interruptions begin.

Neither pattern is necessarily bad if it is compatible with yours. However, a difference in work habits that causes minor problems at the beginning of a relationship may lead increasingly to anger and frustration for both the client and the lawyer. It can even have a harmful effect on the outcome of the case. To avoid this, simply ask whether the lawyer is a morning person or not. If the response shows that the lawyer's schedule is not compatible with your own, ask how flexible the lawyer can be. Then ask yourself how flexible you can be.

Personality

Your personality types should be a good fit as well. Are you a domineering or successful person who knows exactly what you want done and simply want the lawyer to "keep it legal"? Are you going to resent it or get angry when a lawyer offers suggestions on how to conduct yourself in ways that are more operational than legal? Are you going to be even angrier when you get a bill for the time spent in making those suggestions? Alternatively, are you the kind of person who will do unquestioningly what the lawyer says to do? Will you welcome unsolicited suggestions on how you might improve your results? Are you willing to pay for these suggestions? Are you somewhere in between these extreme positions? Tell the lawyer what your position is, and see how the lawyer reacts. Can the lawyer function within the framework of what you want? Be wary if the lawyer says the extra nonlegal advice is "free." Someone, somewhere (probably you) will be paying for the time expended in giving unsolicited "free" advice.

Is the lawyer a good listener or egocentric, domineering, and rude? Does the lawyer interrupt you and tell you that he or she really doesn't need to hear everything? Does the lawyer tell you to go home and write everything out, rather than listen to you? (The lawyer will probably never read what you write. At most, the lawyer will give it to a clerk to read and digest. This will deprive you of the lawyer's experience in getting all the relevant facts, including hidden ones that didn't seem obvious or relevant to you.)

Does the lawyer spend a lot of your time regaling you with war stories of past victories? If you enjoy the war stories, and if this is the type of lawyer you want and need, you've hit pay dirt. On the other hand, if this is not what you want or are willing to accept and pay for, a stormy voyage awaits you. Your relationship may end on the rocks, regardless of whether the legal results are good or bad.

Also observe whether the lawyer discusses the facts of the case, or just dwells upon how much better his or her firm is than the firm on the other side? Some lawyers try to oversell their ability or pump the client up to expect large fees by emphasizing the lawyers or law firms involved, rather than the law and facts.

127

This can be a sign of lack of confidence in knowing the subject matter or law in the case before them. It also can be a technique to seek a larger fee. You can get an interesting reaction to this dwelling upon the other side's lawyers by saying, "Well, if you're afraid of the other firm, perhaps I should be interviewing another law firm to represent me." A good lawyer or firm with a lot of experience may or may not know something about the other firm or lawyer. If the lawyer does, a few words of comment are reassuring, but not a long harangue.

Philosophy and Beliefs

If it is important to you that you share the lawyer's personal or political beliefs, you should test the lawyer early on. If you don't like or appreciate what the lawyer stands for, you may not like or appreciate what the lawyer does for you. If you are an extremely conservative person and the lawyer is extremely liberal, or vice versa, it may have an effect on your relations and ability to work together.

In most cases, political and personal differences should be ignored so the parties can stick to the professional problems involved. If you are the kind of person who has to eat, sleep, and breathe your beliefs and transmit them to the whole world, then be sure you are compatible with the lawyer, or that you and the lawyer can sublimate the differences to work together. Failure to face and solve this problem, if it is a problem, can have disastrous results.

Do you and the lawyer have similar attitudes about meeting time deadlines? Some people are procrastinators who need frequent reminders of approaching deadlines. Are you the kind of person who does their best work at the last minute under pressure? On the other hand, do you like to do the work as soon as it has to be done in order to get it reviewed several times to be sure it's perfect and out of the way? Ask the lawyer which kind of person he or she is, or tell the lawyer what kind of person you are. In litigation, which will have many, many time deadlines over a period of years, procrastination can pose problems. Every routine matter can become a super crisis because it was left to the last minute. You may be less appreciative when the work has to be done a second time or a third time because it was wrong or incomplete due to waiting until the last minute. You may be even less appreciative when you get the bills for the extra work.

I once heard a judge chastise a lawyer by asking, "Why is it that your firm never has time to do it right, but you always have time to do it over? Don't your clients get tired of paying for the extra work?" Judges don't like their time being wasted by lawyers who repeatedly seek extensions and even then turn in incomplete work. Eventually it will affect the outcome of the case.

But, if you like watching routine matters become crises due to procrastination because you live that way, then you may be happy to have a firm or lawyer that does things the way you do. Efficient lawyers prevent such problems by making good use of tickler systems and assistants to prevent a routine matter's becoming a crisis due to procrastination, neglect, or overwork.

Tell the lawyer frankly that you do or don't like the excitement and exhilaration of last-minute crisis situations, and ask what the lawyer's own feeling is.

Ask the lawyer why he or she is a lawyer. Note that the questions is not why the lawyer *became* a lawyer, but why he or she *is* a lawyer. You want an upbeat answer. Hopefully, the response will be that law is an intellectually stimulating profession that gives the lawyer the opportunity to help people. If you get answers such as "I can make a lot of money" or "It's all I know how to do," be careful. You can reasonably anticipate that you and your legal problem will be treated with the same lack of enthusiasm as the lawyer feels about the law.

Availability

Ask if the lawyer is available or can be reached nights and weekends, and if you may call at home in an emergency. Ask for the lawyer's home phone number, promising that you won't use it except in an emergency. If the lawyer is willing to be accessible only from 9:00 A.M. to 5:00 P.M., Monday through Friday, be

129

sure to have all your emergencies Monday through Friday from nine to five. Remember that you won't get any help for yourself or a member of your family from this lawyer or this firm in the 77 percent of the week that is outside these hours.

Ask the lawyer if you will automatically get copies of all incoming and outgoing correspondence. The answer should be yes. If the answer is no or that the firm is "selective," ask if the lawyer will undertake in representing you to send you copies of everything. A firm that won't send you copies may be hiding something or may be defective in its internal management.

If you really are not comfortable that you and the lawyer are compatible, then interview another lawyer. You may have to pay for the time of each interview, but it's better to pay a little to find out what you don't want than it is to pay a lot to get what you don't want. You probably won't have to go through more than two interviews to select a firm you feel compatible with.

If you still aren't happy after three interviews, there's a good chance that the problem is not the lawyer but that what you want simply doesn't exist. At that point, you'll have to accept the best you can get from among the firms with which you have met.

What kind of listener is the lawyer? You want a lawyer who knows the law and who knows what to do with your situation. You do not want a lawyer who doesn't know how to listen to you. Lawyers who do not listen to their clients often are simply afraid that if they stop talking long enough for the client to ask a question, the client might ask a question they can't answer.

Lawyers who do not listen to their clients at the outset of the relationship usually don't listen to their clients during the case. They sometimes lose cases for the client because they are so busy self-aggrandizing they don't hear the client when he or she is trying to convey important, relevant information about the case. The client ends up unhappy no matter how the problem turns out. Further, they sometimes alienate judges and juries with their arrogance.

If you are going to hire this type of lawyer, be sure that you write out everything the lawyer didn't want to hear. Mail or otherwise give the information to the lawyer. Then hound the lawyer until you're comfortable he or she has read and knows what's in the writing. You can work with this type of lawyer, but you'll have to work harder to be sure the lawyer doesn't ignore the facts of the case in the quest to prove how great he or she is.

In general, avoid using lawyers, no matter how competent they might seem to be, who don't have a sincere interest in your case and in you. If a lawyer comes across as uncaring, arrogant, and insensitive to your particular needs, the lawyer is probably the wrong one for you. You will never be happy, and the lawyer really won't care whether or not you're happy. Look further.

Confidentiality

Does the lawyer practice confidentiality? Ask what other people the lawyer represents in your industry or geographic area. If you were recommended by a client, pump the lawyer for some information about the other client and his or her case. Ask about the kind and size of case it was. A good lawyer will politely decline to answer. A lawyer who talks about other clients' legal affairs to you will talk about your legal affairs to other clients and even nonclients when given the opportunity.

Look for other signs of the firm's concern for confidentiality. If you can see the names of other clients on files and on documents in the lawyer's office, the lawyer probably won't be sensitive to protecting your confidence.

As mentioned earlier, if the receptionist answers the telephone and announces the names of calling clients in the presence of those in the reception area, then the receptionist may repeat your name in front of people in the reception area when you call. This is a symptom of failure to train staff in confidentiality.

If you hear lawyers discussing their clients' cases in elevators and rest rooms, you can be assured they will also discuss your confidences in elevators and rest rooms.

Be wary of law firms that are sloppy in protecting client confidences. They may also be sloppy in the handling of legal work.

131

If you feel that a law firm seeks publicity by discussing client names and cases and is not careful about protecting confidentiality, then you should go to another firm.

Gender

Is it important that your lawyer be the same gender as yourself? You may be more or less comfortable with a female lawyer or a male lawyer representing you depending on the specific type of case. After many years' of practice, I can tell you of both male and female lawyers I wouldn't want representing me in a case and I can list both male female lawyers I would hire in a minute to represent me. I have promoted males over females, and vice versa.

I personally do not think it is fair or accurate to generalize that males or females are "better" or "worse" for certain types of cases or for juries or judges. I have appeared before female judges who were notoriously anti-male to the point of prejudicing a litigant's case, and I've appeared before male judges who were anti-female to the point of affecting the litigant's case.

If a lawyer tells you that a judge is anti-male or anti-female, the lawyer is probably telling you the truth. It is my experience that gender-biased judges are usually biased against both the lawyers and their clients. You should think twice about using a female lawyer who tells you that a given judge doesn't like women, and additionally about using a male lawyer who says that a judge doesn't like men.

Some clients may feel they need or want a male or a female lawyer to assume an authoritarian, commanding role to guide them, or may feel that only a male or only a female lawyer can truly understand the demands of motherhood or fatherhood and the needs of children. I think such beliefs are erroneous, but if they are your beliefs, by all means look for the lawyer you will have confidence in.

If you are going to feel more comfortable with a lawyer who is male or a lawyer who is female, you should make known your preferences immediately.

Many lawyers go out of their way to let you know their gender either by their name or by a photo. Other lawyers hide their gender by using only initials in their professional listings.

CONFLICTS OF INTEREST

Whole books have been written on what constitutes a conflict of interest. I will try to give just a brief overview of what you should look out for in this regard when selecting a lawyer.

Oversimplified, a conflict of interest exists when there are facts that could impair the loyalty of the lawyer to a client. Thus, a law firm cannot represent both sides of a dispute or negotiation at the same time. If it did, the law firm's loyalty to one person could be impaired by its loyalty to the other person. A lawyer or firm is supposed to use all its skills and resources to help a client. The law firm should not hold back information that one client needs to protect the interests of another client.

Sometimes these conflicts are subtle and indirect. Suppose that a law firm is being paid to defend a claim that cigarettes cause lung cancer. That firm might not be the right firm to prove for another client that cigarettes do cause lung cancer. If two people are insured in the same car accident and there is only enough insurance money for one person, who should get it? If a husband and wife are in the same accident, should the lawyer advise them that, in the event of divorce, the settlement will or won't be divided between them, depending on how the settlement is drawn up? The divorce could occur many years in the future. The potential conflict is not obvious. However, the world being practical, multiple parties often use the same law firm to save legal fees, even though the clients could have independent lawyers.

The lawyer and law firm have an ethical and professional responsibility to disclose actual and potential conflicts of interest. Every law firm has a system of checking for conflicts. The responsibility to be ethical is held by the firm and the lawyer. A law firm cannot keep itself ignorant by one lawyer's hiding information from another lawyer or department in the firm.

A client may waive a conflict of interest. In other words, if there is a conflict, the client must decide whether to proceed to use a firm or go to another law firm for advice before waiving any conflicts. Unethical law firms that are hungry for business sometimes tell a client not to be concerned about potential conflicts. These firms may tell the client to waive the conflict without getting independent advice from another law firm concerning the waiver.

There is no harm in asking a law firm, especially one of the larger firms, if there are existing or potential conflicts of interest that it wishes to disclose. In such situations, you are at the mercy of the law firm to tell the full truth.

If you suspect a conflict, immediately demand reassurances in writing. If you get any double-talk or mumbling, or if the firm tells you don't need independent advice from another law firm, you should immediately consider changing lawyers. If, indeed, there is a conflict and the firm knew or should have known of the conflict, you should demand a refund of all fees paid and a surrender of your entire file without the firm making copies of anything in it. Do not be afraid to ask for help from the bar disciplinary authorities, if necessary. It is important that you get your new firm on the case as soon as possible to protect your interests. Do not sign any release of the initial firm without independent legal advice.

TEN QUESTIONS TO ASK BEFORE HIRING A LAWYER

1. **How many matters like mine have you handled before?**
   - How many cases like mine are you now handling?
   - When was the last time you concluded a case like mine? What were the similarities and differences?
2. **Who will in fact do each stage of the work? You or some other person?**
   - If the case goes to trial, who will the trial lawyer in the courtroom be?
   - How many judge or jury trials has that person tried to verdict? What were the results?

- Who will in fact review all documents to be sure they are correct before asking me to sign?
- Who will be doing the negotiating for me?
- Who will take and defend the depositions?

3. **How much will this cost?**
   - What is the absolute maximum fee?
   - Are you expecting a blank check if the amount of work exceeds your estimate because of unanticipated behavior of the other side or other unanticipated difficulties with the case?
   - How will you keep me updated as to running costs?
   - What happens if I run out of money during the case and cannot pay you?
   - What do I have to pay if the case is lost?

4. **What about additional costs such as payments to experts, court reporters, investigators, economists, accountants, and appraisers?**
   - How much are they likely to cost, and who advances it?
   - Will my case come to a halt if I can't pay these experts in advance?
   - Do all costs come out of my share after your percentage fee? Or are they deducted from the gross recovery before calculating your percentage fee?

5. **How long is this matter likely to take? What is the process and how long should each stage of the process take?**

6. **What will you do if I am not satisfied with the best settlement you can obtain and I am willing to take my chances in court before a judge and jury?**
   - Will you honor my wishes or will you threaten to withdraw and sue me for a fee?
   - If not, will you release me from my agreement and let me go to another lawyer who is willing to go to trial?

7. **Will you keep be updated?**
   - Will you send me a copy of all documents and correspondence in my case, as they are generated or re-

135

ceived, and inform me of your contacts with the other side?

- Will you advise me of deadlines as soon as you know of them?

8. How do I contact you if there is an emergency outside of regular office hours? If you are not available when I call, with whom can I speak about questions or information concerning my matter?

9. What are your office policy and your personal policy on returning telephone calls? Within how much time should I expect a return call?

10. Which bar associations and professional associations do you belong to, and in which ones are you active?

CHAPTER 10

How Businesses and Insurance Companies Find the Right Lawyer

THIS CHAPTER IS intended primarily for corporations and businesses. It is, however, worthwhile for others to read or skim this chapter to see if there are sections or considerations that apply to their own situation and needs.

SIMILARITIES AND DIFFERENCES BETWEEN BUSINESSES AND INDIVIDUALS

Businesses and insurance companies often have some of the same problems as individuals in selecting and hiring the right law firm.

The major problem with businesses and insurance companies is not finding a lawyer since the lawyers and especially the larger law firms aggressively hound corporations and insurance companies to get them as clients. Some clients welcome the solicitations, some find them distasteful, and most businesses and insurance companies are somewhere in between. The major problem of the client is not finding a lawyer, but rather selecting the right lawyer.

Businesses are able to place a greater emphasis on selection than on finding because they normally are more sophisticated and experienced in their ability to classify exactly what they need from a lawyer. Businesses are also more experienced because they have an ongoing need for legal help rather than a occasional need. Businesses have more resources available to obtain recommendations and they are experienced in negotiating their own agreements with a law firm.

When businesses and insurance companies select lawyers there is much more emphasis on controlling costs and treating the entire problem calmly and dispassionately. The emotional and ego elements are not as important to a business as they are to an individual.

POPULAR RECOMMENDATION SOURCES

Businesses rely very heavily on recommendations to select the right lawyer for their legal needs, although they must also be more careful in evaluating recommendations. Present law firms rate very high as a source of recommendations because the present firm understands the client's business and the client's legal needs and lawyers are better qualified to judge the abilities of other lawyers. On the other hand, a law firm may not recommend the most appropriate firm if the present law firm regards the most appropriate firm as being a competitor for all of the client's legal work. The present law firm may recommend a specialty or "niche" firm that cannot handle the client's other legal needs rather than recommend the department or lawyer in a firm regarded as a competitor for the client's total business. The present law firm might recommend a firm in the same city or another city whose principal qualification is that they don't try to steal the clients. The existing firm might even try to dissuade the client from seeking a better qualified or more experienced law firm in order not to appear as being limited in legal ability. The present firm will often undertake work it really shouldn't undertake in an attempt to prevent other law firms from getting exposure to the client.

Judges

Judges often are prohibited from giving recommendations but sometimes can be induced to do so. Their recommendations, when obtainable, may be the best. They see many lawyers and know the good ones.

CPAs and Bankers

The client's CPAs and bankers are probably ranked second and third after the client's present law firms for recommendations. These groups are trusted by businesses. Unfortunately, CPAs and bankers often are not able to truly judge the professional quality of a law firm's legal work.

In routine matters, law firms are fairly similar and professional skill is almost the same in all firms. When the unusual or serious problem arises, the skill level of the lawyer or firm becomes critical, and only another lawyer or a judge is in a position to distinguish firms based on technical skills.

In some cases the client's CPA firm or the client's bank may compete with lawyers for business and, accordingly, may not recommend the best law firm for fear of losing business from the client. Common areas where CPAs and bankers compete with law firms are taxation, wills, trusts, employee benefits, estate planning and litigation management. Since CPAs and bankers compete with law firms for this business, the CPA or the banker may only recommend a law firm which cannot compete for that type of business.

On balance, however, CPAs and bankers can inform clients about the "name" firms in the given area of law or in a given geographic area. CPAs and bankers can pass on to their client their present clients' satisfaction or dissatisfaction with a law firm without really knowing if the law firm is the best for the client's legal needs.

Other Businesses and Trade Associations

A business is very likely to turn to other businesses or to trade associations of similar businesses for recommendations for law firms. The business, however, may be concerned over a "leak" which could be harmful. For example, a business normally might not ask a competitor or trade association for a recommendation to a bankruptcy firm or to a law firm for a grand jury investigation. Additionally, there is frequently a serious problem of conflicts of interest when one law firm represents several different clients who are in the same business or industry. (See the section on "Conflicts of Interest" in Chapter 9.) The problem of conflicts of interest is often ignored or rationalized by larger law firms in order to get and keep business.

Friends, Relatives, Consultants, Directories, and Bar Association Referral Services

Friends, relatives, consultants, directories, bar association referral services, and many of the other sources listed in this book are typically used by businesses only after going through the above described recommendation procedure, or when there is a time urgency.

Lawyer-to-Lawyer Referral Panels

Many bar associations maintain lawyer-to-lawyer referral panels, which are not open to the general public as are other types of lawyer referral services. Lawyers typically volunteer to help other lawyers with clients' legal problems. Lawyers on these panels are not directly seeking business. They are volunteers who want to help other lawyers be sure that the clients get the best possible legal advice even if there is nothing in it for the law firm giving the help. The volunteer law firm on the panel may from time to time get some recommendations or be brought in to associate on a specific problem, but generally they are simply trying to help other lawyers do a good job.

You should consider asking your lawyer to help you by using the services of the lawyer-to-lawyer referral panels. You must, however, first determine your exact legal needs because the lawyer-to-lawyer referral panels are very narrowly defined in terms of the nature of the legal work involved.

The Martindale-Hubbell Law Directory

The Martindale-Hubbell Law Directory is described in great detail in Chapter 4. That section should be read again.

HOW BUSINESSES RESPOND TO HARD SELL DIRECT SOLICITATION FROM LAW FIRMS

Many law firms now hire nonlawyers (and sometimes lawyers) to cold call business clients in an effort to get the prospective clients' legal business away from another law firm. (Cold call refers to telephoning a prospect where there is no preexisting connection or relationship between the prospect being called and the person calling. It is commonly used by stockbrokers and is euphemistically called telemarketing.) The caller will sometimes offer one of many inducements to interest the potential client. Typical inducements are:

1. Inviting a prospect to a firm-sponsored seminar.
2. Offering to do a seminar at the prospect's place of business (sometimes referred to as a "dog and pony show").
3. Offering to put the prospect on a firm mailing list to receive firm mailings.
4. Offering to come over and meet with the client to discuss fees and services available (sometimes referred to as a "beauty contest").
5. Offering to bid for legal work through the request for proposal procedure (RFP).

Some clients are offended and insulted by these hard sell direct solicitations. Some clients regard solicitations as unethical and unprofessional and would never consider using a firm or being identified as the client of a firm that uses aggressive hard sell/cold call solicitations. Those clients are often especially offended when they tell the caller that they are satisfied with their present counsel and the caller continues to harangue them.

I have received reports of law firms hiring outside "consultants" who hire public relations firms to do the calling. The public relations firm then subcontracts the telemarketing to a telemarketing firm that subcontracts with individuals who are often incomprehensible over the telephone and seem to be illiterate as well. The telephone telemarketers sometimes can't even read or pronounce the words in their script as put in front of them on computer screens.

On the other hand, some businesses which are potential clients may regard the legal profession as "just another business" and welcome the opportunity to receive contacts and information and solicitations from a company that appears to really want the business. The hard sell/cold calls may actually be welcome and well received. The potential client may admire aggressiveness in seeking business.

I personally have a low regard for those law firms which would use lawyers or nonlawyers to attempt to interfere with existing attorney-client relationships. That interference may impair the client's receiving the best legal representation by creating doubts in the client's mind about the quality of the representation. The soliciting law firm, through its nonlawyer hustlers, may be willing to sacrifice the client's professional needs to their own economic interests by attempting to create dissatisfaction with the legal advice received from the existing counsel.

If you want and welcome cold call/hard sell aggressive solicitations from law firms or those hired by the law firms, then you should inform the receptionist where to route the calls when they come.

HOW BUSINESSES DECIDE WHETHER TO LITIGATE OR SETTLE A MATTER

Businesses have greater latitude and control over their own legal destinies than do individuals. Businesses can more easily and better control legal costs and have more options with respect to settling disputes.

There are factors that businesses can and must consider that are beyond the scope of individuals. Every business should consider economic and noneconomic factors in deciding whether to litigate or settle a dispute. These criteria should be examined *before* seeking the appropriate lawyer or law firm.

Some of the noneconomic factors may include the time away from business preparing for depositions and trials, spending long hours in lawyers' offices, attending endless meetings to review the case and discovery procedures, and attending the depositions of other persons. There can be bad publicity (or good publicity) egos get ruffled, reputations and careers can be damaged. A business must consider alternative uses and investment of the time and money involved in litigation.

To focus on the question of estimating the economic costs of a case, I have developed a system which can help a business decide whether to litigate or settle a matter and, if to litigate, how to anticipate and control the legal costs involved.

HOW BUSINESSES USE COST ESTIMATE FORMS TO CONTROL LEGAL COSTS

This section is based on a presentation I made to the American Corporate Counsel Association at its annual meeting. While the information is intended primarily for corporate counsel and clients managing legal fees on larger cases, the same format can be used by any government agency, or even by an individual whose control of legal costs is important. Reviewing this section may give you some new approaches to managing a legal matter and may give you some basis for discussing representation with a law firm.

Based on my experiences in serving as an arbitrator and lawyer in fee disputes, on my past experience as a CPA, and on my having practiced law since 1964, I've noted that most clients and corporate counsel fail to think about the cost and importance of a case *before* authorizing settlement or litigation or other solutions. To emphasize, I've found that most clients and corporate counsel fail to set appropriate terms for the engagement of outside law firms *before* selecting the appropriate firm for the particular problem. Unfortunately, clients and corporate counsel too often wait for a catastrophe to happen before asking the questions of themselves—questions that should have been asked *before* the disaster occurred.

The legal fees cost estimate form that begins below will help you focus on how much to budget for a case, and then to decide if an alternative is available. This form will also help show the true costs of a case for the purpose of allocating corporate resources. Although it is not always possible to control or monitor the work and cost of a legal matter, the following system nonetheless will help in many instances to reduce and control costs.

LEGAL FEES COST ESTIMATE FORM ....

1. What are our objectives and the other side's objectives in this case? What do we and the other side want? Check all applicable objectives.

	WE	THEY
Money? (Maximize recovery or minimize costs?)	☐	☐
Minimum Time? (To resolve as rapidly as possible?)	☐	☐
Maximum Time? (To delay as long as possible?)	☐	☐
Vengeance? (To right a perceived wrong?)	☐	☐
Publicity? (A public forum to tell a story?)	☐	☐
Conduct? (To set a precedent to or to force a change in conduct?)	☐	☐
Other? _____	☐	☐

2. Is there an alternative which can give both sides what they want without the expense of litigation?
   - ☐ Face-to-face meeting?
   - ☐ Arbitration?
   - ☐ Mediation?
   - ☐ Contribute money to a charity?
   - ☐ Receive or make an apology?
   - ☐ Other? _____

3. **What is the importance of this case to us?**
   - ☐ Our very existence is involved.
   - ☐ A serious impact on our earnings, either long-term or short-term, is involved.
   - ☐ A monetary or other award for or against us could seriously help or hurt us.
   - ☐ A monetary or other award for or against us would probably not seriously help or hurt us.
   - ☐ A fundamental policy of the company is involved.
   - ☐ The case is a nuisance.
   - ☐ Lack of monetary recovery by us would seriously impact our earnings or position.
   - ☐ Lack of monetary recovery by us would not seriously impact our earnings or position.

4. **Monetary valuation of the case (if we commence the case).**
   - a. Recovery sought (net of offsets) $ _____
   - b. Probable attorney's fees if won $ _____
   - c. Probable interest if won $ _____
   - d. Probable costs if won. $ _____
     -      Total $ _____
   - e. Probability of winning   _____ %
   - f. Probability of collection   _____ %
   - g. Dollar value of case if won = Total × (e) × (f) = $ _____

5. **Monetary valuation of the case if lost.**
   - a. Probable median judgment (principal) if lost $ _____
   - b. Probable attorney's fees if lost $ _____
   - c. Probable interest if lost. $ _____
   - d. Probable costs if lost $ _____
     -      Total $ _____
   - e. Probability of losing   _____ %
   - f. Dollar value of case if lost = Total × (e) = $ _____

6. **Estimated costs and resources required. (Subject to revision and modification.) Be sure to include fringe costs in indirect costs hourly rates.**

   Direct Costs
   - Outside counsel—attorney's cost $ _____
   - Outside counsel—non-attorney's cost $ _____
   - Deposition reporter costs $ _____
   - Photocopy costs $ _____
   - Outside expert's cost $ _____
   - Other direct costs $ _____

Indirect Costs—Legal

Senior corporate counsel	$ _____	per hour
Intermediate corporate counsel	$ _____	per hour
Junior corporate counsel	$ _____	per hour
Paralegals	$ _____	per hour
Other indirect legal costs	$ _____	

Indirect Costs—Corporate

Senior executives (officers and directors)	$ _____	per hour
Department heads	$ _____	per hour
Intermediate personnel	$ _____	per hour
Accounting personnel	$ _____	per hour
Data processing personnel	$ _____	per hour
Other indirect corporate costs	$ _____	

Other Costs

Other internal and external costs and resources required	$ _____

For each of the foregoing categories, it will be necessary to accumulate actual historic costs and to make best estimates. A 12- or 14-columnar format is recommended, but space limitations don't permit it to be fully spread out on this page. The cost amounts can be maintained manually or with a simple computer spreadsheet. The following format may enable the reader to visualize the finished product.

	Costs to Date	Estimated Minimum Costs to Complete	Estimated Maximum Costs to Complete
Direct Costs	$_____	$_____	$_____
Indirect Costs—Legal	$_____	$_____	$_____
Indirect Costs—Corporate	$_____	$_____	$_____
Other Costs	$_____	$_____	$_____
Totals	$_____	$_____	$_____

7. Company participation in case—personnel probably required (availability of nonlegal company executives and staff for interviews and discovery).

a. Mary Jones, Treasurer
b. John Smith, Executive Vice President
c. Arthur Doe, Vice President, Engineering
d. Jane Roe, Vice President, Personnel
e. William Thomas, District Sales Manager
f. Tom Slick, Salesman, Former Employee
g. Slip Stick, Engineer, Former Employee
h. Joe Schtick, Marketing Director, Former Employee

	Has Been Contacted	Has Not Been Contacted	Easily Available	Available With Difficulty	Not Available	Estimated Hours Required
7a.	_____	_____	_____	_____	_____	_____
7b.	_____	_____	_____	_____	_____	_____
7c.	_____	_____	_____	_____	_____	_____
7d.	_____	_____	_____	_____	_____	_____
7e.	_____	_____	_____	_____	_____	_____
7f.	_____	_____	_____	_____	_____	_____
7g.	_____	_____	_____	_____	_____	_____
7h.	_____	_____	_____	_____	_____	_____

HOW BUSINESSES AND INSURANCE COMPANIES USE THEIR FEE AGREEMENTS TO CONTROL BILLING ABUSES

Since a business or insurance company is normally better able to negotiate its engagement terms than an individual, the business can and should put provisions into its fee agreements which can reduce or eliminate unintended billing abuses. I don't wish to infer that billing abuses are intentional or malicious or that law firms are cheating clients. Billing abuses by a law firm are normally not intentional. Law firms sometimes lose control of the management of a case. It is common for a law firm to react to client emergencies, causing disruption in the management of cases and personnel. People and resources are reassigned and juggled on a last-minute crisis basis. Priorities get shifted and often cases get lost in the shuffle. This is a normal event in law firms and it should be anticipated and expected. Clients, however, should not be subject to billing abuses when this occurs.

Listed below are some of the more common abuses which can be anticipated and controlled in the fee agreement between the business and the law firm and which should be considered *before* using the law firm for a matter.

1. The law firm uses the case as a revolving door for new associates to receive training. The client or corporate counsel should specify which lawyers they are willing to pay for to work on the matter. That is, the firm can use any number of lawyers

147

on the case to get legal education, but the client pays only for pre-approved lawyers.

2. The law firm bills for multiple conferences between several lawyers who have multiple conferences on a daily basis. General counsel should insist on a description of the conferences (who, when, what, why, where, etc). Requiring a full description of conferences will cut down both the number of conferences billed for and the length of the conferences. Too many conferences with vague descriptions may indicate inexperienced or unsupervised people on the case.

3. The law firm should require that a designated partner review and sign off on the bill before it goes to the client. Insisting on a personal review by a responsible person will reduce the number of "computer errors" and unexplained charges in the bill.

4. The law firm should designate who is going to take and review depositions. In some cases, personnel used are too expensive for routine depositions. In other cases they are too inexperienced. The law firm must use its best judgment, but the client should know whether associates or partners or paralegals are going to review depositions on the particular case. The law firm also should indicate whether it is buying electronic deposition disks or media from court reporters for more economic assistance in deposition analysis.

5. On major photocopy matters, the law firm should have a policy (and let the client know) regarding when it uses internal people at law office rates, when it sends the work to commercial copy services, and when the client is to do the copying. This policy should be communicated to the client.

6. Firms often pour time and resources into a case far out of proportion to the value of the case. The client should explain to the law firm (after filling out forms and after consultation with the firm) what the budget for legal fees and costs will be for the specific matter.

7. The firm's bills are late, causing the client to run up big legal fees without knowing about it until well into another

month's billing. The client should insist on periodic, timely billing.

8. The firm fails to advise the client when unanticipated legal fees may make the case uneconomical. The firm and corporate counsel should pre-establish "flash points" when the case will be reviewed and discussed by counsel and the firm (for example, when legal fees reach 15 percent of the amount involved in the case or when some procedural point in the case is reached).

9. The firm should require lawyers who are new to the case to identify clearly how much time they spent learning the facts or law of the case. If other lawyers in the firm already knew the facts, but didn't do the work, the client should not be charged for the unnecessary duplication.

10. The firm is simply the wrong firm for the legal matter. Firms will sometimes do work for a good client that they shouldn't handle. The firm may be afraid of upsetting the client or be afraid the client may be exposed to a "competitor" if another firm is suggested. The firm will waste a lot of its time and the client's money learning an area of law another firm knows well. The client should ask the firm to make it known in the fee agreement the firm's level of experience in the area of law. As such, the client knows what they are getting.

11. The firm is often too large or too small for a particular case. Small cases often get overworked by lower-level lawyers in big firms. The lawyers may have a poor attitude toward "small" cases. This abuse can be prevented by agreeing to a maximum fee for the particular matter.

12. The most common error made by law firms is to not ask corporate counsel or clients what they are expecting from the law firm. The firm and the client sometimes start treating every case as being fungible, without making allowances for treating cases differently because of the sum involved, the company personnel involved, or the importance of the case to its client or to corporate counsel. (This includes identifying when a case is not important.) This abuse can be prevented by having a separate

149

fee agreement for each matter, even though most of the agreements will contain identical terms.

Hopefully, consideration of the foregoing more common fee abuse problems will encourage the client and the lawyer to pay more attention to their fee agreements before fees and costs are unnecessarily expended.

COMMON QUESTIONS ASKED BY INSURANCE COMPANIES IN SELECTING OR KEEPING THEIR LAW FIRMS

This section may be of value to you with the process of finding the right law firm for your needs. It is a composite list of questions used by insurance companies in the process of selecting law firms.

Insurance companies are perhaps the largest institutional purchasers of legal services in the United States. As a group, insurance companies probably spend more money for legal services than either business or individuals. Insurance companies have hundreds of years of experience in finding and selecting lawyers. It is worth looking at the concerns of insurance companies and adapting them to your needs where applicable.

Insurance companies pay lawyers to represent the insured when the company is obligated to provide a lawyer. This type of legal work is variously called defense work and insurance defense work. An insurance company's only interest is to keep its defense costs down, with the least possible monetary exposure at time of trial.

Insurance carriers regularly send out questionnaires asking questions about the law firms they use and prospective law firms. I personally feel that some of the information sought is proprietary and unnecessary to selecting the right lawyer or firm for the client. Some insurance companies involved might not willingly give the same information to a prospective policy purchaser or to a state insurance commissioner. Not all law firms will be willing to answer all of the questions. Each law firm must decide how much information it is willing to give to a prospective client. Some of the questions may even invade the attorney-client relationship of other clients.

Again, it is worthwhile to review these questions asked by major insurance companies if only to prepare your questions in advance, or to examine a firm's marketing activities and materials to see which questions are answered to your satisfaction.

In looking for or considering a law firm, this list of fifty questions could be considered as a "due diligence" checklist, meaning that you will have exercised due diligence in searching for the right firm(s) by asking the right questions.

1. In what specialty areas does the firm claim to possess unique expertise?
2. Who are the senior lawyers in those areas?
3. Have they been involved in any cases of particular note?
4. At what points in time do you evaluate files?
5. How do you establish a value to a case?
6. How many cases did you try before judge trials, jury trials, and arbitration during the last 12 months?
7. What lines of insurance did those cases apply to? (Auto, products, etc.)
8. What percentage of your total pending cases are insurance cases?
9. In how many of these cases were juries selected?
10. How many of these cases were tried to conclusion?
11. How many of these cases resulted in defense verdicts?
12. What was the average, high, and low for plaintiff's verdicts in these cases?
13. If the firm has been involved in any major structured settlements, give details.
14. Describe what you consider to be the proper role of your firm in settlement negotiations.
15. What is the starting salary of your entry level lawyers?
16. What are the going rates for practices similar to yours in your geographical area?
17. How many lawyers are in your firm?
18. How many lawyers were in your firm three years ago?
19. How many lawyers were in your firm five years ago?

20. What is the ratio of equity partners to all lawyers?
21. What is the turnover rate for nonequity partners?
22. How long has each of your present lawyers been with the firm?
23. What is your average caseload per lawyer?
24. How many hours do you expect each of the firm's lawyers to bill each year?
25. What is your existing capacity to take on new clients?
26. Do you employ paralegals or legal assistants?
27. What types of work do your paralegals and legal assistants do?
28. Has your firm been involved in a spin-off or acquisition in the last five years? If so, give details.
29. Describe the size and functions of your clerical staff.
30. What is the ratio of clerical staff to lawyers?
31. What training do you provide for your lawyers?
32. Is your firm organized into a team structure? If so, how are your teams structured? Type of law, industry area, type of legal skills required, client responsibility?
33. How many lawyers are on each of your teams and what are their experience levels?
34. By what process are team leaders selected?
35. What are the requisite qualities for team leaders?
36. What is the paralegal support level provided for each team?
37. How do senior lawyers review and supervise the work of junior lawyers?
38. Describe who does what on a typical case.
39. What specific measures have you adopted to reduce the cost of handling cases?
40. To what extent do you pass on cost savings to your clients?
41. What statistics and data do you use to analyze and review the performance of the firm and the performance of the people in the firm?
42. What is your proposed rate schedule?

43. When was the last time you raised the rates of each category of charge?
44. How frequently have you raised each category of charge during the last five years?
45. Do you shift lawyers to different rates on the same case dependent on what they are doing on the case?
46. Have you read our document entitled "Litigation Management and Billing Practices"? Does your firm agree to be bound by its terms?
47. Does your firm have a written or oral general statement of case-handling philosophy?
48. Who is responsible for implementing and enforcing your firms philosophy?
49. Have you ever sued a client for fees? If so, give details.
50. Do you have an "affirmative action" program for women and minorities? If so, give details.

Some lawyers consider many of these questions intrusive and would not answer many of them, even at the risk of not getting the legal business. On the other hand, there is no harm in asking. It should also be noted that some insurance companies often regard themselves rather than the insured as the client.

FINDING THE RIGHT LAWYER THROUGH THE AMERICAN CORPORATE COUNSEL ASSOCIATION

Corporate counsel are lawyers who are employed by corporations and institutions rather than by traditional "outside" law firms. These lawyers are typically organized by their employing institution to meet and handle the specific needs and concerns of their employer. It has been said that an "outside" lawyer has a large variety of clients with a large variety of problems, while a corporate counsel has a single client with a large variety of problems. In general, corporate counsel tend to do work which is repetitive to their company or which requires a very specialized knowledge. (I once knew a corporate tax lawyer who did nothing but deal with the property taxation of telephone poles used by his employer.) For various reasons, they tend not to do major litigation and often need recommendations as to lawyers for litigation or lawyers in the areas of law they don't handle.

The American Corporate Counsel Association (ACCA), an organization of corporate counsel, is located in Washington, D.C. ACCA goes out of its way to systematically exclude outside counsel from its membership and meetings unless specially invited by the association. I have been told, but have never verified, that the reason for the exclusion of the outside counsel is that outside counsel spend so much time "hustling" the members to get legal business that the outside counsel are an interference with ACCA's getting its own business done. The ACCA also has chapters in various cities throughout the United States. A corporate lawyer seeking a recommendation could contact and join ACCA to find other corporate lawyers to make a recommendation.

I have had the experience with working with ACCA and some of its members and I recommend that businesses join and use it as a resource in finding the right lawyer.

FINDING THE RIGHT LAWYER THROUGH THE AMERICAN ASSOCIATION OF ATTORNEY-CERTIFIED PUBLIC ACCOUNTANTS

The American Association of Attorney Certified Public Accountants (AAA-CPA) is a small national organization (about 3,000 members) headquartered in Valencia, California. I list this organization purely for personal reasons. The AAA-CPA has affiliated chapters in several states. Every member is both a lawyer and a Certified Public Accountant. It will never be a big organization, because there simply are not many lawyers who are also CPAs. Lawyers who are also CPAs are not necessarily better lawyers than lawyers who are not also CPAs, but it is my experience that Attorney-CPAs are good at understanding complex business, financial, and tax problems. For that reason I have listed this organization in this section of this book. The fact that they are CPAs guarantees at least two years' practical experience (in most cases) in dealing with accounting concepts. Attorney-CPAs, in my opinion, tend to be very analytical, making decisions based on facts rather than emotions. This tendency to be nonemotional may or may not be what a client needs or wants. I had the honor and privilege of being one of the six founders of the AAA-CPA in 1964. I've held every office in the organization and have served as the president. I also served as the president of the allied California Association of Attorney-CPAs, which actually is a predecessor to the AAA-CPA. If you need or want a lawyer with business and accounting skills, or tax or financial ability, I recommend you contact the AAA-CPA through their 800 number for a referral to a member in your area.

11

Finding the Right Lawyer in a Foreign Country

WHEN YOU OR ANOTHER need a lawyer in another country, you may feel totally at sea. Someone who wants legal help probably could do much or most of what has to be done without help from you in the United States, but if the person is distraught, hysterical, or just unable to function in a complicated situation, it would be better to find someone who can do the work on your behalf.

There are two steps in finding legal help in a foreign country. First, find a lawyer. This chapter addresses that step. The second step is to decide whether the lawyer is right for the particular problem. This two-step process is no different from that of finding a lawyer in your own community. Finding the *right* lawyer may be much more difficult than merely finding *a* lawyer, and there is always an element of chance involved. You may have to spend a lot of time and resources checking out the lawyer you find or alternatively just hope for the best.

As with a medical problem, legal problems can range from a crisis emergency, to being critical but not a crisis, to being neither a crisis nor an emergency, but rather just a problem which must be addressed before it gets worse.

THE U.S. DEPARTMENT OF STATE, WASHINGTON, D.C.

The U.S. Department of State often can be of great help, especially in an emergency. Eventually, you will be on your own, of course, but they'll help you get started.

I wish to acknowledge the excellent assistance provided me by the U.S. Department of State. It goes without saying that nothing in this chapter represents the official position of the U.S. government. Additionally, I wish to caution the reader that in the world of government, nothing is permanent. Organizational charts change and personnel move upward and onward, both into and out of Washington. I have been working with the U.S. Department of State for more than thirty years, and I can assure you that the general picture presented here hasn't changed much, except for personnel movement. But that doesn't mean it won't change in the future.

It is easier for you to begin with the U.S. Department of State for several reasons. One is that personnel there speak American English, and you can understand each other when communicating by telephone. Once you reach the department in Washington, D.C., it can contact any of more than 250 overseas U.S. government posts throughout the world on a twenty-four-hour, seven-day basis.

Office of Emergency Services and Office of Citizens Consular Affairs

Remember the magic words "State Department" and "emergency." When you reach the information telephone operator in Washington, D.C., ask for the State Department and the office that handles emergencies. Eventually, you will get one or both numbers. The "emergency" number will be the Office of Emergency Services for U. S. Citizens Overseas, (202) 647-5225 (in 1995). Through a series of voice messages and touch tones, you will learn that two types of help are available. One type of help is for true emergencies, such as a medical problem, death, kidnapping, or arrest on a criminal charge (what I call a crisis emergency). Someone will be on duty during regular Washington office hours as well as outside office hours. Additionally, someone will be available "on call" twenty-four hours a day, seven days a week. The difficulty in reaching that person will depend on the degree of the emergency.

If your need for legal or governmental assistance is not a true emergency, you will be referred to the Office of Citizens Consular Affairs. This office normally will be available to you during Washington business hours.

Within both of these offices, there may be further subdivisions, depending on the country involved.

Country Desk

In addition to these two offices, you can call the general State Department at (202) 647-4000 (1995 number) and ask for the "country desk" of the country in which you need help. The amount of help you do or don't get may depend on the workload of the person you are speaking with and the nature of the matter. In addition, assistance may depend upon whether you are friendly, understanding, and patient, or whether you are arrogant, demanding, and impatient.

The country desk is normally not supposed to get involved unless the problem is so severe that it could impact the overall diplomatic and political relationship of the United States with the country involved. The country desk may or may not be equipped to provide you with current information on the legal system or lawyers or be able to act as an intermediary between the overseas person with the problem and the concerned persons in the United States. On the other hand, it is my personal experience that although the client's problem may not technically be within their jurisdiction or skills, State Department personnel are caring people who will try to help you to the extent they would help any human being with a problem. Even if they can only direct you back to the proper chain of communications, you will feel much better knowing you've done all you can.

Any one of these governmental agencies may be able to provide you or the person in trouble with some or all of the resources described in the remainder of this chapter.

GETTING A VISIT TO A FOREIGN JAIL

Under the Vienna Convention, the foreign nation is supposed to notify the local U.S. consul of the arrest or detention of a U.S. citizen. It must provide the consul with access to the prisoner. Some nations are prompt and others are not. If the arresting authorities have never heard of the Vienna Convention, it can take a long time for official notification to be made. To add further complications, some countries are not signatories to the Vienna Convention. They have no legal obligation even to notify the U.S. government. By your notifying Washington and even by your notifying the U.S. overseas consulate, you may be able to shorten the time involved in getting a visit from the overseas U.S. consul. The consul can't do much from a lawyer's point of view, other than be sure the prisoner gets at least the same rights as a national of the foreign country. (These may not be many.) However, it is very important for the prisoner's mental and physical health to know that the U.S. government is aware of his or her arrest. The visit by the consul may offer some protection against beatings, maltreatment, or execution. A local jailer may be more subdued, knowing that the case has international implications and that he may be accountable for what happens to the prisoner.

GETTING A LIST OF FOREIGN LAWYERS

Overseas consular officers maintain a list of foreign lawyers on a geographic basis. The list is simply one of foreign lawyers who want business. There is no way of knowing whether they are good or bad, honest or dishonest, or the right lawyer or the wrong lawyer for the case. If the consulate gets any negative feedback on the lawyer, the name will be removed from the list. These lists are updated about once every two years on a rotating country-by-country basis. Washington and the overseas consulate usually have the same list unless the consulate has just finished its biennial update. You will have to communicate directly with the lawyers on the list to ascertain whether they can help under the circumstances.

If you have any option, I recommend that you try to limit yourself to lawyers who have and use a fax machine. Fax gives instantaneous hard copy delivered twenty-four hours a day, seven days a week, without regard to local time differences. The hard copy allows you and the other lawyer to study and translate the communications at a more leisurely pace and with greater accuracy. Foreign mail is slow and also can get lost or stolen, sometimes for the postage stamp on the envelope. Fax is cheaper and easier to use than telex or messengers, although telex is still sometimes used.

ACCESSING U.S. CONSULATES AND EMBASSIES

The U.S. Department of State in Washington can provide you with the local mailing address, telephone number, fax number, and names and titles of the people in the consulate or embassy you need to reach. In most cases you will want to deal with the consular officer. You run a calculated risk when you address your communications to a particular person. The benefit is that you may get faster responses from someone who is familiar with you and the case. The detriment is that if the person is out of the office traveling (a very common situation), your communication may languish in an Inbox until the individual returns. Therefore, it is more prudent to address communications simply to "consular officer."

Incidentally, be aware that a "consular officer" can be found in consulates, consulates general, and embassies, as well as in other representative offices. Don't be confused by the fact that consuls are found both in and out of consulates.

161

Money Transfers and Loans

Although this is not technically legal help, the U.S. consul can arrange transfers of money to prisoners from concerned people in the U.S. The consul sometimes can also arrange for small loans from the government for certain limited emergencies. In some cases, the consular officer can even arrange for medical care and for dietary supplements.

It is a fact of life that in some overseas jails, whether a prisoner is fed or not depends on the amount of bribes paid to the jailers. Money can sometimes buy special privileges and immunity from mistreatment. On the other hand, sending the money may simply set the person up to be detained for a longer period in order for the jailer to continue to receive bribes. You may have no way of knowing what will happen to your money after it arrives. You will have to either establish your own line of communications or trust the consular officer to give you the best information available under the circumstances.

Collect Calls

Always offer to accept collect calls from the overseas consulate. Local budgetary problems may prohibit their calling you until authorization is obtained. This can take time or even be denied. Giving them collect-call privileges may solve the problem. Hopefully, their operator and your receptionist can combine their talents for the consulate to call you on a telephone line for you to accept the charges and then switch on the two fax machines. (Many State Department staff refer to all electronic written communication as a "cable," whether it is a telegram, telex, or fax.)

Use of the Diplomatic Pouch

If your communication is highly confidential or involves governmental issues, you can ask to use the "diplomatic pouch." This mail cannot be intercepted, read, or censored by the foreign government. Typically, it will be sent through a post office box in a U.S. city. The post office box is referred to as an APO or FPO box number. (I believe, but am not certain, that the letters refer to the old Fleet Post Office and Army Post Office designations used for military mail.) I personally am familiar with APOs and FPOs in Miami, New York, and San Francisco. The diplomatic mail for most overseas posts goes through Washington, D.C. The current (1995) mailing address is Consular Officer, American Embassy, or American Consulate, Overseas City, Washington, D.C. 20521-xxxx. The "xxxx" refers to the four-digit extension of the zip code which has been assigned to each diplomatic post. If you don't have it, leave it off, but you may save a day or two if you use it.

The U.S. local consular officer decides whether to allow you to use the diplomatic pouch for your mail or their answers. Diplomatic mail usually goes by commercial air service. However, it can take weeks for the mail to arrive after being accumulated with other diplomatic mail. Although your mail will arrive unread or unconfiscated by the local government, it may take a long time. Again, a fax is the best way to communicate if you can get a fax number. In some places, local telephone regulations prohibit private use of faxes. In others, fax lines are limited because consulates want to keep them open.

You can buy a booklet from the U.S. Government Printing Office entitled "Key Officers of Foreign Service Posts," often referred to as the "Key Officers Book." It provides names, communications methods, and positions of key personnel in U.S. embassies and consulates. However, this information is sometimes outdated because of changes in phone numbers. The booklet contains information on about 150 American embassies and about 100 American consulates and consulates general. The booklet costs a few dollars.

U.S. DEPARTMENT OF COMMERCE LOCAL FIELD OFFICES

Another source of help, if the legal problem is a commercial one, is the U.S. Department of Commerce. It may or may not have a representative in a particular city or country. It sometimes uses its own people and sometimes has an arrangement with an economic officer of the State Department.

The Commerce Department has local field offices throughout the United States. The level of help you can get varies greatly, depending on the workload of the office you contact. Often the most knowledgeable people are in the field (where they are supposed to be) and hard to contact. The information you can get may depend on the level of the person with whom you are able to establish contact. If you don't succeed at the local level or district office of the Department of Commerce, you can try the Bureau of Economic and Business Affairs of the State Department in Washington, D.C., currently (202) 647-1942. The overseas representative of the Commerce Department may not be able to direct you to either a lawyer or an organization that can recommend a lawyer.

OVERSEAS AMERICAN CHAMBERS OF COMMERCE

Obviously, the sources of information for finding the right lawyer will depend on the local situation at the time. If there is a local American Chamber of Commerce (sometimes called an "AmCham"), it normally has English-speaking lawyers with American clients. The consulate will normally give you that information or get it for you. The U.S. Chamber of Commerce in Washington, D.C., has a section dealing with overseas chambers of commerce and may be able to help you find an AmCham.

In addition to U.S. governmental agencies and groups, there are other sources inside and outside the United States which can offer help in finding a lawyer in a foreign country:

THE MARTINDALE-HUBBELL LAW DIRECTORY

Most American lawyers are familiar with the Martindale-Hubbell Law Directory, but their clients may not be. (See the section "Finding the Right Lawyer by Using the Martindale-Hubbell Law Directory" in Chapter 4.) In addition to being in many law offices, Martindale-Hubbell can be found in most law school libraries, governmental libraries (including U.S. government offices overseas), and many public libraries. In addition to containing a free listing for every lawyer who wants to be included, it rates lawyers according to their reputation in their communities. It also accepts paid advertising under "Biographical Listings." Most larger firms and many smaller firms are included in these biographical listings, which are arranged geographically.

Martindale-Hubbell has a foreign lawyer section. It may have a listing for the geographic area in which you are interested. These lawyers want business from American clients. They tend to be on the expensive side, but generally their level of English is good, and many of the lawyers have studied comparative law in U.S. law schools. Accordingly, they have some understanding of the U.S. system and of American values. These firms tend to fall into and out of favor because they often are tied politically to the power structure. When the power structure changes, and they are on the outside, using them can be a mistake due to their identification with the old government. The U.S. consular officer or the American Chamber of Commerce may tell you whether the firms are currently "in" or "out."

LOCAL EMBASSIES AND CONSULATES OF FOREIGN GOVERNMENTS

You may or may not find local embassies and consulates of foreign governments to be helpful. The firms they recommend are sometimes politically well-connected because the consul is politically well-connected with the current government. On the other hand, if you need legal skills rather than political connections, the referral may be more of a detriment than a help. Additionally, the foreign consul may have been away from home for so long that he or she doesn't know the current situation or procedures. Over a period of more than twenty-five years, I've had good and bad experiences with law firms recommended by foreign embassies and consulates. Certainly, it is worthwhile getting the recommendations and then making further inquiry.

OVERSEAS BRANCH OFFICES AND AFFILIATES OF U.S. LAW FIRMS

In recent years, many U.S. firms have opened overseas branch offices or formed various types of affiliations with overseas law firms. (I have had affiliations with overseas firms for more than thirty years.) These firms tend to serve commercial interests of multinational clients. They sometimes will not accept employment when a client has a "personal problem" or can't afford a very large fee. But, even if they won't handle your matter, they may try to find you a local lawyer for the cases they won't handle.

LAWYER MARKETING NETWORKS

Many local firms of various sizes and legal specialties have formed national and international marketing networks. There are various reasons for these networks, ranging from a desire to refer their clients to competent lawyers to a desire to simply make more money by getting more business. I do not yet have enough disinterested information or feedback to advise that one should or should not use any particular marketing network. I would expect that with the passage of time, an experience factor will begin to emerge and that some of these networks will flourish while others will fail.

BANKS

Every major U.S. bank has correspondent banks throughout most of the world. You can ask your bank's international department to contact its correspondent bank in the country or city of your concern in order to get the name of the foreign bank's lawyer. That lawyer or firm may be able to help you or to suggest a lawyer who could handle a matter such as yours. If your bank does not have an international department with correspondent banks, it will use the international department of another bank. That bank may or may not be willing to help your bank get the name of the foreign bank's lawyers.

BAR ASSOCIATIONS

Chapter 4 of this book contains a section on finding a lawyer through bar associations. In this section, I simply wish to remind the reader that the American Bar Association and other bar associations have associate members from foreign countries. Also, there are bar associations which by their nature are constituted with foreign lawyers and have published directories of members. I personally am a member of the International Bar Association, located in London, which has a worldwide membership of lawyers who speak, read, and write English. It is an old, established organization with heavy membership in Europe and the British Commonwealth. I also belong to the Inter-American Bar Association, located in Washington, D.C., which has members throughout North America, South and Central America, and the Caribbean. Unfortunately, some of their members have little or no English-language ability. You may have to communicate with these lawyers in Spanish or Portuguese.

PART

....

Foonberg's Glossary of Legal Specialties

....

CHAPTER

Foonberg's Glossary of Legal Specialties

WHAT KIND OF LAWYER DO YOU NEED?

The purpose of including this glossary is to help you find the right lawyer and to be able to know what kind of lawyer you need. To the best of my knowledge, this is the most comprehensive digest of legal practice areas in existence. It has taken me many years to accumulate these descriptions from all over the U.S. and several foreign countries and to narrow the number down to nearly 1,000. This glossary describes legal practice areas as listed by lawyers themselves and others in various legal directories and other publications. By skimming through, reading, and studying this list, you'll be better able to understand lawyers' language and terminology for describing the areas of law your needs might involve. It is most important that you understand that the facts of your situation may involve many different areas of law practice at the same time. For example, you conceivably may need a lawyer or firm of lawyers who knows about auto accidents, medical negligence, breach of contract, warranty law, the trucking industry, the carpet industry, federal law, workers' compensation, Social Security, disability, and insurance policy interpretation from the defendant's side or from the plaintiff's side. Of course, as you increase the number of areas of law involved, you decrease the number of lawyers and firms who know most or all of what you need. On the other hand, when you find lawyers who know the greatest number of areas described in this list, you are more likely to find the right lawyer or firm for your needs.

Learning which areas of law your situation involves is like learning the medical terminology for your medical situation. With a medical problem, you usually know whether you need a dentist or a proctologist. It's not difficult to determine tentatively that you need an ear, nose, and throat specialist rather than a dermatologist. Even then, unknown to you, you may need an orthopedist and a neurologist, as well. If you knew what each *did* it would be easier to ask for a recommendation. Similarly, if you can understand just what is meant by the legalese which describes the types of law a particular lawyer practices, it will be of assistance to you.

Some legal problems are so rare or unusual that you can't find the right lawyer through traditional sources within the legal profession. The following glossary lists practices, problems, and areas of law. This list will help you recognize and determine which type of lawyer(s) or firm can most likely help you or the individual or entity requiring help. Determining the kind of lawyer or firm you need can be a major step in finding the right lawyer with the least amount of wasted time and energy. The references to "Finding the Right Lawyer by Using the Advertisements of Experts and Consultants" can help you find the right lawyer with experience where you need it. Using nonlawyer advertising can be time consuming, but may be the only way you or your lawyer can find the right lawyer.

As indicated elsewhere in this book, the word "specialty" in law is not well defined and its meaning and usage varies greatly from state to state and from lawyer to lawyer. In medicine, there are clearly defined specialty areas with uniform experience and testing standards. In law, this unfortunately does not exist. Accordingly, as used here the definition of "specialty" can range from a lawyer being board certified with experience and examinations to a lawyer having only minimal experience or knowledge in the area. Due to the lack of consistency in defining "specialty," there's no shame or harm or embarrassment involved in asking a lawyer what their experience is in the area of law which interests you. It is most important that you feel comfortable that the individual lawyer(s) handling your problem is competent in the area of law involved.

The term "specialty" as used in this list is intended only to indicate that there are lawyers and law firms doing the kinds of legal work indicated. In some states, a lawyer is prohibited from calling himself or herself a "specialist." In some states there are board-certified specialists with minimum educational and experience testing and with review boards and periodic requalification as a specialist. In some states there are no requirements and anyone can call themselves a "specialist" or claim that they "practice in a specialty area." I have tried to indicate in this list those areas of law where there is some form of a board certification or regulation of recognized "specialty" areas of law practice.

After you feel comfortable that you have an idea of the legal areas that probably are involved, you will be better able to recognize and understand the words used to describe legal problems in the Yellow Pages or other directories. And you can more clearly see which lawyers can handle one or more of the areas where you need help.

FOONBERG'S GLOSSARY OF LEGAL SPECIALTIES

Abandonment. Consult with a family lawyer if a person or family has been abandoned; see a criminal lawyer or a juvenile lawyer if a child has been abandoned; see a business lawyer or a general practitioner if property was abandoned. If a case or client was abandoned by a lawyer, see **Legal Malpractice.**

Abogado. Abogado is Spanish for lawyer. This word in an ad or listing indicates that someone in the office (not necessarily the lawyer) can speak Spanish and interpret for Spanish-speaking clients. See also *Licenciado.*

Abogado Hispano. *Abogado Hispano* is Spanish for Hispanic lawyer. See **Abogado.**

Accident, Depression, and Suicide. See "Finding the Right Lawyer by Using the Advertisements of Experts and Consultants" in Chapter 4 of this book.

Accident Law. Accident law and accident lawyer are the two common ways to refer to lawyers who handle motor vehicle accident cases. Accident lawyers also handle accidents where no motor vehicle is involved. Accident law is so broad that if the case doesn't involve a motor vehicle, you may have to seek a specialist in the type of accident involved. See also **Auto Accidents; Personal Injury Law.**

Accidental Falls. See **Slip and Fall.**

Accountant's Malpractice. See **Malpractice.**

Accountings. Accountings can be secured by business lawyers or litigation lawyers. Probate accountings can be secured by probate or estate-planning lawyers.

Accreditation and Licensing. For accreditation of an individual in a business or profession, one would normally start with a lawyer who does administrative law, since most accreditations involve an administrative process. For accreditation of an educational institution, see **College and University Law.**

ADA. Abbreviation for Americans with Disabilities Act, the federal law that prohibits discrimination against employees with disabilities. Certain categories of disabilities, such as disabilities in seeing, hearing, AIDS, mental retardation, epilepsy, paralysis, etc., are covered. See also **Civil Rights Law; Employment Law.**

Administrative and Government Law. See **Administrative Law.**

Administrative and Regulatory Law. See **Administrative Law.**

Administrative Law. Administrative law deals with representing people and organizations before nonjudicial governmental agencies. It is sometimes called administrative and agency law. Typical agencies would include federal, state, and local hearings for zoning cases, licensing, accreditation, license revocations, permits, etc. The firm you select to represent you should have some knowledge of the government agency involved, including its rules of procedure. Give serious thought to selecting lawyers who know the people on the administrative boards and agencies. Membership on these administrative boards may be by election or appointment. It is also important for the lawyer to know the local political situation and whether what you want is unrealistic because of the local interests involved. A good lawyer can give you practical advice as to what you will have to do to accomplish your goals.

Administrative law firms sometimes do lobbying. Administrative law can be at the application level, the hearing level, or the appeal level. A party who is not satisfied with the results of the administrative-level proceedings can sometimes go further and seek relief in the courts by way of judicial review or begin all over again in court. When a matter is so serious that you expect appeals to the judicial system, if necessary, then also involve a litigation lawyer from the beginning. See also **Political Law.**

Admiralty and Maritime Law. See **Admiralty Law.** See also **Maritime Law.**

Admiralty Law. Admiralty law is normally practiced in the federal courts under very special rules. Admiralty law is also called shipping law and maritime law. In some cases there is a choice between taking a case to a federal district court, sitting as an admiralty court, or taking the same case to a state court. Be sure that your lawyer(s) can advise you if you have this option. Ask what the relative advantages or disadvantages would be in either court. Admiralty law practice in the federal court is a rather specialized type of practice. You should begin with a lawyer who knows admiralty court practice as well as admiralty law. A general practitioner or a business lawyer may be able to help you find the right lawyer to advise you of your options in prosecuting or defending an admiralty matter in a state court or admiralty court. See also **Maritime Law.**

Adoption as an Option Attorney. Lawyers advertising this area of practice often arrange for birth mothers to have all expenses paid by adoptive mothers. See also **Adoption; Family Law.**

Adoptions. Adoptions are very closely monitored where there is any suspicion of buying and selling babies for large profits. Be careful and seek a second opinion if the fee seems exceptionally high for some routine forms and court appearances. If the baby is located or obtained through a charitable or governmental agency, the adoption is sometimes referred to as an agency adoption. If the baby is located or obtained as a private matter without the services of a charitable or governmental agency, the adoption is sometimes referred to as a private adoption or independent adoption, even though there ultimately will be some sort of participation or approval by a governmental agency. Most adoptions can by handled by either a family lawyer or a general practitioner. Some lawyers do only adoption law and claim to have sources of babies for adoption. See also **Family Law; General Practice Law; Surrogate Parenting Law.**

Adverse Drug Reactions. See "Finding the Right Lawyer by Using the Advertisements of Experts and Consultants" in Chapter 4 of this book. See also **Medical Malpractice.**

Adverse Possession. Doctrine of law under which a person who "squats on" or occupies land that he or she knows doesn't belong to him or her can, under certain circumstances, acquire rights in the property. Real estate lawyers handle this area of law.

Advertising Law. See **Entertainment and Sports Law.** See also **Deceptive Trade Practices; Publishing Law; Trade Regulation Law; Unfair Competition Law.**

Aerospace Law. See **Government Contracts Law.** See also **Space and Aviation Law.**

Age Discrimination. See **Civil Rights Law; Employment Law.**

Agricultural Labor Relations. Firms which practice agricultural labor relations are limiting their work in labor law and employment law to agricultural situations.

Agricultural Law. See **Farm and Ranch Law.**

AIDS. Abbreviation for Acquired Immune Deficiency Syndrome. AIDS is a newly developing area of law. The rights of persons with AIDS may be handled under gay and lesbian law or under employment law. Infliction of AIDS is normally handled by personal injury or medical malpractice lawyers. Intentional infliction of AIDS can be a criminal law matter.

AIDS Litigation. See "Finding the Right Lawyer by Using the Advertisements of Experts and Consultants" in Chapter 4 of this book. See also **Employment Law; Gay and Lesbian Law; Medical Malpractice Experts.** For AIDS discrimination, see **Civil Rights Law.**

Aircraft Crash Litigation. See **Airplane Accidents.** See also **Aviation Law.**

Aircraft Financing. See **UCC Law.** See also **Aircraft Title Law.**

Aircraft Leasing. See **UCC Law.** See also **Aircraft Title Law.**

Aircraft Manufacture. Manufacturing quality control. See "Finding the Right Lawyer by Using the Advertisements of Experts and Consultants" in Chapter 4 of this book.

Aircraft Title Law. I'm not aware of any law firms which specialize only in aircraft title work. An aircraft broker may be able to recommend the firm or lawyer which does the title work of the broker. There may be state, federal, and international considerations. For problems of aircraft financing, see **UCC Law.**

Airplane Accidents. A type of personal-injury case that is often considered the most profitable of all personal injury cases. The damages are normally high and the passenger certainly is not at fault. The lawyer representing a passenger may sometimes sit back and wait as the airline, the manufacturer, and the government fight it out as to whose fault caused the accident. See also **Aviation Law.**

Airplane Crashes. See **Aviation Law.** See also **Airplane Accidents.**

Airport Safety, Compliance. See "Finding the Right Lawyer by Using the Advertisements of Experts and Consultants" in Chapter 4 of this book.

Alcoholic Beverage Law. A law in some states under which the seller or provider of liquor to an intoxicated person may have both civil and criminal responsibility if the intoxicated person causes damage or injury. See also **Dram Shop Law; Innkeepers Law; Personal Injury Law.** For licensing, see **Administrative Law.**

Alcohol Tests and Refusals. See **Driving Under the Influence; Driving While Intoxicated; Drunk Driving; DUI; DWI.**

Alternative Dispute Resolution. See **Arbitration.** See also **Mediation.**

Alternatives to Jail. See **Sentencing Alternatives.**

American Indian Law. See **Native American Law.**

Amnesty. See **Immigration Law.**

Amputations. See **Serious Injuries.** See also **Personal Injury Law.**

Amusement Law. Many years ago, amusement law covered carnivals, circuses, and amusement parks. These activities are now treated as other businesses. See **Entertainment and Sports Law.**

Anatomical Gifts. See **Organ Donation.**

Anesthesia Error. See **Malpractice.**

Animal Bites. See **Dog Bite Cases.**

Annexation. See **Land Use Regulation.** See also **Administrative Law; Political Law.**

Annulment. A decree that more or less says that the marriage is unwound back to the beginning and that the parties' original marriage was not valid. Annulment is sometimes an alternative to divorce. It is sometimes applicable where parties were under the legal age of marriage or where some sort of fraud was involved. Annulments may protect the parties' right of support from prior marriages or have other legal consequences not present in divorce cases. There may be religious reasons for an annulment rather than a divorce. This type of law is normally handled by general practitioners, family lawyers, and divorce lawyers. See also **Divorce; Family Law.**

Antitrust Law. Business law concerned with practices that may unfairly restrain competition. Antitrust law is very complex and requires a specialist. Antitrust law is sometimes lumped together with trade regulation law. Antitrust law can either be a private matter or a government matter. It can either be civil or criminal. It can be state or federal. It can stand alone or be combined with other legal areas such as unfair competition, franchise law, class actions, or breach of contract.

Antitrust law deals with economic price fixing so that the marketplace is not truly free and open, but is being "fixed" or "rigged." The price fixing can be in the form of competitors agreeing on prices or rigging public bidding or applying pressure through commercial dealings or litigation to keep retailers and distributors and others in line. It may involve commercial practices called "tying," and "diversion," and "grey market," "discounting," "franchising," and "boycott." The antitrust activity can be intentional and secretive, such as meetings in hotel rooms or on golf courses, or at resorts or conventions, with no records being kept; or it can be open and unintended, such as the merger of two leading companies in a given area of activity. In most countries of the world this activity is called a "cartel" or a "combine" and is legal. Conduct which is legal in one state can be criminal or give rise to civil liability in another state.

Very few lawyers truly have a good understanding of the extent of antitrust law unless they have had cases in it. If a person or company thinks they might have an antitrust problem they should get an opinion from a lawyer who specializes in antitrust.

Appeals. See **Civil Appeals; Criminal Appeals.**

Appellate Practice. See **Civil Appeals; Criminal Appeals.**

Arbitration. Arbitration is a type of procedure which is normally less formal than a regular trial and without a jury. After hearing the facts and legal arguments, the arbitrator or panel of arbitrators renders a judgment, called an award, which can have all the legal effect of a court judgment after a trial. Arbitrations are good when both parties want to resolve their problems and get on with their corporate or personal lives.

Often, the arbitrator is an expert in the technical area that is the subject of the dispute. Accordingly, unlike other general litigation, expertise in the subject matter of the dispute may be as important as, or more important than, general trial or litigation skills. Lawyers who rarely or seldom do regular litigation may be able to do an excellent job in arbitrations if they and the arbitrator are both knowledgeable in the subject matter. Lawyers who do arbitrations may be found within the area of subject matter expertise, the area of legal expertise, or the area of trials or alternative dispute resolution. See also **Church Law; Mediation; Rent-a-Judge.**

Arbitration and Mediation. See **Arbitration.** See also **Meditation.**

Architectural Malpractice Law. See **Malpractice Law.**

Armed Forces Law. See **Military Law.** See also **Veterans' Benefits.**

Arson and Insurance Fraud. See **Insurance Coverage.** See also "Finding the Right Lawyer by Using the Advertisements of Experts and Consultants" in Chapter 4 of this book.

Arson Defense in Insurance Cases. See Insurance Coverage. See also "Finding the Right Lawyer by Using the Advertisements of Experts and Consultants" in Chapter 4 of this book.

Art Law. Some lawyers claim to be experts in the law of art. Art appraisals, taxation of artists, and gifts of artworks are sometimes included in tax law. Museum law is often included within art law.

Asbestos and Lead Consulting. See "Finding the Right Lawyer by Using the Advertisements of Experts and Consultants" in Chapter 4 of this book.

Asbestos Cases. Cases where there has been or may be injury arising out of exposure to asbestos. These cases are normally handled as class-action cases, which means that a few lawyers are handling most of the cases. You or your lawyer will have to search around until you find one of these lawyers. Asbestos cases are sometimes handled by lawyers who handle silicosis cases, and sometimes by workers' compensation lawyers. See also **Class Actions; Workers' Compensation Law.**

Assault and Battery. Assault and battery cases can be either civil or criminal, or both. Technically, an assault is when one person threatens another. (Examples include raising your fist, aiming a gun, raising your arm with a weapon in it, or using threatening words or gestures.) A battery occurs when there is a touching of the threatened person. There can be criminal consequences to a civil case, and vice versa. A general practitioner, general criminal lawyer, or personal injury lawyer would be a good starting point in locating a lawyer.

Asset-Based Lending. Asset-based lending is lending (and borrowing) which is based on the strength of the collateral rather than the income stream of the borrower. This area can include anything from pawn shops to real estate projects. See also **Banking Law; UCC Law.**

Asset Protection Law. An area of law sought by people who want to insulate all or some of their assets from creditors. Professionals concerned about possible malpractice exposure are common clients in this area. People and companies facing imminent bankruptcy may need this help. Elder care and estate planning lawyers often help plan to protect assets in the event of catastrophic or long-term illness. Such an illness could deplete an estate, leaving the spouse or heirs penniless. Some people confuse asset protection, which is perfectly legal, with hiding assets from spouses, tax authorities, and bona fide creditors, which is not always legal. International lawyers can often help in the creation and use of offshore companies and trusts. See also **Estate Planning.**

Asset Protection Trusts. See Asset Protection Law.

Assignments for the Benefit of Creditors. Cases where a debtor, normally a business, simply turns over its assets to a reviewer for the benefit of creditors without the delays, expenses, benefits, and burdens of a formal bankruptcy. Business lawyers, general practitioners, and bankruptcy lawyers can assist in this work.

Association Law. Association law normally deals with the law of clubs and organizations of all sizes, ranging from a local luncheon club to an international charity or service organization. It is a specialty area of law. It happens to be one of my specialty areas. Association law typically deals with the creation and maintenance of what people call "nonprofit" organizations, such as trade associations and charitable organizations. This area of law is actually much broader than this, and includes just about any organization that might be or want to be tax-exempt or nonprofit. This area also includes the relationships and liabilities of members, directors, officers, and executives of these organizations. Association law is normally a subdivision of tax law and is sometimes called the law of "tax-exempts" or "nonprofits." See also **Nonprofit Organizations.**

Asylum. See Immigration Law.

Athletic Helmet Injuries. See "Finding the Right Lawyer by Using the Advertisements of Experts and Consultants" in Chapter 4 of this book.

Atomic Energy Law. This area is sometimes included in natural resources law and sometimes included in public utilities law, among other areas. Accidents involving atomic energy are handled by negligence lawyers and personal injury lawyers.

Attachments. Court-ordered liens against property and property rights. Attachments are created before a judgment is obtained. Executions are court-ordered proceedings against property after a judgment has been obtained. Attachments and executions are sometimes both lumped together as garnishments.

To get an attachment against another, consult a business lawyer, a collections lawyer, or creditors rights lawyer. To get help when an attachment is levied against you, consult the same types of lawyers and also consult with a bankruptcy lawyer. See also **Garnishments.**

Attorney Disciplining and Admissions. See **Lawyer Disciplining and Licensing.**

Attorney-CPA. Lawyers who are also licensed as Certified Public Accountants. They often have excellent tax law and business law backgrounds and qualifications. I am an Attorney-CPA. Being an Attorney-CPA is not a specialty. Such lawyers are found in all areas of law practice. They typically work well with businesses.

Attractive Nuisance. A dangerous condition, such as a deserted machine or real estate, that is attractive to children. The children are "attracted" onto a dangerous place and are injured. See a real estate lawyer or a personal injury lawyer. See also **Dangerous Premises.**

ATV (All Terrain Vehicle) Accidents. Accidents involving ATVs. These usually are handled either by personal injury lawyers or lawyers who specialize in motorcycle and recreational vehicle accidents. See also **Motorcycle Accidents.**

Auto Accidents. Auto accident cases normally are handled by claimants' personal injury lawyers. Normally "auto accidents" describes legal matters where there has been a collision between an auto and another object or person. Most personal injury lawyers can handle most auto accident cases involving a couple of vehicles, and involving injuries that were incurred during an auto accident which have completely healed or that normally will completely heal.

If an auto accident involves multiple vehicles, if it involves (or might involve) defective auto parts, engineering, or improper or inadequate safety procedure, or if it involves permanent, serious, or unusual injuries, then a team of lawyers may be necessary to handle the case properly. A major case may require the skills of many different legal specialists and significant financing of experts and investigation. The words "auto accidents" is only the beginning. Therefore, look for a single law firm with enough varied experts in the firm to handle a complex or complicated case. Some solo practitioners or small firms might be reluctant to bring in other experts for fear of diluting their own fee, or they might not realize that they need more expertise than they have. There are many different possible fields of legal expertise that could be involved in an auto accident. See also **Personal Injury Law; Warranty Law.**

Auto Insurance Claims. See **Auto Accidents; Insurance Claims.**

Autopac Claims. In some parts of Canada this refers to claims arising out of auto accidents. See **Auto Accidents.**

Aviation and Space Law. See Aviation Law. See also **Space and Aviation Law.**

Aviation and Space Technology. See Aviation Law. See also **High Technology Law; Space and Aviation Law.**

Aviation Law. Aviation law is a broad term which can apply to representing people and organizations before the various boards and agencies involved in aviation. It can also apply to representing plaintiffs or defendants in personal injury suits arising out of air crashes and disappearances. Aviation law is sometimes considered part of space and aviation law. See also **Administrative Law; Personal Injury Law; Space and Aviation Law.**

Avoid Court. "Avoid court" usually means the lawyer does mediations and arbitrations. See **Mediation.** See also **Arbitration.**

Avoiding Probate. While avoiding probate can be a legitimate estate-planning objective that is appropriate and best for the client, it can also be just a pitch to peddle unnecessary or inappropriate living wills, universal trusts, insurance policies, life insurance trusts, charitable trusts, mutual funds, stocks, and other gimmicks and products to the vulnerable and unwary. Many companies, including many nonlawyers, try to hustle business by peddling the "avoid probate" theme. Try to get advice from experienced probate and estate planning lawyers before accepting or rejecting the various schemes to avoid probate.

Bad Checks. "Bad checks" normally refers to criminal charges arising out of a bad check. A criminal lawyer is normally required. Bad checks can also have civil consequences. In some states, one has to be very careful in collecting a bad check with regard to promises of no criminal prosecution if the check is made good.

Bad Faith Cases. Bad faith cases normally involve claims or suits against your own insurance company for unfair claims handling (technically, breach of the implied covenant of good faith), because the insurance company did not exercise good faith in the way it handled your claim or case. These cases are normally brought by insureds against their own insurance companies. In some cases, the insureds assign their claim for bad faith damages to the person suing the insured. See also **Insurance Coverage; Insurance Law.**

Bail. Bail is money, property, or some form of guarantee given to a court to ensure that a prisoner will attend the court at a future date. If the person does not show up, the bail is forfeited, and the person may or may not be deemed a fugitive, depending on the facts of the case. If the person does show up as agreed, the bail can be exonerated.

The procedure for getting someone out of jail on bail varies greatly from place to place, depending on the underlying offense for which the person is charged and on the overcrowding of the local jails and prisons. Persons arrested are "booked," finger printed, photographed, and run through the computers to see if they really are who they say they are. At the same time, they are checked to see if they are wanted for a more serious crime. This booking process can take anywhere from a few minutes to many hours, in some cases even days.

Understandably, the person in jail is normally very unhappy about being in jail, especially when he or she doesn't know the procedure for getting released. In many cases, a person will be turned loose without bail after having been booked due to jail overcrowding. In some cases, there will be a preprinted schedule of "indicated bail" showing how much the bail is for different offenses charged. Sometimes it is necessary to set the amount of bail by a proceeding before a magistrate or judge. In some cases, a bail bond company may be able to do everything using its lawyers and personnel. In cases where you do not want to pay a bail-bond premium, you may wish to use your own lawyer. Sometimes any relative or friend can post indicated bail without a lawyer.

A local criminal lawyer will be able to advise you on the local situation and whether or not you need a lawyer to get someone out of jail.

Bakery Machine Accidents. See "Finding the Right Lawyer by Using the Advertisements of Experts and Consultants" in Chapter 4 of this book.

Banking Law. Banking law normally refers to representing banks before regulatory boards and agencies. It sometimes can be extended into general business law as applied to banks. It also is used to describe doing collection work for banks. Banking law is sometimes called financial institution law because the laws affecting banks often affect other financial lending institutions. Banking law is normally a department in a larger law firm, although some smaller firms specialize in it.

Bank Lending Practices. See "Finding the Right Lawyer by Using the Advertisements of Experts and Consultants" in Chapter 4 of this book.

Bankruptcy. The term "bankruptcy" is so broad that it is not possible to describe it adequately in less than another book. In this section, I will give you an overview of some of areas of bankruptcy.

As a practical matter you need to have a bankruptcy lawyer representing you or at least have a bankruptcy lawyer working with your lawyer. It is totally false economy to try to handle a matter in bankruptcy court without help from a bankruptcy lawyer. I have seen many otherwise competent lawyers get totally hammered, to the detriment of their client's case, because they tried to represent a client without the help of a local bankruptcy lawyer. The lawyers and the judges in the bankruptcy court all know one another. A relatively tiny number of firms handle most of the work. These firms and the judges work together to speed small cases through the system where appropriate, and to treat big cases with great deliberation and study over a long period of time where appropriate.

Lawyers who are not part of this close-knit group often find that their client's case will suffer due to some minor inconsequential rule of the local court or judge not being observed as the judge would like it observed. Most judges go out of their way to help a person without a lawyer, and will try to be patient with lawyers unfamiliar with the procedure of their court. In any event, the judge doesn't consciously penalize the party without a lawyer or penalize the lawyer to the detriment of the client. Some bankruptcy judges are grossly overworked, have impossible calendars, and simply can't make the time to help or be patient with the nonexpert.

I've heard of many cases in which parties in bankruptcy court have suffered greatly for not having had the services of a bankruptcy specialist. I have heard experienced, nonbankruptcy specialists call the bankruptcy court "Disneyland," "fantasy land," or "the zoo" because of what they perceive to be weird results in cases. In a significant matter, you should insist that a bankruptcy specialist be brought in. Do not rely on your otherwise skilled business or general practice lawyers, unless they can assure you they can protect you and your case in bankruptcy court.

Creditors of companies and individuals that file bankruptcy often find themselves enmeshed in a nightmare of legal expense and wasted time digging out and reconstructing old records because they filed a claim in bankruptcy. Many creditors refuse to file claims in bankruptcy unless so much money is involved that the claim warrants the expense of a lawyer, even if nothing is ever collected. The last date to do something is often called a "bar date" in bankruptcy proceedings.

Bankruptcy is a part of the federal court system. Due to the supremacy of federal law over state law, as well as to the various bankruptcy laws, the federal court system can prevent state courts from hearing or deciding a matter, but not vice versa. A state court cannot stop a federal bankruptcy court. Due to this system, an individual, a company, and even a city can file bankruptcy, and the bankruptcy law will prevent creditors from going after the bankrupt party outside of the bankruptcy court. The moment a petition in bankruptcy is filed and the creditor has notice of the filing, the creditor cannot do anything further without going to bankruptcy court to do it. The creditors must immediately stop (technically called stay) all foreclosures, repossessions, court action, harassment, attachments, receiverships, etc.

Bankruptcy can give a debtor a fresh start free of old debts. There is a system of "priorities" (a technical term) determining which creditors get paid if any are going to get paid.

Bankruptcy law is divided into chapters covering different types of bankruptcies. Accordingly, bankruptcies are often referred to by their chapters. For example, Chapter 7 refers to "straight" bankruptcy, Chapter 11 refers to business reorganizations and workouts, Chapter 12 refers to family farmers, and Chapter 13 refers to wage earners.

If they can file a Chapter 13 proceeding (sometimes called a "13" or Debt Adjustment Plan), wage earners turn over their paycheck to the court-appointed trustee, who pays the creditors according to the system of priorities as they exist in the residence state of the wage earner. The trustee gives the rest to the wage earner for food and spending money. This system continues until all creditors are paid, some settlement is reached, or the wage earner goes to "straight," or Chapter 7, bankruptcy. The wage earner can keep some assets and must surrender others.

In some states, consumer bankruptcy is a board-certified legal practice specialty, as is business bankruptcy. See also **Chapter 7; Chapter 11.**

Bankruptcy, Insolvency, and Reorganization Law. Three areas of law that deal with businesses and people unable to pay their bills or who have other financial problems pending. Depending on the industry of the debtor, the local law and procedures, and whether the client is the debtor or the creditor, there are often many possible approaches. These three areas can be very similar or very different. A bankruptcy lawyer can usually best advise as to what is best for the particular situation. Receiverships and assignments for the benefit of creditors are sometimes included in this area of practice.

Bankruptcy Law. See **Bankruptcy.** See also **Debt Relief.**

Bar Owner Liability. See **Liquor Law.** See also **Dram Shop Law.**

Barrister. Historically, and currently in some countries, barristers did court work and solicitors did office work. Barristers accept cases only from solicitors, not directly from the client. This distinction between barristers and solicitors is disappearing, and "lawyers" now do both court and office work.

Battery Explosions and Fires. See "Finding the Right Lawyer by Using the Advertisements of Experts and Consultants" in Chapter 4 of this book.

B.I. Abbreviation for bodily injury. See **Personal Injury Law.**

Bicycle Accident Reconstruction. See "Finding the Right Lawyer by Using the Advertisements of Experts and Consultants" in Chapter 4 of this book.

Biking Accidents. See **Motorcycle Accidents.**

Bill of Sale. A document that passes legal title to some types of personal property (as differentiated from real property). Different types of personal property require different type of documents and procedures to transfer good title properly to the buyer. Depending on the complexity of the deal, a bill of sale can normally be prepared by a general practitioner or a business or corporate lawyer. Certain kinds of bills of sale require expertise in the legal area involved, such as a bill of sale to an oceangoing ship or an aircraft. A bill of sale for real property (land) is called a deed.

Bio-Reproductive Law. See **Surrogate Parenting.**

Biotech Law. Biotech is a newly developing area of law dealing with genes, chromosomes, bioengineering, and other newly developing technology. There are firms and lawyers which specialize in this area of law. This area of law is normally done by firms which practice intellectual property law because of the interplay of patents, licensing, trade secrets, etc. See **Intellectual Property Law.**

Birth Injuries. See **Medical Malpractice.** See also **Personal Injury Law.**

Black-Lung Law. There are lawyers who specialize in the defense and prosecution of black lung cases. See **Personal Injury Law.**

Blue-Sky Laws. Many states (and the federal government) have laws to regulate the way money is solicited from the public for investment purposes, the uses to which the money is put, and the accountability for the money. Many states also have laws regulating the relationship between a corporation and its investors. Many states don't care what you do to investors, as long as you don't do it to people who live in that particular state. These various laws are called "blue-sky laws." Blue-Sky laws also include federal regulation, where applicable.

Promoters and others often try to run their businesses and get their investors to send or bring money to states that either do not regulate investments or that do so loosely. Nevada, Delaware, and Utah are common examples. In some cases, offshore corporations locate in places such as Switzerland or Panama. The reasons for using these locations may be perfectly valid and have nothing to do with blue-sky laws. Corporate securities lawyers and tax lawyers would be the appropriate beginning points if you are considering starting or investing in one of these companies. See also **Offshore.**

Boating Accidents. There are lawyers with expertise in accidents on boats and accidents between boats. The applicable laws vary as to boating accidents governed by federal law and those governed by state law. See **Admiralty Law.** See also **Maritime Law.**

Boating Design and Construction. See "Finding the Right Lawyer by Using the Advertisements of Experts and Consultants" in Chapter 4 of this book.

Boating Operations. See "Finding the Right Lawyer by Using the Advertisements of Experts and Consultants" in Chapter 4 of this book.

Boilers. See "Finding the Right Lawyer by Using the Advertisements of Experts and Consultants" in Chapter 4 of this book.

Bond Claims. Bond claims usually refers to the various bond claims arising out of construction disputes. See **Construction Law.**

Boundary Lines. See **Real Estate Law.**

Brain Damage. In some situations, the lawyer is seeking cases where there was brain damage, especially to newborn infants as the result of medical malpractice. See also **Malpractice; Serious Injuries.**

Breach of Contract. See **Contract Law.**

Brief Banks. A method of sharing information among law firms. Law firms working on a specific type of case often share research with each other by depositing a copy of the research and briefs into a brief bank. They also withdraw copies of other firms' research and briefs given to the brief bank. Some specialty law associations maintain brief banks. These brief banks can lead you to the lawyer closest to you or to a recommendation for that lawyer.

Brokerage Law. See a business lawyer or a general practitioner for help in classifying your problem needs. For licensing of brokers, see **Administrative Law;** for insurance brokers, see **Insurance Law;** for real estate brokers, see **Real Property Law;** for stockbrokers, see **Securities Law.**

Broker Dealer Law. See **Securities Regulation.** See also **Securities Law.**

Bulk Sales Law. Bulk sales laws apply in some states when the entire inventory or assets of a business are transferred. The bulk sales laws in some states protect the new owner from claims of creditors of the old owner of the goods or the business. This area of law can normally be handled by a general practitioner or a business lawyer. In an exceptionally complex case, it may be worthwhile to consult with a UCC lawyer. See **UCC Law.** See also **Business Law.**

Bus Accidents. See **Subway and Bus Accidents.** See also **Railway Accidents.**

Business Crimes Law. See **White-Collar Crimes.**

Business Divorces. The law firm using this label is indicating it can handle disputes between owners of a business. See also **Business Law; Litigation.**

Business Law. The broad area of law covering the legal needs of businesses rather than the personal legal needs of individuals. This very broad description includes a great many areas of law. The lawyer or firm will have varying degrees of skill in the various areas of law. Recent surveys indicate that about half of all lawyers say they practice business law. I personally tell people that I practice business law. It is important to be sure that the lawyer or firm can handle the particular area of law for which you need a lawyer. General representation, corporate formations, partnerships, agreements, acquisitions, mergers, real estate, leases, debt collection, contract disputes, etc., are among the hundreds of possible areas covered by business law. See also **Corporate Law.**

Business Sales and Purchases. See **Business Law.**

Business Start-Ups. Business start-up lawyers typically are seeking new businesses as clients. New businesses often have no established ties to a lawyer. These firms typically will help with deciding whether a corporation, partnership, or other entity would best suit the needs of the new business and its owners. These lawyers typically can handle simple stock issuances, employment agreements, and buy-sell agreements. They also can help with simple low-level tax questions and with simple literary-property problems. These lawyers usually network with lawyers in other areas of practice. Business start-up work is done by business lawyers, corporate lawyers, tax lawyers, and general practitioners.

Business Valuation. Business valuation is an area within business law. Business valuation is often important for buy-sell agreements; estate, gift, or inheritance taxes; or for divorce cases, among other areas. Some lawyers claim to specialize in the area of business valuation. See **Business Law.**

Cab Accidents. See **Bus Accidents.** See also **Subway and Bus Accidents.**

Cable Television. See **Communications Law.**

Campus Security and Safety. See "Finding the Right Lawyer by Using the Advertisements of Experts and Consultants" in Chapter 4 of this book.

Cancer Diagnosis. Some lawyers specialize in cases involving incorrect diagnosis of cancer or late diagnosis of cancer. These cases are normally handled by medical malpractice lawyers. See **Malpractice.**

Captive Insurance. Captive insurance refers to an insurance company owned by the companies it insures. See **Insurance Law.**

Caregivers. See **Elder Law.**

Casino, Bar, Disco, Hotel, and Restaurant Security and Liability. See "Finding the Right Lawyer by Using the Advertisements of Experts and Consultants" in Chapter 4 of this book. See also **Personal Injury Law.**

Casino Law. See **Gaming Law.**

CC & Rs. "CC & Rs" stands for conditions, covenants, and restrictions that impair or benefit the use and value of real estate. Real estate lawyers and general practitioners can usually advise you on the legal effect of CC & Rs. Just about every lawyer studies CC & Rs in law school.

Ceramics Materials Problems. See "Finding the Right Lawyer by Using the Advertisements of Experts and Consultants" in Chapter 4 of this book.

CERCLA (Comprehensive Environment Response Compensation Act). See **Environmental Law.**

Chancery Practice. Historically, courts were divided between law courts and equity courts. The latter were also called chancery courts. In most states and in the federal system, the same judges and courtrooms are used for chancery cases and law cases, except there is no jury when the court hears equity or chancery cases. To the nonlawyer, the principal difference between the two is whether there is a jury. To a lawyer, there can be very significant differences in the types of cases and the types of relief that can be granted by a court.

In some states, notably Delaware, the chancery courts are still operated as an almost autonomous court system, independent of the law court system. In Delaware and the other states that divide the two systems, the chancery courts typically are busy deciding questions of corporate law and of the rights (or lack of rights) of corporate shareholders, directors, etc. The judges and lawyers who practice in the chancery court system are supposedly more expert in corporate and chancery matters than judges and lawyers who do both law and chancery. See **Corporate Law.**

Chapter 7. Chapter 7 is sometimes called a "straight" bankruptcy. There is no reasonable expectation that the debtor can pay all or most of his or her bills to get a fresh start. The debtor signs over all assets to the court, and the trustee in bankruptcy sells the property to get money to pay the creditors at least in part, depending on the amount and nature of the asset and the amount and claims of the creditors. The debtor then makes a fresh start free of past debt, with certain exceptions a bankruptcy lawyer can explain. Although bankruptcy is provided for under federal law, it is mixed with state law, and the results can be different in different states. See also **Assignments for the Benefit of Creditors; Bankruptcy Law.**

Chapter 11. Chapter 11 normally applies to going businesses. In Chapter 11 cases, the goal is to keep the business open and the employees working. In theory, some sort of arrangement or "workout" will be made with all the creditors to reorganize the ownership and debt structure. There may be negotiation with the key creditors. This negotiation process and resulting deal is called a "workout." The business then "comes out" of the bankruptcy court with a reorganized debt and ownership structure. In some cases, the Chapter 11 proceeding is simply a stall for time until the debtor goes into a straight bankruptcy. In some cases, the Chapter 11 proceeding is simply a business strategy to accomplish some goal with one or more creditors or competitors. If the creditors are unhappy, the plan of reorganization is sometimes called a "cram down."

Chapter 12. See **Assignments for the Benefit of Creditors.** See also **Bankruptcy.**

Chapter 13. See **Bankruptcy.**

Charitable Foundations. "Foundations" are typically single-purpose charities which get or originally got their money from a small number of donors rather than from the general public. Charitable foundation work is normally done by tax lawyers. See also **Nonprofit Organizations; Taxation.**

Charities. See **Nonprofit Organizations.**

Chattel Mortgages. "Chattel mortgages" is the old name for what is now called a "security interest" in states that use the Uniform Commercial Code (UCC). A chattel mortgage normally creates some form of claim or lien on personal property, with possession of the property staying with the owner. In a pledge or pawn situation, there normally is a change in possession away from the owner. A mortgage or deed of trust normally creates a lien on real property. Depending on the particular facts, a general practitioner or a business lawyer is normally a good starting point. See **UCC Law.**

Chemical Poisoning. If a person has been injured, see **Defective Products.** If a toxic tort is involved, see **Environmental Law.**

Child Abuse and Child Neglect. See **Juvenile Law.**

Child Custody. Cases that seek to resolve who will have legal custody of a child. Child custody cases normally arise in a divorce case. Child custody cases also arise when a child's parents are dead or are unfit or unable to take care of a child. Child custody matters are normally handled by divorce or family lawyers. See also **Dependency Law; Grandparent Visitation Rights.**

Child Dependency. Child dependency normally refers to hearings held to determine whether a child should be left in the custody and control of its parents or put into other surroundings for the protection of the child. This is an area of law halfway between family law and criminal law. See also **Child Custody; Dependency Law; Juvenile Law.**

Child Molestation. Child molestation can be both a criminal and a civil matter. The prosecution or defense of a child molestation should be done by a lawyer or team of lawyers working together. They must understand the connection between the criminal prosecution or defense and the civil significance, including the inclusion or exclusion of insurance coverage for defense costs or settlement.

Children's Law. See **Family Law.** See also **Juvenile Law.**

Child Support. The amount of money or support being furnished to a child when the parents are separated or divorced. These cases are usually handled by family lawyers, except when the child has some sort of claim for support against a dead person. In such a claim, a probate lawyer would normally be more appropriate. See also **Divorce; Family Law.**

Chillers. This refers to refrigerators, not to movies. See "Finding the Right Lawyer by Using the Advertisements of Experts and Consultants" in Chapter 4 of this book.

Christian Attorney. The lawyer with this ad is apparently Christian, but one cannot tell if only Christian clients are accepted. I do not think such a lawyer is setting forth qualifications to practice ecclesiastical law.

Church Law. Church law is also called ecclesiastical law. Lawyers who practice church law typically represent the religious organizations with legal problems dealing with the religious beliefs or practices of the church. They also represent either the church or a member of the church in disputes or interpretations that both sides wish to keep out of the civil courts. Divorces, conversions, burials in church-owned cemeteries, marriages, creation of trusts and endowment funds, major gifts to the church, church financing, taxation of the church, and its activities are all common areas within the gambit of church law. I personally have represented clients in church law matters and have recommended use of the church's judicial procedures in lieu of civil courts where appropriate.

Churning. Churning is a type of case in which a stockbroker or other financial planner takes advantage of trust, naivete, or ignorance to cause a client to keep buying and selling securities for the purpose of the broker's or planner's getting commissions on the purchases and sales. Typically, the securities or commodities being bought and sold are inappropriate for the person involved but have high commissions for the broker. This type of case is normally handled by securities lawyers or lawyers who do securities or securities fraud work. The cases may involve federal court, state court, or arbitration, depending on the facts. If possible, such cases should be handled by a lawyer who knows both litigation and securities law. See **Securities Law.**

Civil Appeals. Civil appeals, as the name indicates, is the area of law dealing with appeals after a case is won or lost in the trial court. In some states, this is a board-certified specialty. There are lawyers who do only appeals. In some firms, the appeals are handled by the same trial lawyers who tried the case.

Civil Litigation. See Litigation. See also **Trial Practice.**

Civil Rights Law. Most private civil rights law is practiced within the context of employment law. Some is practiced within the context of personal injury law, criminal law, and education law. Much civil rights law is practiced by lawyers in civil rights organizations. Civil rights issues often arise in connection with other issues. See **ADA (Americans with Disabilities Act).** See also **Employment Law.**

Civil Service Employment Law. In all the Yellow Pages ads, directories, and lists which I reviewed to try to ensure the accuracy and completeness of this glossary, I found only one firm which claimed a specialty in civil service employment law, along with private employment law. The firm was in the Washington, D.C., area and listed the following subdivisions of ability in employment law: Adverse Action, Performance Appraisals, Wrongful Termination, Court of Appeals Review, Removal, Suspension, Security Clearance, Equal Employment Opportunity, Grievance and Arbitration, Reduction in Force, Disability Retirement, and Senior Executive Service. See also **Employment Law.**

Civil Trial Law. In some states, this is a board-certified specialty. See **Litigation.** See also **Trial Law.**

Claim and Delivery. Claim and delivery is one type of lawsuit to get possession of some piece of personal property to which you have a right. Replevin and conversion are also names for legal proceedings to get possession of personal property, as opposed to land or intangible claims. Business lawyers, creditor's rights lawyers, and collection lawyers do this type of work.

Class Actions. Class actions are cases where many people are combined into a single group for purposes of prosecuting a claim. Often, the financial damage suffered by any one of the people does not justify that individual alone protecting his or her rights or claiming damages. For example, a single shareholder who was defrauded or a single person who was injured by a defective or dangerous product could not economically take on large businesses and insurance companies with essentially unlimited funds to spend to protect their market position and reputation. Class actions typically require great expertise and substantial expenditures on both sides. The individual claimants may get little except moral satisfaction (which may be all they really want). There is a tremendous risk that the law firm representing the class will lay out huge sums of money and then not get paid if the case is lost. Often the lawyers' fees eat up most of the recovery, when there is one.

A class action may be the only way a plaintiff can seek redress, but both the plaintiff(s) and the defendant(s) should realize what they are getting into when they begin to prosecute or defend this type of legal proceeding. Expertise, skill, and financing will be required on both sides. These cases are normally handled by personal injury and litigation lawyers for both the plaintiffs and the defendants. See also **Chancery Law; Mergers and Acquisitions.**

Clean Air/Water/Environment. See **Environmental Law.**

Closings. Closings are also referred to in some states as settlements. Normally, closings are transactions where real estate is bought and sold. The real estate normally, but not necessarily, is a private home or farm. In many states, closings are done by lawyers; in others they are done by nonlawyers. Closings are normally done by real estate lawyers and general practitioners.

Coastal Land Use and Activities. Many states with ocean boundaries or lake shorelines have special restrictions concerning the use or development of property within a certain distance of the shoreline. Typically, some sort of coastal commission must give prior approval to the regulated activities. These matters can normally be handled by lawyers who specialize in coastal commission cases, by administrative lawyers, by land use regulation lawyers, or by real property lawyers.

Cohabitation Law. Cohabitation law is a newly developing area of law. Cohabitation law generally includes the rights and liabilities of two unmarried people with respect to each other and to third parties.

When the two people are of the opposite sex, the area usually is handled by family lawyers or general practitioners. When the two people are of the same sex, the legal relationships may also be within the area of law known as gay and lesbian law. See also **Family Law; Gay and Lesbian Law.**

Collection Law. Collection lawyers normally represent commercial enterprises in the collection of money from the enterprises' customers. Collection lawyers are sometimes called "commercial lawyers." Normally, collection lawyers are brought in when a large volume of similar cases allow the collection lawyers to provide lower-cost services using forms, computers, and nonlawyers. A collection lawyer will usually represent a business on a contingency or partial-contingency basis. Most collection lawyers will not represent isolated, nonrepetitive clients or cases on a contingency, unless there is a large sum of money involved.

Many collection lawyers will not represent defendants in debt collection cases for fear that their creditor client would view representing "the other side" as disloyalty.

Collection lawyers sometimes refer to themselves as commercial litigators or commercial lawyers when the cases are not routine, when the cases involve a lot of money, or when there is no element of contingency involved in the fee. See also **Business Litigation; Commercial Law;** and specialty lawyers based on the type of business or industry involved.

Collections. When a lawyer lists "collections" in an advertisement, the lawyer will often take on noncommercial collection cases. Typical noncommercial collections include personal loans, and sometimes include back alimony or back child support. In noncommercial cases, the lawyer may not be willing to attempt collection on a contingency basis.

College and University Law. Some lawyers have a narrow subspecialty in university law. Normally, university law would be handled by a lawyer who does association law or nonprofit organizations or taxation. College and university law can include all of the problems handled by any enterprise and special problems such as accreditation and tenure.

College Campus Security. This area includes rapes, assaults, and robberies. See "Finding the Right Lawyer by Using the Advertisements of Experts and Consultants" in Chapter 4 of this book.

Commercial and Industrial Leasing. See **Real Estate Law.** See also **Landlord and Tenant Law.**

Commercial Law. Until recently, commercial law referred to what is now called collection law. Recently, the term is more often used to describe what lawyers often call business law. It may be difficult to look for or find a commercial lawyer to handle a particular type of case. The term is too vague to be of much help in finding the right lawyer for a client. See also **Business Law; Collection Law.**

Commissioner for Oaths. In some countries, a commissioner for oaths does what an American notary public does (acknowledge signatures, etc.). A commissioner for oaths is normally not a lawyer. See also **Notary.**

Commodities Futures Law. See **Securities Law.** See also **Securities Regulation.**

Commodities Law. See **Securities Law.** See also **Securities Regulation.**

Common Carrier Cases. Common carrier cases typically involve a railroad, an airline, a shipping company, a bus company, a taxi company, and other companies which carry goods or passengers. Typically personal injury or general practice attorneys are a good starting point, although there are lawyers who do specialty transportation law work such as rate-setting cases.

Communications Law. An area of law that usually deals with obtaining and keeping government licenses, commonly from the Federal Communications Commission (FCC). In some cases, state and local governments are involved. Cable TV and cellular telephones are areas where local governments are commonly involved. Some communications lawyers deal with international communications systems involving satellites or fiber optic communications. Lawyers and law firms doing communications work are often located near the locations of the licensing authorities or near high-tech centers. See also **High Technology Law; Intellectual Property Law; Space and Aviation Law.**

Community Associations. See **Association Law.** See also **Condominium Law; Nonprofit Organizations.**

Community Property Law. Community property law is simply a form of marital property law in states which have a form of community property. It is a serious mistake to assume that the community property law of one state is similar to or the same as that of any other state. See also **Divorce Law; Family Law; Probate.**

Competency. For mental capacity, see **Estate Planning;** for incompetent professional care, see **Malpractice.**

Complex Civil Litigation. Complex civil litigation can either be complex cases involving many lawyers and much evidence, or a case that is pending in several different courts at the same time. These cases are handled by lawyers specializing in litigation or trial law. See also **Litigation; Trial Law.**

Computer Law. Computer law is a very general term which can cover the manufacture, licensing, and copying of software and hardware. It can also cover disputes between those who sell hardware and software and those who buy it, as well as disputes concerning computer consultants. Most computer law lawyers and firms have, or claim to have, the engineering and scientific skills and knowledge necessary to understand the facts and the technology in order to apply the law. Many lawyers and firms claim to "specialize" in computer law, although it is not yet a generally accepted specialty. See also **High Technology Law; Intellectual Property Law.**

Computer Related Cases. See "Finding the Right Lawyer by Using the Advertisements of Experts and Consultants" in Chapter 4 of this book.

Condemnation. Condemnation cases involve a government agency's taking property and then paying for it. The dispute could involve the government's right or need to take the property or the amount of compensation being paid. There are lawyers who specialize in these cases but they may be difficult to find. Some of them practice in municipal law firms. You may have to ask for help from your general practitioner or real estate lawyer. Condemnation also normally includes inverse condemnation law. Condemnation work is sometimes called "eminent domain."

Condominium Law. Some lawyers specialize in the construction and sale of condominiums and condominium developments. Some lawyers have a specialty in condominium associations. See also **Homeowners' Association Dues.**

Conflict of Interest. For conflicts involving lawyers, see **Fee Disputes; Legal Malpractice; Malpractice.** For conflicts involving corporations or associations and their officers and directors, see **Association Law.** For conflicts involving elected or appointed government officials, see **Criminal Law; Political Law.** See also "Conflicts of Interest" in Chapter 9 of this book.

Conservatorship. See **Family Law.**

Constitutional Law. Constitutional law is sometimes used to describe the conflicts between state and federal laws. Constitutional law is also procedures used to describe individual rights and used in criminal and other governmental proceedings. The term "constitutional rights" normally refers to rights and limitations under the federal constitution. In some cases, the term "constitutional law" refers to the constitution of a state. See **Civil Rights Law.**

Constitutional Law (Freedom of Speech). This is often involved in libel and slander cases. See also **Defamation Law; Libel and Slander; Publications Law.**

Construction Accidents. Accidents involving cranes, hoists, rigging, or forklifts. See "Finding the Right Lawyer by Using the Advertisements of Experts and Consultants" in Chapter 4 of this book.

Construction Injuries. See **Workers' Compensation Law.**

Construction Law. Construction law can be a very broad field of law encompassing just about every phase of construction and the problems of injuries, accidents, and damages which arise during construction. Much construction law is, in the final analysis, a fight between insurance companies which have posted completion and surety bonds for various contractors. For this reason, many firms which practice construction law also do surety work and various forms of insurance law. See also **Insurance Coverage; Insurance Law.**

Construction Litigation. See **Construction Law.**

Consular Law. See **International Law.** See also **Immigration Law.**

Consumer Credit Laws. Most states and the federal government have laws to assist individuals and companies who believe their credit has been unfairly reported. In some cases, only a correction to the credit rating can be made. In some cases, the other side of the dispute can be told. In other cases, the person injured by the erroneous credit reporting can collect damages. See **Consumer Laws.**

Consumer Laws. Consumer laws are sometimes called consumer protection laws. This area of law deals with various protections and remedies offered consumers. It is a very broad area of law and crosses over into many other areas, such as litigation, personal injury, class actions, etc. Consumer laws generally are designed to give remedies and rights (often including attorney's fees) to consumers to encourage them to prosecute when laws affecting safety, honesty, or accuracy are involved. Typical areas include credit reporting, defective products, unsafe products, false advertising, deceptive packaging, and lemon laws (for purchases of defective products). Lawyers who seek consumer law cases typically advertise this in their Yellow Pages ads.

Consumer Protection Laws. See **Consumer Laws.**

Contempt. Contempt normally arises in the context of a specific type of case, most commonly domestic relations. Contempt can be criminal, civil, or both. A general practitioner is normally a good starting point when there is a contempt problem. Depending on the specifics of the case, a family lawyer or divorce lawyer may be more appropriate.

Contingent Fees. Fees linked to the amount recovered. Lawyers who list contingent fees typically will accept high-risk, high-reward cases where they earn a fee only if they win. Contingent fee cases are common in claimants' personal injury and will contests, consumer-oriented cases, and class-action cases.

Contract Law. There is no recognized specialty known as contract law. Lawyers who list this area of law are saying they can either draft contracts or litigate breach-of-contract matters. See also **Litigation Law; Transactional Law.**

Contract Negotiation. Depending on the difficulties of the contract, contracts can be negotiated by almost any experienced lawyer who really understands the underlying object of the contract. Lawyers in general practice and business law normally do contract negotiation. Government contract negotiation and renegotiation is a specialized field of contract negotiation.

Contract Review. Some lawyers advertise that they are willing to review a contract and advise you of its legal effect, even though they didn't participate in the negotiating or drafting of the contract. It is usually a good idea to get a contract review before signing any significant contract or any contract you don't fully understand. Even though you may not be able to change anything, you will at least understand what you are signing and what your legal rights and responsibilities will be after signing. General practitioners are a good starting place. If the contract is specialized, the general practitioner can assist in finding the right lawyer to review the contract.

Convenience Store Robbery Deterrence and Crisis Management. See "Finding the Right Lawyer by Using the Advertisements of Experts and Consultants" in Chapter 4 of this book.

Convenience Store Security. See "Finding the Right Lawyer by Using the Advertisements of Experts and Consultants" in Chapter 4 of this book.

Conversion. See **Claim and Delivery; Theft.**

Copyrights. See **Intellectual Property Law.**

Corporate Control. See **Mergers and Acquisitions.** See also **Chancery Practice.**

Corporate Counsel. See **In-House Counsel.**

Corporate Finance and Securities Law. See **Securities Law.**

Corporate Finance Law. See **Securities Law.**

Corporate Law. In most practices, when the lawyer uses the term "corporate law" it is just another way of saying business law, as opposed to what some lawyers call "people law." In business law or corporate law, the firm concerns itself with the problems of commercial enterprises rather than the personal problems of individual people. Many lawyers who list corporate law or corporations are indicating they can advise and help in the creation of new corporations. They may be indicating they can advise between the advisability of a corporation as opposed to a partnership or other form of organization.

True corporate law deals with the rights and problems of corporations and their shareholders, directors, officers, and employees, as well as stock issuance, securities laws, compliance with procedures and laws applicable to corporations, etc. If you have a situation involving true corporate law, such as a shareholder dispute, you should make that clear to the lawyer you speak with. The lawyer may not realize that you need a lawyer knowledgeable in corporate matters rather than a lawyer knowledgeable in general business matters. Business law and corporate law divide into hundreds of subspecialties. Generally, a general practitioner or business lawyer is a good starting point. See also **Business Law; Chancery Practice.**

Corporate Lawyer. See **In-House Counsel.**

Corporate Recovery. Corporate recovery is a fancy way of saying bankruptcy and receiverships. See also **Assignments for the Benefit of Creditors; Bankruptcy.**

Corporate Securities Law. See **Securities Law.**

Corporations. See **Corporations and Partnership Law.** See also **Business Law; General Practice.**

Corporations and Partnership Law. An indication the lawyer can advise on the creation of a new corporation, as well as the advisability of a corporation as opposed to other forms of business enterprise. Common alternatives to corporations include partnerships, trusts, and sole proprietorships. Common types of corporations include public corporations, "close" corporations, Subchapter S corporations, Delaware and Nevada corporations, and offshore corporations. Common types of partnerships include general partnerships and limited partnerships. A general practitioner may be a good starting point for finding the lawyer to advise you as to choice of business entity.

Cosigner Protection. See **Bankruptcy.** See also **Creditors' Rights.**

Costs. Reference to "costs" can either refer to the monies which must be advanced during the case or to monies which a court may order to be paid.

Costs May Be Required. "Costs may be required" means that although the lawyer is willing to work on a contingent-fee basis, in some cases the client will be required to pay out-of-pocket costs.

Country Club Law. See **Association Law.** See also **Nonprofit Organizations.**

Court-Martial. See **Military Law.**

Courtroom Design and Safety. See "Finding the Right Lawyer by Using the Advertisements of Experts and Consultants" in Chapter 4 of this book.

Covenants Not to Compete. Covenants not to compete usually arise out of an employment agreement or contract for the sale of a business. Such covenants can be created, negotiated, or interpreted by either a business lawyer or an employment lawyer. If there is a problem, a litigation lawyer should be involved.

Coverage. See **Insurance Coverage.**

Creditors' Rights. A broad area of law dealing generally with seeking money from someone who is claimed to owe it (debtor) in a business contract (as opposed to tort) situation. In most cases you should start with a general practice or business litigation lawyer, who can then further direct you if some special expertise is needed. Obviously, different skill levels are required in this area of law. For example, it takes less skill or experience to sue an individual or to repossess an auto or an overdue consumer loan than would be required for a creditor to take possession of an oceangoing vessel with a crew of 800 and 1,700 passengers on board.

Credit Reporting. Consumer credit reporting is governed by layers of state and federal regulation setting forth detailed procedures and remedies. Trade or business credit reporting is normally a matter of trade defamation or libel. See also **Consumer Credit Laws; Consumer Laws.**

Criminal Appeals. An appeal takes place after a trial is lost in whole or in part. In some states, all criminal cases are automatically appealed. In some states, only certain types of serious cases are automatically appealed. There are lawyers who only handle criminal appeals. In some cases, the appeal can be handled by the same lawyer or firm that handled the original case. In some jurisdictions, criminal appeals are a board-certified specialty.

Criminal Assaults on Premises. See **Personal Injury Law.** See also **Campus Security and Safety; Unsafe Premises.**

Criminal Law. Criminal law is a very broad area of law. In some jurisdictions, it is a board-certified specialty. It would take an entire book just to list the areas of law included within this broad area. Everything from murder to spitting on the sidewalk is included. Criminal lawyers tend to develop subspecialties in specific areas of the law. They usually network with one another and can find the right sub-specialist for the case. Drug and drug-related cases take up a large part of the world of criminal law. White-collar crime is usually classified as crime committed with a pen and without physical violence. It has been estimated that as much as one-half of all prisoners never committed an act of violence. White-collar defendants get a lot of media coverage and public interest, and judges often give sentences to first offenders longer than sentences given to repeat offenders for crimes of violence.

All criminal accusations should be taken most seriously. It is most important that the lawyer know the idiosyncrasies of the local judges and juries. As well, to negotiate a deal where advisable, the lawyer should know the local prosecutors. I know of no area of law where it is more important to get the right lawyer. If you have the time and money, check out carefully who you will be hiring to defend you or another in a criminal case. A few extra days in jail until the right lawyer is hired will be time well spent. Don't be in a rush to hire the lawyer who paid the most to get TV coverage. Ask your general practitioner: "Who would you hire to represent your son or daughter?" Rely heavily on the advice given you by other lawyers as to who is the right lawyer for the case. In most cases, when a lawyer says or lists criminal law as an area of practice, he or she is referring to defending criminal prosecutions as opposed to being the prosecutor, although technically, prosecutors also practice criminal law. See also **Private Criminal Law.**

Criminal Law and Traffic Offenses. Criminal law and traffic offenses are sometimes lumped together as a single area of practice. See also **Criminal Law; Traffic Offenses.**

Criminal Law Defense. See **Criminal Law.**

Criminal Law Prosecution. See **Criminal Law.**

Criminal Tax Law. A specialty within white-collar crime, sometimes called tax fraud. When a tax matter has criminal implications, it is important to get a criminal tax lawyer immediately. Civil tax lawyers often do not understand the criminal aspects and procedures of criminal tax cases. CPAs may have no attorney-client privilege and no ability to raise the privilege against self-incrimination for the taxpayer, when applicable. A white-collar criminal lawyer or a civil trial lawyer without actual tax fraud experience can sometimes damage the case. This is a very narrow subspecialty requiring very specific experience. Unfortunately, the defendant or person under investigation often thinks the whole thing is a civil tax matter that will go away when a check for back taxes is written. Often, the person's civil tax lawyer or

CPA treats the matter lightly because the accused doesn't tell the whole story to the lawyer or CPA. In most of the cases I've handled, the accused was a sophisticated, educated business or professional person who erroneously thought he or she was smarter than the government, the lawyer, or the accountant. Such people usually think they will get away with it and frequently lie to the IRS, the grand jury, their own lawyer, and their own CPA. Start your search for a lawyer immediately with either tax law or white-collar crimes. See also **Taxation; White-Collar Crimes.**

Crowd Control in Public Places. See "Finding the Right Lawyer by Using the Advertisements of Experts and Consultants" in Chapter 4 of this book.

Cruise Ships and Cruise Ship Accidents. See **Admiralty Law.** See also **Maritime Law; Personal Injury Law.**

Curators. In some states, the person who manages the finances of an elderly or incompetent person is called a "curator." See also **Elder Law; Estate Planning.**

Currency Seizures and Forfeitures. See **Forfeitures.** See also **Customs Law.**

Custody. Normally refers to child custody matters connected with a divorce. Also it refers to modifications of prior child custody orders. Custody matters are often connected with matters of alimony or child support. Custody matters are normally handled by general practitioners, family lawyers, and divorce lawyers. See also **Child Dependency; Divorce; Family Law; Grandparent Visitation Rights.**

Customer List Protection. See **Unfair Competition Law.** See also **Copyrights; Deceptive Trade Practices.**

Customs Law. Customs law normally deals with one of three areas. Few people know that a person bringing money into or taking money out of the United States sometimes has to declare the money on arriving or leaving. Customs inspectors routinely "sweep" an airplane arriving or leaving, looking for undeclared money. If they find undeclared money that should have been declared, they often seize it and will later forfeit it or negotiate a settlement. I personally have had success in this type of law, but have never known another lawyer to take these cases when they are meritorious. Not declaring currency or property can be a form of smuggling.

A second area of customs law deals with the traditional matters of classification of goods for taxation or quota purposes. This area is handled by customs brokers for simple matters. The customs brokers may or may not be lawyers. Only a small number of lawyers do the traditional customs law of duties, quotas, and tariffs. They call themselves customs lawyers and typically are located in major port cities. Sometimes a customs broker will recommend a lawyer when the matter is too complicated for the customs broker. In some customs cases, a criminal lawyer is necessary.

Another area of customs law involves drugs. This area is handled by criminal lawyers. See **Criminal Law.**

Dalkon Shield IUD Cases. An entire network of lawyers handles these cases. Many of the lawyers simply forward the claims to other lawyers. It would probably be worthwhile to associate with a lawyer already handling this specialized area rather than to start from ground zero.

Dangerous Premises. An area of law that can include swimming pool accidents, failure to supply guards or lighting, failure to properly or adequately maintain or repair premises, or maintaining an unsafe work area. Escalator accidents and slips and falls also are included. When children are involved, this type of law is sometimes referred to as "attractive nuisance." In some cases, a lawyer who does landlord and tenant law will be knowledgeable. When a person suffers an injury while on the premises for a job-connected reason, a lawyer who handles workers' compensation would be involved. This area of law is also done by personal injury or negligence lawyers. A general practitioner is a good place to start. See also **Attractive Nuisance; Lack of Security; Slip and Fall; Unsafe Premises.**

Dangerous Work Area. See **Dangerous Premises.** See also **Slip and Fall; Unsafe Premises; Workers' Compensation Law.**

Death Cases. The words "death cases" really are not very informative about what the lawyer or firm does or does not do. In most cases, lawyers who handle "death cases" are simply fishing for personal injury cases or workers' compensation cases where there might be a lot of money involved. Normally, these lawyers are not looking for probate cases or estates or death tax cases. A more accurate description is "wrongful death cases." In such cases the death of a person is possibly caused by something other than from old age. See also **Wrongful Death Cases.**

Death Claims. See **Death Cases.** See also **Wrongful Death Cases.**

Debt Collections. See **Bankruptcy.** See also **Collections; Commercial Law.**

Debt Negotiation Services. Debt negotiation services are typically advertised by law firms that do bankruptcy work. These firms are sometimes able to convince creditors to renegotiate debts to avoid a bankruptcy situation. See also **Assignments for the Benefit of Creditors; Bankruptcy; Negotiations.**

Debt Relief. Protection from creditors. Typically refers to lawyers who file bankruptcy for debtors under various chapters of the U.S. bankruptcy laws.

Deceptive Trade Practices. Deceptive trade practices or deceptive trade can include false advertising, unfair competition (sometimes called "dirty tricks"), false packaging, false labeling, mislabeling of goods or services, "bait and switch" advertising, as well as a large variety of deceptive conduct. Some form of advertising, labeling or business competition is normally involved. See also **Advertising Law; Consumer Laws; Unfair Competition Law.**

Deeds. Deeds normally can be prepared by general practice lawyers in most cases or by real estate lawyers.

Defamation Law. Defamation law may or may not be related to employment. Defamation cases can normally be handled by negligence or personal injury lawyers. See also **Employment Law; Libel and Slander.**

Defective Machinery. See **Personal Injury Law.**

Defective Products. Defective products involve the belief that a product caused injury. A personal injury lawyer would normally be the beginning point in finding the right lawyer. Many lawyers specialize in the injuries caused by a specific product. Most personal injury lawyers network with other such lawyers and can find the subspecialist for the particular product, be it a particular type or manufacture of machinery, food, drugs, cosmetics, or whatever. Most clients who believe they have been injured by a defective product do not realize there may be others of similar belief, and that some lawyer, firm, or laboratory has already done research into the area involved. On some occasions, a general practitioner can find the right lawyer, but a personal injury lawyer usually can do the job faster.

Defective Roads. See **Personal Injury Law.**

Defective Vehicles. This could involve consumer law, covering situations where you are not happy with the car you bought from a dealer (also called lemon law cases), or it could describe cases where injury or accident is believed to have been caused by defective manufacture or design of a car. The latter is technically called "warranty liability." These cases are handled by general practice lawyers and personal injury lawyers.

Delaware Corporations. See **Blue-Sky Laws.** See also **Chancery Practice.**

Delinquent Homeowners' Association and Condominium Association Fees. See **Homeowners' Association Dues.** See also **Condominium Law; Real Estate Law.**

Dependency Law. Dependency law is normally the area of practice where a court decides if a child should be removed from its parents and declared to be a dependent of the government. See also **Child Custody.**

Deportation. See **Immigration Law.**

Derivative Actions. Derivative actions are, in theory, suits brought by one person (usually a shareholder) against another (usually a director, officer, or third party) in the name of a corporation. Derivative actions are normally brought by an unhappy shareholder. See also **Chancery Practice; Class Actions; Corporate Law.**

Design Professionals. Design professionals normally refers to architects, engineers, and contractors who give opinions or testimony involved in alleged construction defects cases. See also **Construction Law; Malpractice.**

Diet Fraud. See "Finding the Right Lawyer by Using the Advertisements of Experts and Consultants" in Chapter 4 of this book.

Diplomatic Law. See **International Law.**

Directors' and Officers' Defense and Coverage. The responsibility of a corporation to protect its officers and directors when they are sued—and the obligation, if any, of the corporation's insurance company to defend the corporation's officers and directors—is a very narrow question of insurance coverage law and of corporate law.

Disability Claims. In some states, there is a governmental system of disability benefits for employees who cannot work due to nonjob-related causes. Workers' compensation lawyers are usually knowledgeable in this area of law. See also **Workers' Compensation Law; Work Injuries.**

Disabled Persons. Hiring and employment of disabled persons is normally included within employment law. See also **ADA (Americans with Disabilities Act); Civil Rights Law; Employment Law.**

Dischargeable Debt. Dischargeable debts are normally those which have been eliminated by a bankruptcy. Nondischargeable debts are those which survive or are not discharged by a bankruptcy. See also **Bankruptcy.**

Disco Liability. See "Finding the Right Lawyer by Using the Advertisements of Experts and Consultants" in Chapter 4 of this book.

Discrimination Law. See Civil Rights Law. See also ADA (Americans with Disabilities Act); Employment Law.

Disfigurement. See Serious Injuries. See also Personal Injury Law.

Dissolution. Dissolution is a modern word for what used to be called divorce. Historically, people divorced each other and there was an element of fault or right and wrong involved. The current trend is to say the marriage or marital status should be dissolved without the stigma and emotion of proving that someone was wrong, at fault, or guilty. This area of law is usually handled by general practitioners, family lawyers, and divorce lawyers. See also Divorce.

Diversion. See Antitrust Law.

Divers. Some firms advertise for cases involving injuries to divers. Although in theory these could be scuba or sports divers, in practice this is a form of workers' compensation dealing with offshore oil exploration and oil rigs. See also Offshore Injuries; Scuba Accidents; Workers' Compensation Law.

Divestitures. See Mergers and Acquisitions. See also Antitrust Law; Corporate Law; Reorganizations; Taxation.

Divorce. A divorce is usually the legal end of a marriage other than by death. Divorce doesn't happen automatically; a court proceeding and decree is required. The modern tendency is to use a process called dissolution, rather than the divorce. In most cases, a divorce and a dissolution are legally about the same thing, although there can be differences. A divorce usually has meant that one party divorced the other and it was necessary to prove that one person or the other was in some manner "guilty" of some act such as adultery, desertion, failure to support, physical violence, etc. In a dissolution, the legal state of marriage is dissolved and it may not involve finding anyone "at fault." Divorce law can also include alternatives to divorce such as annulment or legal separation.

Divorce and all the legal matters incident to divorce, such as property settlement or division, child custody, alimony (sometimes called spousal support), child support, payment of bills, inheritance rights, modifications of prior court orders, etc., are normally handled by lawyers who may identify themselves as general practitioners, family lawyers, or divorce lawyers. See also Dissolution; Family Law.

Divorce for Men Only. One firm advertises "Divorce for Men Only." I haven't seen anyone advertise "Divorce for Women Only." See also Family Law.

Document Examination. See "Finding the Right Lawyer by Using the Advertisements of Experts and Consultants" in Chapter 4 of this book.

Dog Bite Cases. Cases where the plaintiff was bit or harmed by a dog or other animal. Dog bite cases are normally civil cases handled by personal injury lawyers. However, if a dog bite results in death or serious injury, there can be criminal consequences. Your postal letter carriers can often recommend a lawyer who has handled a dog bite case for themselves or for another letter carrier. If your dog or animal is involved, check whether your homeowners, general liability, or other insurance policy will cover costs of defending and paying claims. Lawyers handling dog bite cases often handle other animal bite cases as well.

Domestic Violence. See **Family Law.**

Dominican Divorces. In the Dominican Republic, it is sometimes possible to get a divorce by proxy with little or no waiting before or after the judicial decree. There are lawyers throughout the United States who have relationships with firms in the Dominican Republic. For various reasons, most U.S. family lawyers advise against getting a Dominican divorce or any other foreign divorce, except under very special circumstances for very specialized reasons. These cases are usually referred by U.S. lawyers who practice international law. See also **International Law.**

Doors. See "Finding the Right Lawyer by Using the Advertisements of Experts and Consultants" in Chapter 4 of this book.

Dram Shop Law. Dram shop law is an isolated area dealing with the liability of the seller of liquor (the dram shop) for damages caused by the buyer of liquor. Typically, the buyer becomes or is drunk and injures or kills while drunk. This area of law is also called Dram Act. See also **Innkeepers Law; Liquor Law; Personal Injury Law.**

Driver's License Suspension. Driver's license suspension cases are normally handled by lawyers who do either administrative law generally, or who do criminal law involving automobiles or drunk driving or driving under the influence of controlled substances. See also **Drunk Driving; DUI; DWI.**

Driving Offenses. Driving offenses normally refer to traffic tickets or criminal cases related to the use of a motor vehicle. In some cases the lawyer is seeking serious cases such as those involving alcohol, drugs, or death. In other cases, the lawyer is simply indicating a willingness to handle simple, routine traffic cases. If drugs, death, or alcohol is involved you should seek a Criminal lawyer with experience in that area of law. See also **Dram Shop Law; Drunk Driving; DUI; DWI; Traffic Cases.**

Driving Under the Influence. See **DUI.** See also **Dram Shop Law; Drunk Driving; DWI.**

Driving While Intoxicated. See DWI. See also **Drunk Driving; DUI.**

Driving While Suspended or Revoked. Technically, driving while suspended or revoked should be called driving with a suspended or revoked license, since it is the license, not the driver, which is suspended. See also **Traffic Offenses.**

Drug and Alcohol Testing. See **Employment Law.**

Drug Cases. Cases that involve the possession, sale, manufacture, or cultivation of narcotics or controlled substances such as steroids. Drug cases sometimes involve a person's being in a place where there are drugs or where drugs are sold. Drug cases normally require a criminal lawyer. Many criminal lawyers specialize in drug cases. It is important to know whether a drug case is going to be prosecuted by state or federal authorities, or both. Some lawyers only know defense of federal crimes, some only know defense of state crimes, and some claim to know both. I've seen ads which specifically refer to cocaine, heroin, marijuana, Dilaudid, and Methamphetamine, although I don't know why it is necessary or helpful to list the specific drug cases the lawyer handles. Drug cases are sometimes called "substance abuse" cases.

Drug cases sometimes are civil or administrative matters involving the licenses or practice restrictions of people who use or dispense drugs.

Ask the lawyer which type of drug matters the lawyer can handle as the needs of a case can be very different. The words "drug cases" are a good beginning but not the end in finding the right lawyer for the case.

Drug Offenses. See **Drug Cases.**

Drug Reaction. Cases involving bad reactions to drugs and medicines can be handled by medical malpractice lawyers, product liability lawyers, and general personal injury lawyers.

Drunk Driver Injuries. Firms that seek personal injury cases where the other party was drunk (or the equivalent) are seeking cases that are easier to win. Some people are tolerant toward drunk driving or driving under the influence (DUI). These people may become violently anti-drunk driving when they or a member of their family is killed or injured by a drunk driver. These ads seek to capitalize of this feeling of anger and rage. See also **Dram Shop Law; Personal Injury Law.**

Drunk Driving. Historically, and still today in some jurisdictions, drunk driving was charged or proved based on observable conduct alone. Typical conduct included erratic driving, inability to walk a straight line, slurred speech, etc. Today, drunk driving is often proven based on blood-alcohol percentages. Rather than debate whether a person was in fact drunk, police officers and prosecutors depend on chemical blood tests to prove their case.

Drunk driving is normally a very serious offense, especially when it is a second or third offense or if an accident or injury was involved. Always try to find a local lawyer who specializes in drunk driving cases or who does criminal law generally, and who knows how local judges are likely to treat the case. See also **DUI; DWI; Reckless Driving; Traffic Offenses.**

DUI. DUI normally stands for "driving under the influence" of either alcohol or other substances to an extent the law considers unsafe for the other people using the roads. Normally chemical tests of urine, blood, or breath are used to support the personal observations of the arresting officers or witnesses. Often the penalties for a second or third conviction can be very heavy, including jail or prison as well as heavy fines and loss or restriction of driving privileges. For this reason, lawyers often provide such descriptions as "Second Offense." See also **Dram Shop Law; Drunk Driving; DUI; DWI.**

Durable Powers of Attorney. A document giving a person (the agent) the power to make health care and medical care decisions for another (the principal) when the principal is not able to make to make decisions. The power can even extend to life or death decisions. Durable powers of attorney are normally prepared by lawyers who practice estate planning, wills, general practice, elder law, probate law, conservatorships, and family law. See these various headings.

DWI. DWI stands for "driving while intoxicated." In some jurisdictions, DWI only applies to alcohol intoxication. In other jurisdictions, it includes other chemicals. DWI is normally proven by blood-alcohol content rather than by proving that a person was or was not influenced or intoxicated. See also **Drunk Driving; DUI; Traffic Offenses.**

Earth Subsidence and Movement. See **Land-Use Regulation.** See also **Construction Law.**

Easements. See **Real Estate Law.** See also **Title Insurance.**

Ecclesiastical Law. See **Church Law.**

Education Law. Education law normally refers to the representation of schools, colleges, universities, and school districts. Education law sometimes confines itself to labor law matters at a school. It can also include the variety of legal needs of a school, including taxation. See also **College and University Law; Municipal Law.**

Elder Law. Elder law is a newly developing specialty that tries to bring under one lawyer or firm the many different areas of legal abilities and specialties needed by the elderly, and those who have responsibility for the elderly. (Those who take care of the elderly are sometimes called "caregivers.") It sometimes takes a very special type of lawyer or legal assistant to help the elderly. Many lawyers don't have the patience to interview the elderly, or are not willing to go to hospitals, nursing homes or retirement centers when the client can't get to and from a law office. Elder law lawyers often are skilled in establishing competency, which might later become an issue. They often have appropriate videotaping equipment and facilities to record the client in an effort to establish the client's competency.

Most of the problems of the elderly are traditional problems that can be handled by a general practitioner. If not, they can be referred by a general practitioner to appropriate specialists where required. Some of the more common areas of elder law are estate planning, conservatorships, wills, trusts, living trusts, life care contracts, Medicare, Social Security, guardianships, conservatorships, consumer law, competency, estate and gift taxation, etc.

With advances in modern medicine, people are living longer than they used to. They often have special needs such as durable powers of attorney, living wills, etc, which are intended to give guidance to those who must make decisions for the elderly person when the individual is no longer capable of making decisions. See also **Durable Power of Attorney; Estate Planning; Organ Donation.**

Elderly/Injuries to the Elderly. See "Finding the Right Lawyer by Using the Advertisements of Experts and Consultants" in Chapter 4 of this book.

Election and Redistricting Law. See **Political Law.**

Electrical Piping. See "Finding the Right Lawyer by Using the Advertisements of Experts and Consultants" in Chapter 4 of this book.

Elevators and Escalators. See "Finding the Right Lawyer by Using the Advertisements of Experts and Consultants" in Chapter 4 of this book.

Embezzlement. Embezzlement is a special form of theft that normally involves stealing from someone where there is a special relationship, such as employer and employee. An accusation of embezzlement would require the services of a criminal lawyer.

Eminent Domain. See **Condemnation.**

Emotional Injury. Emotional injury is sometimes compensable. A personal injury, workers' compensation, or general practice lawyer is normally a good starting point to determine one's right to compensation, if any.

Employee Benefits. See **Employment Law.**

Employee Rights. See Civil Rights Law; Discrimination Law; Employment Law.

Employee Stock Option Plans (ESOPs). An employee stock option plan is known as an ESOP. ESOPs are usually created by tax lawyers. Occasionally an employment lawyer, an employee benefits lawyer, an accountant, or even nonlawyer consultants from pension plan administrators are involved in the plan creation or application.

Employee Stock Options. Employee stock options are normally created by tax lawyers. Estate planning lawyers and employee benefit lawyers often advise employees whether or not to exercise these stock options.

Employer-Employee Law. See Employment Law. See also Civil Rights Law; Discrimination Law.

Employer-Employee Relations. See Employment Law.

Employer Penalties. See Immigration Law.

Employer Sanctions. See Immigration Law.

Employment Contracts. Most employment contracts can be written by either a general practitioner, a corporate lawyer, or a business lawyer. Unless there are some very sophisticated issues involved, it is rarely worth the expense to have a simple employment contract drafted or negotiated by an employment law firm.

Employment Law. Cases that involve an employee's suing an employer or former employer for a claimed breach of the terms of employment. The case often involves a claimed firing or other penalizing of an employee based on some form of discrimination, such as age or sex discrimination. Employment law can also encompass matters such as pension plans, retirement benefits and medical insurance problems. Employment law does not ordinarily include physical injuries that are included under workers' compensation. In some cases, employment law claims are handled as discrimination cases.

Areas commonly included in employment law include wrongful termination, breach of contract, "whistle blowing," customer lists and confidential information, trade secrets, prohibition of employees from working for competitors, privacy, sexual harassment, rights of disabled or handicapped employees, maternity or parenting rights, wages and hours laws (overtime), occupational safety and health (OSHA), equal employment, grievance procedures, employee discipline and discharge, unions, collective bargaining, strikes, boycotts, lockouts, lie detector tests (polygraphs), drug testing, HIV testing, health insurance, plant closings, security clearance, equal opportunity, age bias, gender bias, affirmative action compliance, promotion, hiring, evaluation, discharge, employment of aliens, discipline, selection, and disciplinary procedures.

In some areas of the country, federal employment law is considered a separate subspecialty

Historically, law firms that represent employers would never represent employees and vice versa. If you find a firm that does employment law for one side, it will often recommend a firm for the other side. See also **Breach of Contract; Civil Service Employment Law; Contract Law; Discrimination Law;** "Finding the Right Lawyer by Using the Advertisements of Experts and Consultants" in Chapter 4 of this book.

Energy Law. See **Oil and Gas Law.** See also **Natural Resources Law.**

Energy Project Development. A lawyer specializing in energy project development would have to know natural resources law, municipal financing law, administrative law, utility law, and about ten other fields of law. I would expect to find this much expertise in a special department of a very large law firm.

Enforcing Mortgages and Liens. See **Mortgages.**

English Language, Syntax, Grammar, and Vocabulary. In some cases involving advertisements or common or special meaning of language, there is a need for an "English language specialist." See "Finding the Right Lawyer by Using the Advertisements of Experts and Consultants" in Chapter 4 of this book.

Entertainment and Music Litigation. There are firms and departments of firms specializing in the area of litigation. See also **Intellectual Property Law.**

Entertainment and Sports Law. A large area of law. There are very few firms that do this kind of work, yet many firms and individuals want to do this kind of work because of the perceived glamour and excitement as seen on various TV series. Typically included in this area of law are motion picture law, television law, contract law, labor law with emphasis on the guilds, and several other niche lawyering areas found only in entertainment law. Representation may be institutional, such as studios, financing, distribution agreements, etc., or may be individual, representing the performer. It takes many years to learn enough about entertainment law to be able to deal intelligently with the people involved in the industry on a take-charge basis.

Entertainment law is often lumped together with sports law, as there is a great deal of similarity when negotiating on behalf of an entertainer and athlete. See also **Literary Property.**

Entertainment and Sports Representation. Some law firms are also licensed as employment agencies or talent agencies. They network for their clients as agents, charging an agent's commission in addition to or instead of charging a fee for legal services.

Entertainment Financing. See **Entertainment and Sports Law.**

Entertainment Law. See **Entertainment and Sports Law.**

Entrepreneurship Law. See **Business Law.** See also **Business Start-Ups.**

Environmental Law. An area of law that includes many subspecialties in the general area of what is called clean air, clean water, or clean environment. This area of law is also called toxic waste disposal, hazardous waste disposal, and toxic torts. Environmental problems can be state or federal, civil or criminal, private or public.

Since much of environmental law is the result of specific legislation, the legal areas are often referred to by the acronyms of the law creating the legislation. Common examples include CERCLA (Comprehensive Environmental Response, Compensation, and Liability Act), CWA (Clean Water Acts) and CAA (Clean Air Act).

Most lawyers who do this kind of work are found in large firms. They are sometimes found in the real estate department, the litigation department, or sometimes the land use and regulation department. This area of law is relatively new and is not fully institutionalized. Environmental impact reports (EIRs) and studies are included in this area of law. See also **Land-Use Regulation.**

Equine Law. Specialization in the law regarding horses. These lawyers are especially common in Kentucky. They handle cases involving syndications of racehorses and just about any question of law involving a horse or, in some cases, horse races. If you can't find a local equine lawyer, it may be worthwhile for you to find a Kentucky law firm by looking in the Martindale-Hubbell Law Directory and calling that firm for a recommendation to a local lawyer. You could also call your general practitioner and ask that person to find an equine lawyer for you.

Equity Law. See **Chancery Practice.**

ERISA and Fiduciary Responsibility. See **ERISA Law.** See also "Finding the Right Lawyer by Using the Advertisements of Experts and Consultants" in Chapter 4 of this book.

ERISA Law. ERISA is an acronym for a pension law dealing with employee pension plans and retirement plans and employee rights under those plans. Lawyers who do this kind of work typically are employee benefit or employment law or tax lawyers.

Escalators. See "Finding the Right Lawyer by Using the Advertisements of Experts and Consultants" in Chapter 4 of this book.

Escheats. A process whereby the state or other governmental entity takes ownership of property when it has been abandoned or unclaimed for a certain number of years. Dormant bank accounts are a common example. Escheat problems can normally be handled by a general practitioner. The area of law called unclaimed credits also is within escheat law.

Escrows. See "Finding the Right Lawyer by Using the Advertisements of Experts and Consultants" in Chapter 4 of this book.

Eskimo Law. See **Native American Law.**

ESOP. See **Employee Stock Option Plans (ESOPs).**

Espionage. I have only found one lawyer in America who claims espionage defense as a specialty. Normally one would turn to a criminal lawyer for help.

Estate Planning. This is a very broad description of several different areas of law, each of which is described as a separate category elsewhere in this glossary. Estate planning and probate is a board-certified specialty in some jurisdictions. See also **Asset Protection Law; Charitable Foundations; Competency; Conservatorship; Durable Powers of Attorney; Elder Law; Gifts; Guardianships; Incapacity; Life Care Contracts; Living Trusts; Nursing Home Contracts; Organ Donation; Probate Contests; Trust Law; Wills.**

Evaluations of Closely Held Businesses. See "Finding the Right Lawyer by Using the Advertisements of Experts and Consultants" in Chapter 4 of this book.

Evaluations of Professional Practices. See "Finding the Right Lawyer by Using the Advertisements of Experts and Consultants" in Chapter 4 of this book.

Eviction. See **Landlord and Tenant Law.**

Excessive Force. This normally refers to allegations of unnecessary police brutality. See also **Police Malpractice.**

Executive Compensation. Executive compensation is normally a matter of tax law. It can also be a matter of securities law or of corporate law. In some law firms, it is included within employment law. See also **Tax Law.**

Exempt Organizations. See **Nonprofit Organizations.**

Experts. To find lists of nonlawyer experts in various areas, see "Finding the Right Lawyer by Using the Advertisements of Experts and Consultants" in Chapter 4 of this book.

Explosives. See "Finding the Right Lawyer by Using the Advertisements of Experts and Consultants" in Chapter 4 of this book.

Expungements. Oversimplified, expungement involve "cleaning up" unfavorable public records. See also **Criminal Law; Record Sealing.**

Extradition. Extradition can either be a state matter (from one state to another) or a federal matter (to a country outside the United States). Extradition normally is a matter of criminal law. If the criminal lawyer is not familiar with international law and custom and applicable treaties, he or she should work with an international lawyer on the matter. Some lawyers specialize in extradition. In some cases, there is a connection between deportation (an immigration matter) and deportation (a criminal matter). See also **Immigration Law.**

Failure to Appear. A failure to appear charge is normally the result of a defendant's not showing up at a trial or other proceeding. A failure to appear is sometimes minor, resulting in a forfeiture of bail, and that's the end of it. A failure to appear can also be serious, resulting in the issuance of an arrest warrant for the felony crime of failure to appear. In many cases, the failure to appear is a more serious offense than the underlying origin of the proceedings. Anyone contemplating not showing up at a trial or hearing should first get advice from a criminal lawyer on the consequences of failing to appear.

Failure to Diagnose. Failure to diagnose can be a form of medical malpractice. A common failure to diagnose claim is failure to diagnose cancer. These cases are handled by medical malpractice and personal injury lawyers. See also **Malpractice.**

Failure to Provide Safety Equipment. See **Safety Equipment.** See also **Workers' Compensation Law.**

Falamos Portuguese. Portuguese for "we speak Portuguese." The law office will have a person available to translate Portuguese, not but necessarily a lawyer. These words in an ad mean that the firm accepts and welcomes clients who speak Portuguese. These ads often seek immigration cases. I speak Portuguese but do not put this in any ads or listings because I don't do immigration work.

False Advertising. See **Advertising.** See also **Consumer Protection Laws; Deceptive Trade Practices; Unfair Competition Law.**

False Arrest. Involves the wrongful detention of a person. Can be civil or criminal. Begin with a criminal lawyer or general practicioner.

False Imprisonment. See **False Arrest.**

False Labeling. See **Deceptive Trade Practices.**

Family Law. An area of law that can include just about anything involving the rights and responsibilities of members of a family to one another or to outsiders. Divorce, annulments, separations, adoptions, guardianships, conservatorships, custody disputes, surrogate parenting, and elder law could all be included in family law. In practice, family lawyers tend to concentrate on divorce cases. Cohabitation is a newly developing area of family law. In some states, family law is a regulated specialty area of law. The lawyer is required to pass exams and demonstrate expertise in becoming a family lawyer. A family lawyer or a general practitioner is a good starting point to find what you need. Family law is a board-certified specialty in some jurisdictions.

Family Violence. Family violence is both a criminal law matter, if one is either a victim or charged with the crime, and a family law matter, if one is the victim.

Farm and Ranch Law. An area of law that deals with the special problem of farmers and ranchers. This area is sometimes called agricultural or "Ag" law. Farm and ranch law is a board-certified specialty in some jurisdictions.

Federal Employment Law. See **Employment Law.**

Federal Injury Law. In a great many areas of practice, the handling of injuries under federal law and under state law are very different. Dockworkers' cases, and seamen's cases, and railway workers' cases are examples. There are lawyers who specialize in prosecuting and defending injury cases brought under federal law.

Fee Disputes. Fee disputes could refer to any type of dispute over a professional fee, but normally refers to disputes over lawyer's fees. The dispute could be between two lawyers or between a client and one or more lawyers. Business lawyers and trial lawyers do this type of work. A few lawyers, such as myself, are relatively knowledgeable in this area due to a secondary skill in law office management and knowledge of conflicts of interest laws.

FELA. An acronym for Federal Employers Liability Act, the law governing workers' compensation injuries to railroad workers. Most workers' compensation lawyers can do FELA. See also **Railway Injuries.**

Felonies. A rather more serious group of crimes than are misdemeanors. Misdemeanor refers to those crimes which are not felonies. Usually, but not always, a given prosecution can be either a misdemeanor or a felony depending on the facts and depending on the skills of the prosecutors or defense lawyers. In some jurisdictions, the term "misdemeanor" refers to the penalties, which historically could not exceed one year in a local jail, as opposed to being a felony, which could be punishable by more than one year in a state prison. In some jurisdictions, the allegation of the crime as being a felony or a misdemeanor determines the court in which the trial will take place. See **Criminal Law.**

Fidelity and Blanket Bond Litigation. See **Insurance.**

Fidelity and Surety. See **Insurance Law.**

Fifth Amendment Rights. See **Grand Jury Investigations.** See also **Criminal Law.**

Financial Institution Law. See **Banking Law.**

Firearms and Explosives. See "Finding the Right Lawyer by Using the Advertisements of Experts and Consultants" in Chapter 4 of this book.

Fire Loss Litigation. There are lawyers who specialize in negotiating and litigating fire loss claims, both for the claimant and for the insurance carrier. Lawyers handling this area of law often work on a contingency basis. To find such a lawyer, you might ask a nonlawyer fire loss adjuster for a recommendation. Personal injury lawyers and negligence defense lawyers can usually handle routine cases.

When an insurance company pays a fire loss claim to an insured, it may seek to recover what it paid out from a negligent party who caused the fire. This is done by a process called "subrogation." The prosecution and defense of arson matters is a different area of law. See also **Arson Defense in Insurance Cases; Subrogation Law.**

Firing. See **Employment Law.**

First Amendment and Media Law. Law firms which do First Amendment and media law typically represent newspapers, radio and television stations, etc. See also **Defamation Law; Libel and Slander; Publishing Law.**

First Offenders. The term "first offenders" really doesn't add anything to describing what the lawyer does that is different from other cases. Normally, this term is applied in drunk driving or DUI cases where there is a significantly lesser sentence or fine for first offenders. See also **Drunk Driving; DUI.**

Foreclosures. The type of lawyer you need may depend on the nature of the property being foreclosed upon or to be foreclosed upon, or the nature of the underlying debt. Either a litigation lawyer who knows writs and injunctions or a bankruptcy lawyer may be the right place to start if you are the debtor. A collection lawyer, a creditors' rights lawyer, or a real estate lawyer may be the right lawyer if you are the creditor. A general practitioner could be of help in some cases and would be a good starting point. See **Real Estate Law.**

Foreign Judgments/Foreign Law/Foreign Corporations. The word "foreign" simply means outside the state. It does not mean outside the United States. Accordingly, a Massachusetts corporation is a foreign corporation in New York. Similarly, an Indiana or New York court order is a foreign judgment in California.

Forfeitures. Forfeitures involve the government's taking possession of an accused's assets before or after conviction. The forfeiture may prevent the accused from hiring a specialized private-practice lawyer the accused would otherwise want. Accordingly, many otherwise qualified, competent lawyers are nervous or hesitant about accepting a case where the accused may have no way to pay. They know that the government may attempt to take the legal fees away from the lawyer as a form of forfeiture. In effect, the lawyer will become a defendant and the lawyer getting paid may depend of the accused being acquitted. This system of fee forfeitures turns the criminal defense into a contingency fee arrangement, which is normally forbidden by the ethics of the profession.

Forfeitures are usually done under federal law, but some states also have forfeiture laws. Forfeitures should not be confused with IRS seizures for taxes, nor with customs seizures and subsequent forfeitures for currency importation and exportation. Forfeitures are normally handled by criminal lawyers. IRS seizures are normally handled by tax lawyers. See also **Customs Law; Tax Law.**

Former Administrative Law Judge. In some cases, an administrative law judge is a judge like any other. In some proceedings, the administrative law judge is an ordinary lawyer who acts as a hearing officer in the case. Sometimes these administrative law "judges" leave the bench and go into, or back to, private practice. They often list their former employment in phone directories, etc. They normally are very knowledgeable in the narrow, limited areas where they served as an administrative law judge. They often have experience in labor law, social security law, and other specialty areas.

Former Claims Adjuster. In most cases, a former claims adjuster with this directory listing used to work for an insurance company. Putting this fact in a directory listing implies that with their knowledge of insurance companies they can get bigger settlements. It is possible, however, that they used to work as a claims adjuster for a law firm.

Fractures. See **Serious Injuries.**

Franchise Law. There are lawyers who specialize in the state and federal law applicable to franchises and distributorships. Franchise law lawyers are typically in business and corporate law firms.

Fresh Start. See **Debt Relief.** See also **Bankruptcy.**

Full-Service Firm. The words "full-service firm" indicate that you can bring any legal need to the firm and lawyers there will try to help you if they can. If they do not have the ability within their firm, they will try to find you a lawyer, firm, or agency that may be able to help you. A full-service firm is similar to a general practice firm, except that a general practice firm may or may not be as willing to help you find the right lawyer when it can't handle the case. General practice firms without a network of other lawyers is a general practice firm, but not a "full service" firm. See also **General Practice.**

Furnaces. See "Finding the Right Lawyer by Using the Advertisements of Experts and Consultants" in Chapter 4 of this book.

Gambling. See **Gaming Law.**

Gaming Law. Law covering gambling where gambling is legal. Gaming lawyers usually represent gambling casinos and other businesses that operate legalized gambling. Gaming lawyers normally devote their energies to getting and keeping gaming licenses. Gaming law does not normally include the collection of gambling debts, which is done by collection lawyers. Gaming does not ordinarily include routine criminal gambling prosecutions such as bookmaking, which is done by criminal lawyers. As you might expect, there is a large concentration of lawyers with expertise in gaming law in the states of Nevada and New Jersey.

Garnishments. Garnishments are typically claims against wages and bank accounts, often as the result of a tax lien or a civil judgment. If you are a debtor, usually a bankruptcy lawyer or a debt renegotiation lawyer is the proper lawyer to begin with if you are the debtor. If you are the creditor who wishes to get a garnishment, you would want a lawyer who does collections or creditors' rights. See also **Attachments; Bankruptcy.**

Gas Transmission. Gas transmission is normally included within oil and gas law, energy law or natural resources law.

Gay and Lesbian Law. A newly developing area of law that may be involved when two people of the same sex are cohabiting. There may be questions of legal relations arising out of written or oral agreements; questions with respect to rights and liabilities and with respect to third parties; and questions of inheritance, joint property rights, rights to employee benefits, etc. In some cases, lawyers who handle gay and lesbian rights also deal with employment and housing discrimination and with AIDS-related cases. I personally have never seen this listing in any recognized list of legal specialties, but I have seen it advertised in newspaper ads and in the Yellow Pages. See also **Cohabitation Law; Employment Law; Family Law.**

Gay Rights. See **Employment Law.** See also **Gay and Lesbian Law.**

General Practice. General practice is the backbone of the American legal system. General practice is the logical entry point into the legal system when there is any question as to whether there is a need for a specialist, and, if so, which specialist. As should be apparent by this glossary of legal practice descriptions, no one lawyer or law firm in the world can do everything a client might need and do it at the highest level of competence. If you wish to analogize law to medicine, think of the legal general practitioner as being like a medical general practitioner, internist, or family doctor. The general practitioner will treat you if possible, and will refer you to a specialist if one is called for.

General practice can include hundreds of areas of law. The extent to which a general practitioner will handle a problem or seek help from a specialist will depend on the level of difficulty of the case and the level of experience of the general practitioner. A few of the more common areas included are auto accidents, bankruptcy, business law, business planning, civil litigation, collections, creditors' rights, criminal law, defective products, divorce, DUI, DWI, wills, estate planning, family law, real estate, personal injury, zoning, etc. The list has no end. This is simply a limited example of some of the areas.

The general practitioner often can help even in the most complex areas of law by doing research or asking for help from other experts. If after you read this glossary of legal practice areas you are confused or not clear on what type of lawyer(s) you need, then get help from a general practitioner.

Interesting enough, many of the largest, oldest, most prestigious law firms in the world list only general practice in their practice description rather than list the many areas of law they practice. See also **Full-Service Firm.**

Getting Out of Jail. This is normally done by criminal lawyers. See also **Bail.**

Gifts. The area of gifts and gift taxes is normally handled by tax lawyers or by estate planning lawyers with tax ability.

Glass Materials Problems. See "Finding the Right Lawyer by Using the Advertisements of Experts and Consultants" in Chapter 4 of this book.

Government Contract Claims. See "Finding the Right Lawyer by Using the Advertisements of Experts and Consultants" in Chapter 4 of this book.

Government Contract Negotiation. See **Contract Negotiations.**

Government Contracts Law. Government contracts law is a specialty area of law. It is a very broad area and can be either civil, crim-

inal, or both. It can involve employment termination or purely negotiations, renegotiations, and audits of government contracts. Most of
the lawyers with this expertise are employed as corporate counsel by
the companies that need this specialized service. Those in private practice tend to be in large law firms and large cities, and especially in
Washington, D.C. If you need help involving government contracts or
have a matter in this area of law, you should spend the time looking for
a lawyer who has this expertise.

Government Contracts Litigation. See **Government Contracts Law.**

Government Employment Law. There are firms that specialize in
labor law as applied to government employment, in addition to labor
law as applied to private employment. See also **Employment Law.**

Government Law. See **Administrative Law.** See also **Government
Employment Law.**

Government Procurement Law. See **Government Contracts Law.**

Grand Jury Investigations. In most cases a criminal lawyer should
be immediately hired when a person or company is summoned to
appear before a state or federal grand jury. It may be necessary to
assert Fifth Amendment rights, or to negotiate a deal resulting in par-
tial or total immunity. The underlying investigation may require the
help of a second lawyer or firm familiar with the type of conduct being
investigated.

Grandparent Visitation Rights. Rights, in some states, of grandparents to visit their grandchildren when the grandchild's parents are
deceased or divorced. The rights of grandparents vary greatly from
state to state. In some states, grandparents have no visitation rights.
This area of law is normally handled by a family lawyer or general
practitioner. See also **Divorce; Family Law.**

Gray Markets. See **Antitrust Law.**

Green Cards. See **Immigration Law.**

Guardianships. Guardianships normally are over the person's health
and care, over the persons assets and affairs, or over both the person's
assets and care. Guardianships can be a matter of juvenile law for
minors, or of elder law, or of family law.

Habitual Offender. See **Traffic Offenses.**

Handicapped Children. See **Special Education.**

Handicapped Rights. There are lawyers who specialize in the rights
of handicapped or disabled persons as they may pertain to employment, public facilities, or educational situations. These lawyers can

sometimes best be located by calling organizations that advocate the rights of the particular handicap involved (blindness, hearing, AIDS, learning disabilities, etc.) and asking those organizations for recommendations. The rights of the handicapped or disabled in employment and hiring situations is included within employment law. See also **ADA (Americans with Disabilities Act).**

Harassment. See **Injunctions.** See also **Employment Law; Family Law.**

Hate Crimes. Hate crimes are normally acts of violence directed at people based on race, religion, or origin, etc. There are state and federal laws providing for civil and criminal responsibility for committing hate crimes. Those laws often provide for monetary damages, penalties, and attorneys' fees. A general practitioner on a personal injury lawyer can be a good starting point for finding a lawyer in this area. See also **Victims of Crimes.**

Hazardous Waste Law. See **Environmental Law.**

Health Care and Hospital Law. See **Health Care Law.**

Health Care Law. Health care law normally refers to the legal affairs of the providers of health care rather than the legal affairs of the recipients of health care. Health care law is very heavily a matter of tax and corporate law rather than the medical aspects of negligence, etc. The tax and business legal affairs of doctors, medical groups, HMOs, hospitals, laboratories, etc.; pension plans, estate planning, antitrust, personal matters such as divorce; and criminal tax fraud, medicare fraud, and insurance fraud are sometimes included within health care law. These legal services are normally provided within the framework of complying with state and federal regulations and insurance company payment regulations. Health care law also encompasses third-party payment programs and hospital licensing and certification issues.

Health Law. See **Health Care Law.** See also **Hospitals.**

Health Providers. See **Health Care Law.**

Hearing Loss. Hearing loss and ringing in the ears is often related to an injury. A knowledgeable personal injury lawyer is the best place to begin to find a lawyer who understands the connection between trauma and hearing loss.

Helicopters. Manufacturing quality control. See "Finding the Right Lawyer by Using the Advertisements of Experts and Consultants" in Chapter 4 of this book.

Herniated Discs. See **Serious Injuries.**

High Technology Law. See **Intellectual Property Law.**

High Technology Litigation. See **Intellectual Property Law.** See also **Litigation; Trial Practice.**

Highway Bridges and Crossings. See "Finding the Right Lawyer by Using the Advertisements of Experts and Consultants" in Chapter 4 of this book.

Hit and Run. An area of law that deals with drivers who cause, or are involved in, an accident and then flee without correctly identifying themselves, as well as with their victims. This area of law can be both civil and criminal. See also **Personal Injury Law; Traffic Offenses.**

HIV Infections. See **AIDS.** See also **Employment Law.**

HIV Testing. See **AIDS.** See also **Employment Law.**

Home Consultations. When a law firm advertises "home consultations," it usually means the lawyer or someone in the firm will come to the hospital to start your case and to give you legal advice on what to do. Elder law and personal injury lawyers normally offer this service when there are significant injuries or significant dollars involved. Typically, the lawyer or someone from the office will ask questions designed to screen the big cases from the smaller and medium-sized ones. The consultation will only be made at the hospital when the case appears to be a "big injury."

Homeowners' Association Dues. Lawyers who deal with problems of homeowners' or condominium associations' dues normally specialize in condominium law or real estate law. See also **Condominium Law.**

Homesteads. Homesteads normally refer to the process whereby someone who owns real property in which he or she lives can protect that property in whole or in part from creditors. This area of law is normally handled by general practitioners or bankruptcy or creditors' rights lawyers. Some law clinics and do-it-yourself vendors sell forms for a person to do his or her own homestead declaration and recording. There normally is too much involved not to use a lawyer.

In some parts of the United States, a homestead refers to a savings institution. Homestead can also refer to a source of title from the U.S. government, in which case the area of law would be handled by real estate lawyers.

Homosexuals. See **Gay and Lesbian Law.**

Honest Lawyer. I have seen this phrase in a few ads. I wonder if the lawyer accepts only honest clients.

Hospital Consultations. See **Home Consultations.**

Hospital Law. See **Health Care Law.**

Hospital Negligence. See **Malpractice.**

Hospitals. The word "hospitals" standing alone usually means a lawyer or firm represents hospitals and is familiar with the various laws and administrative regulations governing them. The representation of hospitals is often included in the category known as health care law. Prosecution and defense of negligence (malpractice) cases is normally not included in this area of law. "Hospital malpractice" normally refers to negligence claims. See also **Malpractice.**

Hotel Food Service. Both hotel and motel food service cases are handles by this "expert." See "Finding the Right Lawyer by Using the Advertisements of Experts and Consultants" in Chapter 4 of this book.

House Counsel. See **In-House Counsel.**

Housing and Development Law. See **Real Estate Law.**

Hydraulics. Hydraulics, hydrology, canals, lakes, storm drainage, dams, steam, ventilation, and coal mining. See "Finding the Right Lawyer by Using the Advertisements of Experts and Consultants" in Chapter 4 of this book.

IG (Inspector General) Inspections. This area of law deals with companies and individuals being investigated by the Inspector General of the United States.

Illegal Arrest. Illegal or false arrest. A matter for a criminal lawyer or a personal injury lawyer. See also **False Arrest; False Imprisonment.**

Illegal Searches. Searches are normally incident to criminal law and the use of evidence uncovered by a search. Illegal searches can also have significance for personal injury, false arrest, police malpractice, and civil rights law.

Immigration and Naturalization. See **Immigration Law.**

Immigration Law. An area of law sometimes referred to as immigration and naturalization law that deals with a foreigner entering, staying in, and/or working in the United States. Immigration law is an area of specialty practice. Most immigration lawyers limit their practice to this specialty. Some larger firms will try to do some immigration work as a convenience to existing clients, but they rarely aggressively seek it except in connection with clients for whom they are already doing other legal work. Also, some immigration firms actively seek related work, such as investor immigration plans and business immigration plans.

Naturalization normally refers to the process of an immigrant's becoming a citizen or resident of the United States. Immigration usually deals with various classes of people who want to enter the United States intending to leave at some point. Immigration also deals with Americans who have or want to have some relationship with a person who is not a U.S. citizen. Common examples are foreign tourists, business visitors, students, and temporary or transient workers. Such people are called "nonimmigrant" because there is no intent to immigrate to the United States. Other types of cases involve foreigners who entered the United States not intending to stay (and then changed their minds). Others wanted some sort of legal right to stay and/or work on an indefinite basis at the time they initially entered. These people, too, are sometimes called "immigrant."

Often the fee-paying client is the person with whom the immigrant has contact, such as an employer, prospective employer, or a relative. When a person other than the alien is paying the fee, the alien and the fee payer should get a letter from the lawyer defining who the client is and to whom the lawyer's professional ethics and responsibility will be directed in the event of a conflict. If a conflict develops, there could be a problem of disclosing confidential information.

Typically, a successful immigrant gets a "green card" or other form of documentation. (Documentation is required to reach a given status.) The immigration work is described by the type of document sought, rather than by the immigration process.

Whenever possible, a person seeking immigration help should seek an immigration lawyer in or as near as possible the city where the immigrant wants to live, as those lawyers know the local examiners and practices. The local lawyer will also know the official position as to areas where there are surpluses or critical shortages of certain types of occupational skills. An occupational skill may be a critical shortage in one state or city so that the "labor certification" can be received while there may be no such shortage at another location.

Some immigration lawyers have specialties in specific occupational areas such as entertainment, high tech, and health care. Some immigration lawyers network with foreign lawyers and consulates to get foreign work visas for U.S. citizens.

"Notarios" often advertise immigration services. Many "notarios" are frauds who take advantage of the similarity between the English word "notary" and the Spanish word "notario" to promise legal assistance. The foreigner often doesn't understand the difference between the "notario" and a notary public and believes that an American notary public can do what the foreign "notario" can do, which simply is not the case. In theory, a nonlawyer can practice limited immigration law, but it would be wiser to use an immigration lawyer.

Common documents or status that may interest a foreigner include permanent residency, labor certifications, transfer visas, bride's visas, work visas, student visas, citizenship, green cards, temporary green cards, work cards, treaty investors, asylum, amnesty, amnesty appeals, employer sanctions, residency and loss of residency, deportation, H-1s (visas for professionals), L-1s (executives and managers), E-1s (traders), E-2s (investors), professionals and international businessmen, political asylum, refugees, change of status, conditional status, relative petition, nonimmigrant visas, temporary workers, investors, I-94 extensions, and business visas.

Immigration fraud, consequences of criminal convictions, and pleas on immigration status also come within immigration law. Immigration and naturalization is a board-certified specialty in some jurisdictions. For historical reasons immigration law is sometimes referred to as immigration and consular law, although very few, if any, immigration lawyers have ever handled a problem involving consular law. (I personally have handled problems involving consular law.) See also **International Law.**

Import-Export Law. See **International Law.** See also **Customs Law.**

Incapacity. See **Estate Planning.**

Incorporations. See **Corporations and Partnership Law.**

Incorrect Cancer Diagnosis. See **Failure to Diagnose.** See also **Medical Malpractice.**

Independent Contractor Law. In many cases, there is a desire by two business people to classify themselves as independent contractors rather than employer-employee with respect to each other for taxation or liability purposes. There is often a third party, such as the government or a creditor, which wants to convert the intended independent contractor relationship into an unintended employer-employee relationship, with resulting serious tax or liability problems. There are lawyers (including myself) who have a subspecialty in this area.

Although it would seem this problem should be an employee law problem, it is normally treated as a taxation problem and is handled by tax lawyers. If you want help in this area, first contact a tax lawyer. Ask that person to help you find a lawyer knowledgeable in independent contractor law, unless the tax lawyer knows that area.

Indian Affairs. See **Native American Law.**

Indian Law. See **Native American Law.**

Industrial Accidents. In theory, industrial accidents could represent any kind of an accident which occurs in an industrial setting. In practice, it refers to matters involving workers' compensation. See also **Workers' Compensation Law.**

Industrial Development Law. Industrial development law is a mixed area of real estate, tax, and municipal law. This area of law deals with putting together real estate development packages where, normally, there is some form of a government subsidy, tax credit, tax holiday, industrial development bond (IDB), or development mortgage on the property involved. To find a lawyer in this highly specialized area, you may have to contact a large number of tax or real estate lawyers. See also **Municipal Law.**

Industrial Financing. See **Industrial Development Law.**

Inheritances. The passage of property from the estate of a person who has died. Some people refer to what they receive as "an inheritance." See also **Estate Planning.**

Inheritance Taxes. The taxes imposed by a state when a person dies and there is a transfer of property. The taxes imposed by the federal government at this time are called estate taxes. These terms are often incorrectly switched around or lumped together. Inheritance tax matters are normally handled by tax lawyers or by estate planning or probate lawyers.

In-House Counsel. In-house counsel are sometimes called corporate counsel or "law discussion." Typically, they are lawyers who work for a single company as an employee. They normally do not have any clients other than their employer. In-house counsel are sometimes called house counsel. Typically, they are experts in the fields of law affecting their employer. They also network with outside counsel and often are excellent sources for recommendations in finding a lawyer. The American Corporate Counsel Association (ACCA), located in Washington, D.C., is an organization of in-house counsel of major organizations.

Injunctions. Injunctions are court orders to require someone to do something or to prohibit them from doing something. They are also called restraining orders. (There are differences in how one gets an injunction or a restraining order, but for purposes of this glossary I won't distinguish the two.) Common situations calling for an injunction are fears of violence or fears of acts that cannot be corrected after they have been committed.

Injunctions are normally incident to some other form of claim, such as one involving family law, corporate law, business law, and real estate law. You have to find a lawyer who is familiar with the underlying type of claim. A good starting point is a litigation law firm.

Injuries. See **Accident Law; Defective Products; Personal Injury Law; Slip and Fall.**

227

Injury of the Elderly. See "Finding the Right Lawyer by Using the Advertisements of Experts and Consultants" in Chapter 4 of this book.

Innkeepers Law. In some states, owners and operators of inns, hotels, and restaurants have special responsibilities to their guests and patrons, to the guests of their guests and patrons, as well as to the invited and noninvited public. In some states, innkeepers may have a responsibility to persons injured by their guests and patrons and for damages caused by intoxicated guests and patrons. See also **Dram Shop Law; Business Law; Personal Injury Law.**

Insider Trading and Violations Law. Law governing individuals and institutions regulated by federal and state securities laws as to what they may and may not do. See also **Securities Law; Securities Regulation; White-Collar Crimes.**

Insolvency. See **Bankruptcy.** See also **Assignments for the Benefit of Creditors; Creditors' Rights; Reorganizations.**

Insurance. The word *insurance*, standing alone, is not very informative. Lawyers selected by insurance companies to represent insureds do "insurance work." In theory, the lawyer represents the insured, but in practical effect, the lawyer represents the financial interests of the insurance company that selected and pays the lawyer. Lawyers who represent clients adverse to the financial interests of the insurance company also do "insurance work." Some lawyers do both kinds of work so long as they are not going against an insured which is insured by one of the insurance companies that use them in other cases. Larger firms tend to represent the insurance companies and insureds and may list themselves in publications not intended for the general public. Smaller firms tend to represent clients with financial interests adverse to the insurance companies. These firms may list themselves in publications intended for the general public.

Lawyers and firms which do work for insurance companies are often excellent technicians who work in a very narrow field of law. Many of these firms and lawyers are not sensitive to client relations and they often are poor at client communications. This is a result of trying to satisfy the insurance company, which pays the bill, rather than the insured, who is legally and ethically the client. If you are forced to use the large "insurance" firms assigned by the insurance company you may get good technical results but be very unhappy at the way you were treated as a client. A company or individual being represented by an insurance company lawyer should not be embarrassed to remind the lawyer that they are paying the legal fees via insurance premiums and expect to be treated as the client, including good communication.

Insurance Claims. Insurance claims typically involve claims against your own insurance company for such areas as fire loss, property damage, theft, commercial, health, disability, life, etc. Uninsured motorist, underinsured motorist, and "bad faith" claims are usually handled by personal injury lawyers. Personal injury lawyers and general practice lawyers are good starting points. If the problem is whether or not there is applicable insurance, then you may need a "coverage" lawyer. See also **Insurance Coverage.**

Insurance Coverage. Insurance coverage lawyers are skilled at reading, understanding, and applying the pages of language in insurance policies. It often happens that because of recent judicial or administrative decisions, the terms of a policy are not valid or are given a special meaning in a special situation. Even the best corporate and business lawyers and the biggest of firms often do not have the skills for doing this very specialized work. Lawyers who do insurance coverage work are often hard to find because they usually do not list their abilities in phone directories. You may have to call several firms or lawyers to find one who knows insurance coverage. Firms that defend cases for insurance companies may have a lawyer available to do coverage work.

Whenever your insurance agent, adjuster, or company tells you that you are "not covered," or that there is a reservation of rights, or that there is limited coverage for the costs of defending a case, settling a claim against you, or paying a judgment against you, consider getting a second opinion from a lawyer who may be more knowledgeable. A good "coverage lawyer" can often assist you in structuring your problem in such a way that your carrier will be contractually obligated to defend you at its expense.

I have even seen situations where insurance carriers pay criminal defense costs because of the possible civil implications of losing or settling the criminal case. In some situations, your insurance carrier has no obligation to pay claims, but does have an obligation to defend you and pay your lawyers' fees.

In some states, there is a type of law known as bad faith law where the lawyers will sue the insurance company after it loses a case. See also **Bad Faith Cases; Insurance Law; Reservation of Rights.**

Insurance Defense. Insurance defense does not normally refer to defending insurance companies. It refers to defending and representing insureds at the expense, direction, and practical control of the insurance company that provides the defense lawyer.

Insurance Disputes. Insurance disputes is a vague term that is not helpful. It could mean claims against your own insurance company. It could also mean any claims where there is insurance to compensate the damaged or injured party.

229

Insurance Fraud. Insurance fraud normally refers to allegations by an insurance company that claims made against it or its insureds were fraudulent. Insurance investigators sometimes document or prove an insurance fraud case and then give the file to criminal authorities for criminal prosecution. The insurance company may follow the criminal prosecution with a civil lawsuit. Accordingly, if insurance fraud is alleged, consult both a civil lawyer and a criminal lawyer.

Insurance Law. Insurance law is a generic term applying to many different situations. It can refer to lawyers selected by insurance companies to defend lawsuits against the company's insureds. It can refer to claims against insured people. It might mean that the lawyer or firm does insurance coverage as described in this book, or claims against one's own insurance company. If you are considering a lawyer who lists that area of law, you will have to ask whether your needs fall within the lawyer's own definition of insurance law. Insurance law can also include such technical areas as reinsurance, excess insurance, primary-secondary insurance questions, and fidelity and blanket bond litigation. See also **Insurance Coverage.**

Insurance Risk Management. A complex system whereby large organizations combine self-insurance, noninsurance, and outside insurance to spread out or reduce their various risks of loss. Insurance risk management as such is not a legal problem but a financial risk taking problem. There are associated legal problems. Typical legal problems in this area include which entity is responsible for costs of defense or levels of indemnity.

Intellectual Property Law. Intellectual property law, sometimes called literary property law, typically includes the areas of patents, trademarks, and copyrights. Lawyers in this area can assist in obtaining legal protection, and sometimes can assist in negotiating or writing up licensing or royalty deals. These areas of legal practice overlap and often include unfair competition, franchising, antitrust, service marks, trade secrets, and high tech and biotech, as well. These lawyers usually can obtain international protection and can network with lawyers in other countries doing similar work. Although some larger firms have intellectual law or literary law departments, most lawyers who specialize in this type of work practice in small specialty firms.

Interference with Business Relations. This area of law is normally handled by business or corporate lawyers. It can also be handled by negligence or personal injury lawyers.

Interference with Contractual Relations. See **Interference with Business Relations.**

Internal Revenue Seizures. Internal Revenue seizures is a narrow subspecialty of tax law and sometimes of bankruptcy law. Lawyers who handle matters related to seizures often also represent taxpayers and third parties in levies, collection and payment arrangements, and settlements. A tax lawyer or CPA, or a lawyer who is also a CPA, may be a good starting point to find the right lawyer. In some cases the IRS actions can be stopped at least temporarily by the filing of a bankruptcy. Often there is a time crisis and a lawyer referral service would be the fastest way to find a bankruptcy lawyer or tax lawyer.

International Law. I personally practice international law. International law typically falls into one or more of these four categories: (1) inbound—a foreign person or company needing legal help in the United States; (2) outbound—a person or company in the United States needing legal help outside the United States; (3) private international law—the legal needs of private companies or individuals, as opposed to those of governments; and (4) public international law— the legal needs of governments and their representatives (ambassadors, consuls, diplomats, etc.). Public international law also refers to the legal needs of international public bodies created by many different countries (for example, a United Nations organization or a bilateral commission). Public international law is sometimes called consular or diplomatic law.

An excellent source of both inbound and outbound lawyers is the Martindale-Hubbell Law Directory. I have devoted a section in Chapter 4 of this book to Martindale-Hubbell and where to find the directories within and outside the United States. The U.S. government can also be of help, within limitations.

A few firms and lawyers who do international law also do immigration, but this is rare.

A bank can be of great help in finding lawyers outside the United States. Almost every bank has a network of "correspondent banks" throughout the world, or they use the correspondent network of another bank. Your bank manager can find out which is the correspondent banker for your bank in a particular location, and find out which lawyer or firm represents the correspondent bank at that location.

Some CPA firms have branch offices or affiliates outside the United States. They can recommend you to their local foreign branch to access the law firm(s) used by or recommended by the foreign branch of the CPA firm.

A handful of U.S. law firms have offices or affiliates outside the country. A few law firms have formal marketing networks with overseas law firms. Some of these networks have been in existence for more than twenty years, but most have come into being in the last few years to do legal marketing. See also **Immigration Law** and Chapter 11 of this book on "Finding the Right Lawyer in a Foreign Country."

International Litigation. Matters involving foreigners who wish to bring or defend litigation in U.S. courts.

International Trade Commission Practice. There is a very specialized administrative body located in Washington, D.C., known as the International Trade Commission. A few law firms regularly practice before it.

International Trade Court Practice. The Court of International Trade hears claims by or against the U.S. government arising out of laws pertaining to international trade. The court also hears cases involving judicial review of administrative agencies' decisions dealing with importation. A great deal of its cases deal with customs matters.

Intestate Succession. See **Succession**.

Inverse Condemnation. Inverse condemnation occurs when a government takes property without intending to condemn it. See **Condemnation**.

Jail Consultations. A lawyer will meet with a potential client in jail. Almost all criminal lawyers will do this.

Jail Injuries. See **Jail Malpractice**.

Jail Malpractice. Jail malpractice includes actions arising out of events while one is confined in a jail and prison. Included are suicides, excessive force, deadly force, handcuffing, overcrowding, lockup management, etc. See also **Police Malpractice** and "Finding the Right Lawyer by Using the Advertisements of Experts and Consultants" in Chapter 4 of this book.

Jail Release. Getting out of jail after arrest. See **Bail**.

Job-Related Accidents. See **Workers' Compensation Law**.

Job-Related Diseases. See **Workers' Compensation Law**.

Job-Related Injuries. See **Workers' Compensation Law**.

Joint Ventures. A joint venture is technically a form of partnership with a specific goal in mind. The term is often loosely used in international law to describe any ongoing relationship between a company inside of a country and a company outside of a country. The term "joint ventures" is also loosely used domestically to describe a situation where one party puts up only the money and the other party exploits a concept. The term joint ventures also has special meaning in oil and gas exploration and development. Accordingly, you would have to know how the term is being used to decide the area of law involved or the type of lawyer skills required. See also **International Law; Venture Capital.**

Jones Act. See **Maritime Injuries.**

Jury Trials. The term "jury trials" simply means the law firm in willing to take on cases where the facts will be presented to a jury. Since juries can be used in both criminal and civil cases, the term "jury trials" tells you nothing about the firm's ability to handle a specific type of case properly before a jury. With the rapidly expanding number of lawyers in America and the often jammed or contested court calendars, many lawyers simply don't have the opportunity to gain jury experience. They call themselves trial lawyers or litigators when in fact they've never tried a case to verdict before a jury. It is common in large law firms that only a few lawyers actually have the necessary experience to represent a client properly in court before a jury.

A firm without jury experience often tries to hide that fact by claiming it is so good it can get good settlements without having to try cases. The firm may claim that its reputation is so good that all others are afraid to go to trial against it. In fact, a small percentage of all litigated cases go to trial before a jury. For a variety of reasons, most litigation ultimately ends up in a settlement of some nature. You should understand that whether your lawyer can negotiate a good settlement for you may depend in part on your lawyer's or your firm's reputation as trial lawyers, including the ability to try cases before a jury. If your firm has little or no jury experience, it may recommend a less favorable settlement to avoid having to bring in another lawyer or firm with jury experience to try or settle the case. Be wary of a "trial" lawyer or a "litigation" firm.

If you are using a large firm, get it in writing that if the matter goes to trial, the firm will, within six months of the trial date, put the case under the direct control and responsibility of a lawyer with recent experience in "first chairing" a jury trial (first chairing means being the lawyer in charge of the case in the courtroom who will make opening and closing argument and who will examine the important witnesses). Also get it in writing that this lawyer will in fact be in the courtroom during the trial. If possible, get the name of the trial lawyer at the time you hire the firm. It won't do you any good if the person in charge of your case is pulled off and assigned to a better-paying case at the last minute, leaving you with a novice in charge.

Juvenile. The word "juvenile" normally means not an adult. Juvenile matters can involve almost any kind of law, ranging from criminal prosecutions in a juvenile court, to approval of contracts made with juveniles, to settlements of civil cases where the rights of a juvenile are involved. There often is a significant difference in procedures (jury or no jury, for example) or punishments, depending on whether a matter will be heard or determined in juvenile court or in juvenile proceedings.

"Juvenile" is not normally an area of law. It is a subdivision of other areas of law. If a case involves a person under the age of majority, one could ask a lawyer whether there is a possibility of the matter being determined to be juvenile matter and, if so, what the advantages and disadvantages are. Juvenile judges normally have more discretion in matters involving juveniles than judges in nonjuvenile cases.

In some communities, juvenile law practice also includes adoptions and child custody. Fitness for custody and disposition of minor children when their parents are incarcerated can also come within the area of juvenile law. Juvenile law is sometimes referred to as children's law. See also **Child Molestation; Dependency Law; Family Law.**

Juvenile Law. Juvenile law normally, but not always, refers to Criminal Law as applied to juveniles. In some jurisdictions, MIP refers to minor in possession of alcohol. See **Juvenile.**

Knee Injuries. See **Serious Injuries.**

Laboratory Negligence. See **Medical Malpractice.** See also **Personal Injury Law.**

Labor Board Hearings. See **Employment Law.** See also **Labor Law.**

Labor Law. Labor law is a board-certified specialty in some jurisdictions. See also **Employment Law.**

Labor-Management Consultants. Labor-management consultants are often nonlawyers. I have been told that by using nonlawyers, both employers and employees can resort to "dirty tricks and tactics" that lawyers are ethically prohibited from doing.

Labor-Management Relations Law. Labor-management relations law can deal with the legal rights or responsibilities of a single employee or of an employee group such as a union. Contract negotiations, strikes, boycotts, and grievances all fall within this area. See **Employment Law.**

Laches. See **Statute of Limitations.**

Lack of Security. These cases normally involve a claimed failure to provide adequate guard service, barriers, or lighting. These cases also involve claimed inadequate barriers or warnings. The injured person has either been assaulted and battered or robbed under circumstances where there was a failure to provide responsible security. These cases are normally handled by personal injury or general practice lawyers. See attractive nuisance. See also **Unsafe Premises.**

Land Development. See **Land-Use Regulation.**

Landlord and Tenant Law. Landlord and tenant law normally deals with rent and eviction suits. Some lawyers represent only landlords in these cases. They are usually employed by or affiliated with various owners' and managers' associations. Other lawyers represent tenants when there is a possibility of the tenants' winning something, as in retaliatory evictions and civil rights violations. In some cases, legal aid will represent a tenant. If significant money is involved, as in commercial property, landlord and tenant law becomes known as real estate litigation.

Land Sales Regulation. Land sales regulation can be a matter of civil law, handled by land-use regulation lawyers or real estate lawyers, or it can be a matter of criminal law. See also **White-Collar Crimes.**

Landslide and Subsidence Law. This is the area of law dealing with houses that come tumbling down the hill after a good rain. Perhaps your neighbor's house slides down the hill into your house, or your house moves several feet because it was built on unsafe soil, or your neighbor weakened your soil support. You may have to look into several different specialty area to find these lawyers. Real property, property damage, and construction are three fields to begin with.

Land-Use Regulation. A catchall term for an area of law that covers just about anything that affects how land can be used. It encompasses zoning, police permits, parking restrictions, and fire department and safety regulations. In recent years, some firms have begun including environmental law and hazardous waste law in this area. Some firms have a land-use regulation department while others simply include land-use regulation in the real estate department. See also **Real Estate Law.**

Lanham Act Law. See **Intellectual Property Law.**

Larceny. Larceny is normally a form of theft and requires the services of a criminal lawyer.

Late Cancer Diagnosis. See **Failure to Diagnose.**

Lawn Mower Accidents. See "Finding the Right Lawyer by Using the Advertisements of Experts and Consultants" in Chapter 4 of this book.

Lawyer Disciplining and Licensing. Some lawyers specialize in the representation of other lawyers faced with licensing or disciplinary problems. Lawyers can be disciplined for matters related to their practice (competency or trust account violations) as well as for matters totally unrelated to the practice of law (conviction of a felony such as possession of narcotics). Many of the lawyers who represent other lawyers with these problems are former prosecutors. These lawyers sometimes practice before administrative bodies called state bar courts.

LCB (Liquor Control Board). See **Alcoholic Beverage Law.** See also **Administrative Law.**

Lead Paint Poisoning. A recent area of law developing on the theory that small children suffer brain damage from ingesting the lead, often from old paint, typically in an older house or a slum type of housing. There are lawyers who specialize in this type of case but you may have to search to find one who really knows this area of law. A good starting point is a personal-injury lawyer, a medical malpractice lawyer, or a general practitioner.

Leasing. See **Real Estate Law.** See also **Landlord and Tenant Law.**

Legal Malpractice. Professional malpractice as applied to the legal profession. There are various forms of legal malpractice claims, including missed deadlines, conflicts of interest, abandonment, etc. Legal malpractice cases are difficult to win because the claimant has to prove both that there was negligence and that the result of the case would have been different without the negligence. Some lawyers specialize in legal malpractice cases.

Legal Research. This listing means the firm will access legal data bases via computer to get copies of laws for a customer.

Legal Separation. An alternative to divorce in which spouses live apart from each other and are free of the financial and other obligations (such as presumptions of paternity) that otherwise would arise out of the fact they are legally married. With a legal separation, the parties remain legally married. People sometimes want a legal separation for religious reasons or because a divorce would eliminate pensions or survivor's benefits. Normally, a family lawyer or a divorce lawyer is the best place to get help. See also **Divorce; Separations.**

Legislative Advocacy. See **Lobbying.**

Lemon Laws. Some cities and states have what are commonly called "lemon laws." These are procedures for consumers to use if they are unhappy with an automobile they bought. Lemon laws sometimes apply to consumer goods other than automobiles. Some lawyers specialize in lemon law cases. This area of law is also covered under consumer laws. See also **Defective Products.**

Lender Liability Law. An area of law in which a lender bank or other financial institution bears some responsibility for the problems or failure of a borrower. The liability may arise from the lender's involvement and supervision (or lack thereof) of the borrower's affairs. Lenders may also have problems concerning environmental or toxic waste damages if they become owners through repossession or foreclosure on a property. See also **Banking Law; Environmental Law.**

Lesbians. See **Gay and Lesbian Law.**

Letters of Credit. Letters of credit are financial documents used for financing trade and for serving as a guarantee of payment. Lawyers who are likely to be knowledgeable in letters of credit include banking lawyers and international lawyers.

Libel and Slander. In general, libel and slander deals with people writing or saying untrue statements that are harmful. Libel and slander cases are normally prosecuted by personal injury lawyers and defended by publications lawyers. In some cases, constitutional lawyers are required. See also **Constitutional Law; Defamation Law; Publishing Law.**

Libel, Slander, Innuendo, Bias. See "Finding the Right Lawyer by Using the Advertisements of Experts and Consultants" in Chapter 4 of this book. See also **Defamation Law.**

Licenciado. In some communities the Spanish word for a practicing lawyer is *licenciado* and the Spanish word for someone with a law degree is *abogado*, whether the individual practices or not. In some communities a *licenciado* is anyone who is educated. This is a matter of regional custom.

License Suspension. For suspension of a driver's license, see **Driver's License Suspension.** For suspension of a liquor license or a professional or business license, see **Administrative Law.**

Licensing. For licensing of an individual in a trade or profession, see **Administrative Law.** For licensing of an individual for a driver's license, see **Driver's License Suspension.**

Liens. Liens against real property may be a matter for a construction lawyer, a tax lawyer, or some other type of lawyer, depending on the underlying cause of the lien.

Life Care Contracts. See **Estate Planning.** See also **Elder Law.**

Lift Stay Motions. In bankruptcy court, creditors are often prevented by law from doing anything to get possession of property, to enforce rights, etc. When the bankruptcy is filed there is "automatic stay" against creditors. When a creditor wants to proceed against the bankrupt, it may be necessary to go to court and file a motion asking the court to lift the stay.

This "lift stay motion" is normally done by bankruptcy lawyers who represent creditors. Some collection lawyers and general practitioners can do a lift stay, but it is generally better to use a bankruptcy specialist who knows the judge and the court procedures. See also **Bankruptcy.**

Limitation Analysis. See **Statute of Limitations.**

Linguistics. See "Finding the Right Lawyer by Using the Advertisements of Experts and Consultants" in Chapter 4 of this book.

Liquor Control Board. See **Alcoholic Beverage Law.** See also **Administrative Law.**

Liquor Law. Some lawyers specialize in liquor law. Normally, liquor law includes the obtaining or retaining of permits or licenses to sell or serve alcoholic beverages. In some cases, these lawyers are also expert in the laws of bar or liquor seller liability for injuries caused by an intoxicated person. Lawyers who specialize in liquor law are usually administrative lawyers with knowledge of local licensing laws and procedures. See also **Administrative Law; Dram Shop Law.**

Literary Property. See **Intellectual Property Law.**

Litigation. The terms "litigation" and "trial" are very broad, general terms which mean the law firm is willing and able to go to court and to trial if a disputed matter cannot be resolved by agreement or settlement. Civil litigation and criminal litigation are often very different, and law firms that do one type sometimes will not do the other.

Some law firms do not go to court and would not, or could not, take your case all the way to trial. These firms must either bring in another firm to try your case or settle your case.

Unfortunately, when a nontrial firm is handling your case, it could be detrimental to you. The nontrial firm may be reluctant to share the fee with another law firm and may tend to recommend a settlement, even when continued litigation would be in your best interest. The opposing law firm may know that your firm does not do litigation, so your position in negotiating a potential settlement may be lowered. When the other side knows your firm is willing and able to go to trial, if necessary, it will communicate this to its client. The client then may be more motivated to settle to avoid further costs of litigation and the uncertainty of results in a court proceeding.

Only a tiny percentage of cases ever go to litigation and an even tinier percentage ever go to trial. It is the possibility of losing a case and the expense of trying a case that prompt lawyers to recommend that a mediocre settlement is better than a good claim. If your law firm never tries cases, you may be sacrificing a large part of your bargaining position if you are willing to go to trial.

True litigation lawyers are current on the rules of court and the particular personalities, likes, and dislikes of the various judges currently sitting in the courts. It can be very prejudicial to your case if your lawyer doesn't know the current rules of the court or angers the judge.

"Litigation" is much broader than "trials." The trial is what occurs in the courtroom. Litigation includes all the work necessary prior to preparing the pleadings, the preparing and filing the pleadings, the discovery (including written and oral questioning), getting evidence from third parties, making appropriate motions before the court, and then actually trying the case in a trial. In other words, litigation is the process by which disputes get tried in court. There is no such thing as an area of law where litigation exists in a void. Litigation is used in connection with a case, and you have to find the lawyer who knows both the kind of case and litigation.

You should always ask your the prospective lawyer if your legal problem requires, or might require, litigation and whether the firm is competent to try the case, if necessary. You should think long and hard about choosing a firm to represent you in a matter which might require litigation when that firm can't do litigation.

In some jurisdictions, lawyers are certified as specialists in litigation or criminal litigation or in various types of litigation inherent in the area involved, such as tax litigation or divorce litigation.

Litigation Support. Litigation support is a part of litigation in which teams of nonlawyers are brought in to help lawyers prepare discovery and trial evidence. See also **Litigation.**

Living Trusts. Living trusts are simply trusts created during your lifetime rather than at your death (testamentary trusts). Also called revocable trusts, they are sometimes appropriate for estate planning in conjunction with a will. They can sometimes save probate fees at death. They can accomplish many goals that can also be accomplished with a good will.

There are many peddlers of living trusts. Some are simply snake-oil salesmen, peddling a product for a profit. A good lawyer can explain both the pros and cons of using a living trust in a particular situation. It is normally a mistake to try to use a living trust without a "back-up" will. It can be a serious mistake to try to use a living trust without help from a probate lawyer. See also **Estate Planning; Probate; Wills.**

Loans. See **Loans and Rental Cars.**

Loans and Rental Cars. Personal injury lawyers in some states advertise that they can arrange loans and low-cost rental cars for their clients. This is intended as an inducement to call that firm if you need a lawyer. In some states this may be unethical or illegal. In other states, it apparently is permitted.

Lobbying. Most law firms that do lobbying are very discreet about it. Other law firms are open about their lobbying. Some law firms solicit legal business by owning a "lobbying affiliate" that aggressively seeks clients for both lobbying and legal business. Lobbying is also called "representation before congress," "representation before federal and state agencies," or "legislative advocacy." Lobbying is often an adjunct to the law practice area called administrative law. Firms that do lobbying sometimes also practice political law.

Lawyers and law firms that do lobbying are usually located in the city or area where the legislative or administrative body is located. Accordingly, capital cities are a good place to begin the search for the administrative law firm that also lobbies before the agency or person you are trying to influence. See also **Administrative Law; Political Law.**

Longshoremen's and Harbor Workers' Injuries. These are specialized areas of workers' compensation law. See **Workers' Compensation Law.**

Look for us in the White Pages. A common phrase in many lawyer advertisements on radio and TV and in other media. The law firm is concerned that if you look for its telephone number in the Yellow Pages, you'll see the names and telephone numbers of competitors.

Lump-Sum Settlements. Lawyers who advertise "lump-sum settlements" are usually workers' compensation lawyers. Many workers' compensation awards for permanent disabilities are paid over a period of many years. The applicant's lawyer can ask for a calculation of a lump-sum award instead of a long-term payout. This is sometimes called a commutation of award. See also **Structured Settlements; Workers' Compensation Law.**

LUSTS (Leaking Underground Storage Tanks). See **Underground Storage Tanks.**

Machinery Injuries. Machinery injuries are normally handled by workers' compensation lawyers if the injury was job-connected, or by personal injury lawyers if the injury was not job-related.

Malpractice. The word "malpractice" is the plain English way of saying "professional negligence" or "professional errors and omissions" and, accordingly, will be treated here. In most malpractice cases, there is a claim against a professional person or institution for negligence. Common examples are lawyers (legal malpractice), health care professionals such as physicians and hospitals (medical malpractice), dentists (dental malpractice), accountants (accounting malpractice), and design professionals (architects and engineers malpractice). The term "malpractice" is also often applied to groups such as morticians, teachers, clergy, pharmacists, police officers, social workers, psychologists, real estate brokers, stockbrokers, and insurance agents. Most malpractice cases are very technical and difficult for the claimant to win.

In choosing or interviewing a lawyer for handling a malpractice case, it normally is not adequate that the lawyer or firm claims to do personal injury, professional negligence, or malpractice work. You should try to find a lawyer or firm with expertise in the specific area of negligence claimed. Lawyers who do this type of work often limit their practice to only this type of work because they have to keep current in two professions, the law and the profession of the claimed malpractice. I am of counsel to a firm with a medical malpractice defense and prosecution department. Each lawyer in the department has a minimum of ten years' experience in malpractice litigation and trials. Accordingly, in choosing a lawyer to represent a claimant, be careful to chose a lawyer with hands-on experience in the field of expertise involved in your case. You can be sure the lawyer representing the professional will be very experienced.

Many lawyers have dual qualifications in that the lawyer may also be trained or licensed as a physician, dentist, CPA, etc. Lawyers who defend malpractice cases typically are hired by insurance companies and do little if anything else.

There is no harm in the lawyer's being licensed or trained in the profession of the claimed negligence, but it isn't critical to the case. Typically, the lawyers and adjusters representing the defendant do not have dual training but they do have extensive experience in the type of case involved, which is usually much more important.

Malpractice cases are hard to win or settle unless there is an excellent case. Many clients whose expectations were not met blame the professional for the unwanted result, when in fact the professional did not commit malpractice. To win a malpractice case, you often have to prove two cases. You must first prove there was malpractice (professional negligence), then you must prove there would have been a different result (to your advantage) if the malpractice had not occurred.

Professional negligence cases often require large sums of money for laboratories, expert opinions, and testimony. Accordingly, many firms will not accept malpractice cases unless they involve serious damages. Many valid claims go unprosecuted because the amount of money involved is too small to justify the large amounts of time and money the lawyer and client will have to spend against defense teams who give no quarter and who are not settlement-minded. You should ask who is going to pay costs if the case is lost. Also ask who is going to advance costs as the case progresses or if the lawyer changes his or her mind about the case and wants to drop it.

Malpractice lawyers normally list themselves as such, and can be found in various areas of law commonly referred to as personal injury, bodily injury, negligence, torts, and insurance claims. A general practitioner may be able to give you a preliminary opinion on your case and then try to find the right specialist for you.

241

Manufacturing Quality Controls for Airplanes and Helicopters. See "Finding the Right Lawyer by Using the Advertisements of Experts and Consultants" in Chapter 4 of this book.

Marine Engineering. See "Finding the Right Lawyer by Using the Advertisements of Experts and Consultants" in Chapter 4 of this book.

Marital Property Law. See **Divorce.** See also **Community Property Law; Family Law.**

Marital Settlement Agreements. Agreements between married couples or cohabitees who are at some point in the process of getting together or splitting up. These agreements typically cover inheritance rights, rights to past and future income, child and spousal support (alimony), pension rights, insurance responsibilities, payment of bills and fees, and many other rights depending on the law of the particular state of the parties.

The agreement tries to contain what the parties have voluntarily agreed to, often without legal advice as to what rights they are giving up or the tax consequences. It is foolish to sign one of these agreements without legal advice. The lawyers who draft these documents normally try to advise at least one of the parties as to rights being given up. These agreements are normally drafted or reviewed by family lawyers. See also **Nuptial Agreements; Prenuptial Agreements.**

Maritime Injuries. Maritime injuries refers to job-connected injuries of seamen under circumstances where U.S. law applies. This area of law is often referred to as "Jones Act" cases. This is a specialized area of workers' compensation law. It can also apply to injuries to ship passengers and to oil workers on offshore platforms and rigs. See also **Workers' Compensation Law.**

Maritime Law. Maritime law is sometimes called shipping law or admiralty law. Maritime Law typically deals with the laws of ocean-going ships, their cargoes, crews, passengers, owners, and creditors. There are often complex questions of mixed state law and federal admiralty law which require specialized knowledge and expertise in state court and federal court litigation as well as skill in understanding the relationship between work-connected injury and compensation rights and liabilities. Injuries of crew members are covered under workers' compensation law. See also **Customs Law.**

Mechanic's Liens. Mechanic's liens, sometimes called workmen's liens, are the rights given to people who repair or work on your real or personal property. Typical mechanic's liens are garagemen's liens against your car and contractor's employee liens against your land. Workers can file liens against your real property to secure payment of claims. They can also take and legally keep possession of personal property as security for payment of claims. A general practitioner should be able to help you in either situation. If the numbers are big enough, you may feel more secure if the general practitioner has backup from a real estate lawyer for liens on real property. If the lien is a possessory lien on personal property, you might want backup from a creditors' rights or bankruptcy lawyer.

Media Law. See **Intellectual Property Law.** See also **Entertainment and Sports Law; Publishing Law.**

Mediation. Mediation, along with arbitration, is a form of alternative dispute resolution. In a mediation, there is no "judge" or arbitrator with the power to make a decision that binds the parties. A mediator practices shuttle diplomacy to get the disputing parties to reach their own decision. The mediator attempts to advise the parties of what the mediator believes to be the strengths and weaknesses of each side's case. The mediator may or may not give an opinion of what a judge or jury would be likely to do. The parties may be in separate rooms outside of each other's presence when the mediator discusses their case with them. The mediator acts as a sort of midwife to get the parties to create their own new agreement to resolve their own problems. The mediation takes place in private with no public audience or records. If the mediation is a failure, the parties simply continue their fighting in court or other forum.

I have studied and practiced mediation and highly recommend it when both sides honestly want to settle a dispute and get on with their personal life or business. It is a waste of time if used as a stall or as an attempt to learn more about the other side's case. Mediation can often be used in employment law, family law, and neighbor law cases. See also **Arbitration; Church Law.**

Medical Collections. There are lawyers who specialize in medical collections. They typically represent doctors, clinics, and hospitals against people without medical insurance. They are a leading cause in driving people into personal bankruptcy. These lawyers typically are knowledgeable in health insurance, government regulation, and malpractice cross-complaints. When sued or threatened with suit in a medical collection case you should seek both the opinion of a medical malpractice lawyer to determine if you have a valid defense and the opinion of a family lawyer as to the responsibility of other family members for the claimed bills. These lawyers may be in health care firms or in collection firms. See also **Health Care Law.**

Medical Devices Failure Analysis. See "Finding the Right Lawyer by Using the Advertisements of Experts and Consultants" in Chapter 4 of this book.

Medical Malpractice. See Malpractice.

Medical Malpractice Experts. Various medical doctors and other experts are available to assist in evaluation and trial of a medical malpractice claim and, in some cases, to help in finding a lawyer. Just a few of the areas of expertise claimed are urology, emergency room procedures, gastroenterology, pediatrics, pediatric emergencies, chart review and maintenance, root canals, dental malpractice, cardiovascular, podiatry, foot and ankle surgery, neurology, oral and maxillofacial surgery, TMJ malpractice, pharmaceutical and medication-related claims, ophthalmology, gynecology, pain medicine, urology, orthopaedic surgery, psychiatry, plastic surgery, addictionists, catheter and suture breakage, hand surgery, geriatrics, AIDS, electric shock therapy, and coronary ICU. See also "Finding the Right Lawyer by Using the Advertisements of Experts and Consultants" in Chapter 4 of this book.

Medical Negligence. See Malpractice. See also **Medical Malpractice Experts.**

Medical Research Law. See **Health Care Law.**

Mergers and Acquisitions. Mergers and acquisitions lawyers normally deal with publicly held companies being bought or sold with the intent of some company's or person's getting control or position. This area is sometimes called "takeovers." In theory, these lawyers (also called M&A lawyers) could deal with any company of any size. In fact, lawyers usually deal only with legal situations where there are complex questions of tax law, securities law, takeover and antitakeover law, antitrust law, intracorporate regulation, minority shareholder rights, freezeouts, etc. Large firms often have an M&A person or department which can handle all of these (and other) areas of law, or can coordinate the various departments in the firm on a single merger or acquisition. Many takeover and antitakeover lawyers are located in Delaware. Those Delaware lawyers are used where there is not agreement to a merger (called hostile takeovers). See also **Chancery Practice.**

Metallurgy. Fracture analysis. See "Finding the Right Lawyer by Using the Advertisements of Experts and Consultants" in Chapter 4 of this book.

Military and Veterans' Law. See **Military Law.** See also **Veterans' Benefits** (sometimes called Veterans' Rights).

Military Law. Military law deals with the rights of persons who are or were members of the military. In some cases, this area includes military procedures such as representation of individuals before courts-martial and before administrative hearings. In some cases, it includes discharges and rights upon discharge. In other cases, it deals with the rights of military people or their families in nonmilitary situations such as nonmilitary civil or criminal claims against people who are or were in the military. Military law also can deal with nonmilitary people accused of crime on a military site. Military law can include ordinary civil disputes or negligence claims involving the military, as well. Veterans' law and veterans' benefits are sometimes included in military law and sometimes are totally separate areas of law practice. See also **Veterans' Benefits** and "Finding the Right Lawyer by Using the Advertisements of Experts and Consultants" in Chapter 4 of this book.

Mineral Rights Law. Mineral rights can include the legal areas of oil and gas, coal, mining of various ores, etc., and in some cases, water law. See also **Environmental Law; Natural Resources Law; Oil and Gas Law; Water Law.**

Mining Law. See **Mineral Rights Law.**

MIP (Minor in Possession). This term refers to a minor in possession of alcohol or other substances. See also **Juvenile Law.**

Misdemeanors. A misdemeanor is usually a crime punishable by less than one year in jail. (A felony is a crime punishable by more than one year of incarceration, usually in a state prison.) The classification of a crime as a misdemeanor or a felony is normally a matter of the punishment sought or imposed rather than what the defendant did. See also **Felonies.**

Misreading of X-Rays. See **Malpractice.** See also **Personal Injury Law.**

Missed Deadlines. See **Malpractice.**

Molestation. The term "molestation" normally refers to child molestation cases. In some communities, molestation also refers to rape and assault on adult women. See also **Child Molestation.**

Monopolies. See **Antitrust Law.**

Mortgages. Mortgages normally covers the putting on or the taking off of a mortgage on real property. It can also deal with foreclosures, litigation involving mortgages, and bankruptcy procedures involving mortgages. In some states, mortgages are rarely used in connection with real estate, and the term "mortgage" is incorrectly used to describe "trust deeds." In some states "mortgages" on personal property are now called "security interests." This type of legal work can be done by a real estate lawyer or a general practitioner. See also **Bankruptcy Law.**

Motion Picture and Television Law. See Entertainment Law.

Motion Picture Financing. See Entertainment Law.

Motorcycle Accidents. Motorcycle accidents and bicycle accidents are normally handled by personal injury lawyers. There are lawyers who specialize in doing only motorcycle accidents, but these lawyers normally will accept only major cases. (I was surprised to learn that in most cases the motorcyclist killed or injured usually had the legal right-of-way but could not be seen.) Major injuries are common and are the kind that juries will gladly compensate for. Arms and legs off, faces mutilated, spinal injuries, and brain damage resulting in paraplegic and coma cases are typical. In a major injury case, you should seek the help of lawyers with experience in handling motorcycle cases. Smaller and medium-sized cases usually can be handled by any experienced personal injury lawyer with experience in valuing and preparing cases. See also **Personal Injury Law.**

Motorcycle Cases. See Motorcycle Accidents.

Motorcycle Helmet Injuries. See "Finding the Right Lawyer by Using the Advertisements of Experts and Consultants" in Chapter 4 of this book.

Mowimy Po Polsku. Polish phrase meaning "Polish spoken here" in Latin letters. These words in an ad mean that the law firm has someone (not necessarily a lawyer) available to interpret for Polish-speaking clients and wants Polish-speaking clients.

Municipal Law. In most parts of the United States, municipal law refers to the representation of cities, districts, and other forms of municipalities and government entities. The lawyer is normally paid as a city employee or under a contract with the city or municipality. In some parts of the United States, lawyers who list municipal law will represent the citizen in an administrative or adversarial matter. Normally, general practitioners who represent citizens rather than governments list municipal law as one of their areas of law. These lawyers sometimes do neighbor law. See also **Industrial Development Law.**

Murder. This is usually the charge for the unlawful killing of a human with malice and premeditation. Murder in some states is broken down between first-degree and second-degree murder. The definition varies from state to state. See also **Criminal Law.**

Museum Law. See Art Law.

Music. See Intellectual Property Law. See also **Entertainment and Sports Law.**

MVA. Abbreviation for motor vehicle accident. This may be a special offense within the drunk driving or the driving under the influence laws of a state. See also **Drunk Driving; DUI; DWI.**

Nakikipag Usap Ng Tagalog. A phrase that means "Tagalog spoken here." Tagalog is the language of the Philippines. These words in an ad mean there is a person available, not necessarily a lawyer, who can interpret Tagalog. The office seeks Tagalog-speaking clients.

Name Changes. For individual name changes, see a general practitioner or family lawyer. For a business name change, see a general practitioner or business lawyer. In problem cases, trademark lawyers or unfair competition lawyers may be necessary.

Narcotics Cases. Narcotics cases are normally handled by criminal lawyers who handle drug cases. Narcotics cases are also called drug cases. See also **Drug Cases.**

Native American Law. Native American law is often called Indian law, Indian affairs, tribal law, or American Indian law. Native American law includes groups which ethnically may not be American Indian, such as Eskimos and Aleuts. Canadians are normally not included in this grouping for political reasons. In Canada, native ethnic groups are sometimes referred to as Inuits. Native American law normally deals with peoples and groups (sometimes called tribes) on the North American continent and docs not include Native Americans in the Central and South Pacific or in the Caribbean. Native American law or Indian law is a specialty. It deals with who is eligible to be considered a member of the group; with who is entitled to what share of the group's income; with inheritance rights to the group's income; and with application of group or tribal law in geographic areas where the law applies (reservations). The law also deals with gaming on the reservations; with oil, gas, and mineral rights belonging to the group, including negotiation for the exploitation of these rights; with taxation rights on and off the reservation; with hunting and fishing rights; with lobbying for legislation and administrative law; and with treaty interpretation. When a question of Native American law arises, seek a law firm familiar with the particular group or tribe involved. Often each group has a totally different set of rules and treaties that apply to it.

Naturalization Law. See **Immigration Law.**

Natural Resources Law. Natural resources law is a broad area which can include traditional oil, gas, and mining law and also what is called energy law and environmental law, including clean air and water. This is probably a result of so many oil and gas and mining companies being involved with environmental law problems.

Neighbor Law. Neighbor law is a newly developing area of legal rights and responsibilities. It deals with the everyday problems of living in a city in close proximity to neighbors, and with what they and you can and cannot do. Noxious odors, noisy children and pets, loud TVs, family fights, weeds, fence heights, overhanging trees and vines, running businesses from homes, animals eliminating on your property, wild parties, and a myriad of other problems are included in this general area.

Truthfully, there are few lawyers who are willing and able to take these cases because often the clients can't or won't pay for the necessary work. In many cases, lawyers who represent cities or practice municipal law will be familiar with the local codes and ordinances that apply. These lawyers may be willing to write a "lawyer's letter" for you, or help you prepare the legal authorities for you to prosecute a small-claims case. See also **Mediation; Municipal Law;** and "Using Small-Claims Court as an Alternative to Finding and Using a Lawyer" in Chapter 3 of this book.

Nevada Corporations. See **Blue-Sky Laws.**

"No Charge for Initial Evaluation." See **"No Fee for Initial Consultation."**

No-Fault Divorce. No-fault divorce usually means that in the particular state, foreign country, or other place where the divorce is going to occur, it is not necessary to prove that anyone was at "fault." In some jurisdictions it is necessary to prove some sort of fault, such as adultery, desertion, or physical violence. If you are going to leave your normal home area to get a divorce, you should first check with a family lawyer to see if the divorce you get in the no-fault jurisdiction will be valid in your case. There are serious questions of inheritance rights, family rights, and liabilities when you go shopping for a divorce. A family lawyer can advise you of your risks, if any, and possibly suggest a reputable lawyer in the area you are interested in. The lawyer may even offer an acceptable alternative under your local laws.

"No Fee for Initial Consultation." A phrase meaning that a lawyer or firm will not charge a prospective client for a consultation to determine whether the potential client has a legal matter that is sufficiently meritorious to pursue from the client's or from the lawyer's point of view. I personally feel that all people should have some access to the legal system and I support the concept of a free initial consultation.

No Fee No Recovery. No fee no recovery, or similar words, usually means that the lawyer will take cases on a contingency basis. The lawyers fees come out of the recovery of damages or benefits received. Be sure to ask who pays out-of-pocket costs and court costs if the case is lost.

Noncompete Agreements. Noncompete agreements are sometimes invalid. Some lawyers are experts in interpreting and applying these clauses. You may find such an expert within an employment law firm or a litigation firm. See also **Employment Law; Unfair Competition Law.**

Nondischargeable Debt. See **Dischargeable Debt.** See also **Bankruptcy.**

Nonprofit Organizations. What most people commonly call nonprofit law is properly called exempt organization law. Exempt organizations do not ordinarily pay income taxes, and payments to them are sometimes tax-deductible as dues or as a contribution. There can be important questions of officer, director, and member liability for taxes and wrongful conduct toward members and others if things are not properly done. Charities and various types of associations fall within this category (I personally do a lot of work in this area). This area of law is normally handled by tax lawyers. See also **Tax Law.**

Nonsolicitation Agreements. See **Noncompete Agreements.** See also **Employment Law; Unfair Competition Law.**

Notario. A *notario*, a Spanish word, should not be confused with a U.S. notary public. In many countries a *notario*, or "notary," is a trained person who performs minor legal services and gives minor legal advice in a few legal areas. Typically, a visit to a *notario* is required to make an agreement legal or to get it entered into the public records. There is no such equivalent in the United States. Many people who do not understand the U.S. legal system seriously damage their legal rights by going to a notary instead of going to a lawyer. See also **Notary Public** and Chapter 11 of this book on "Finding the Right Lawyer in a Foreign Country."

Notary. See *Notario.* See also **Notary Public.**

Notary Public. "Notary public" in an advertisement in the United States usually means that the law office has a notary public available to "notarize" signatures. In the United States, notaries public do other minor functions. Many law offices have a notary public in the office as a public service and as a way to introduce the firm to members of the public.

An American notary public should not be confused with the office of *notario* in other countries. There is an unfortunate similarity of words which causes many people of foreign background erroneously to go to a notary public for legal services and advice which the notary public is not qualified to provide unless the individual is also a lawyer. See also *Notario.*

Nous Parlons Francais. French phrase meaning "We speak French." The firm has someone available to interpret French and English. This person is not necessarily a lawyer. The firm wants French-speaking clients.

Nuclear and Fossil Power. See "Finding the Right Lawyer by Using the Advertisements of Experts and Consultants" in Chapter 4 of this book.

Nuclear Radiation Litigation. See **Atomic Energy Law.**

Nuptial Agreements. Agreements concerning the acquisition and disposition of property and obligations by married couples or cohabitees. These agreements are normally prepared by family lawyers, although they are sometimes prepared by tax lawyers and estate planning lawyers. See also **Marital Settlement Agreements; Prenuptial Agreements.**

Nursing Home Contracts. See **Elder Law.** See also **Estate Planning.**

Nursing Home Neglect. See **Malpractice.** See also **Elder Law.**

Nursing Home Negligence. See **Malpractice.**

Offshore. "Offshore" is a general term referring to outside the United States. Typical uses include offshore trusts, offshore corporations, and offshore manufacturing. Offshore activities are normally handled by either international lawyers or tax lawyers. See also **Blue-Sky Laws; International Law; Tax Law;** and "Finding the Right Lawyer by Using the Advertisements of Experts and Consultants" in Chapter 4 of this book.

Offshore Injuries. A phrase that normally refers to oil rig injuries. See also **Workers' Compensation Law.**

Oil and Gas Law. Oil and gas law is the common name for lawyers who know the law of oil and gas exploration, development, production, and financing, as well as the practical aspects of oil and gas. This area of law is now included in mineral rights law or natural resources law, and in some cases environmental law. It is very important to locate an oil and gas lawyer in the community where the legal question arises, as much oil and gas law depends on custom and trade in the community. Oil, gas, and mineral law is a board-certified specialty in some jurisdictions. See also **Water Law.**

Oil Patch Accidents. See **Oil Rig Injuries and Accidents.**

Oil Rig Injuries and Accidents. This is a specialized form of workers' compensation law. See also **Workers' Compensation Law.**

OMVI (Operating a Motor Vehicle Intoxicated). (Thanks to John Brownrigg of Omaha for this explanation.) See also **Drunk**

Driving; DUI (Driving Under the Influence); DWI (Driving While Intoxicated).

One Hundred Percent Penalty Cases. The one hundred percent represents the penalty the IRS tries to stick onto someone to collect payroll and withholding taxes when a business goes under owing these taxes. The IRS tries to find a "responsible person" to pay the taxes. These cases should be handled by tax lawyers.

On-the-Job Injuries. See **Workers' Compensation Law.**

Organ Donation. People who wish to donate organs or other body parts during their life or at their death often have to execute certain documentation during their lifetime. They can dictate which body parts may or may not be transplanted and the circumstances of their use, such as medical research or donation to an organ bank with no restrictions on use. They also can dictate the circumstances under which the organs or parts may be removed. This area of law is normally handled by lawyers who deal in elder law, estate planning, and general practice.

Out-of-State Personal Injury Cases. Normally a lawyer can practice only in the states where admitted. A lawyer advertising for out-of-state cases probably has some sort of reciprocal or network arrangements with law firms outside the state. See also **Personal Injury Law.**

Overtime Pay. See **Wage and Hour Laws.** See also **Employment Law.**

Paralysis. See **Serious Injuries.**

Paraplegia. See **Serious Injuries.**

Parole Violation. This is usually an area of criminal law. See also **Criminal Law.**

Passports. See **Immigration.**

Patents, Trademarks, and Copyrights. See **Intellectual Property Law.**

Paternity. The status of being a father. Paternity claims are normally handled by family lawyers. If one of the parties is in the military, a lawyer who knows military law may be required.

Patient Neglect. See **Malpractice.**

Pawnshops. See **Pledges.**

Payment Plans. Arrangements to pay off a debt. Payment plans sometimes refer to bankruptcy and debt relief situations. Payment plans can also refer to tax payment plans with the IRS. The debtor works out a payment plan that allows the debtor to live without IRS harassment while making payments on tax debts.

P.D. Slang for property damage or for referring to a public defender. See also **Personal Injury Law; Public Defenders.**

Pension and Profit-Sharing Law. Pension and profit-sharing law is a specialty which has subspecialties. The tax consequences and the advisability of creating or terminating a pension or profit-sharing plan is normally handled by tax lawyers. Valuation and division for divorce purposes is normally handled by divorce or family lawyers. Inheritance distribution of the plan balances is normally handled by estate planning lawyers. Valuation of a plan's assets or liabilities in connection with the purchase or sale of a business is normally handled by a corporate lawyer or a mergers and acquisitions lawyer.

Percentage Basis. Contingency basis for fee calculation, with the fee being a percentage of the recovery obtained. See also **Personal Injury Law.**

Personal Injury Law. Personal injury law encompasses hundreds of different types of cases. Typically, personal injury lawyers will represent an injured person on a contingency fee. The essence of a personal injury case is that a human being has been injured. The contingency fee assures you that you can prosecute a claim you otherwise couldn't afford to pay for. It also assures you that your claim has some merit because a knowledgeable contingency lawyer won't take or keep a case without merit. Lawyers who defend personal injury claims are generally called "defense lawyers." Lawyers who prosecute and/or defend personal injury cases often will represent either side of a case unless there is a conflict of interest with some insurance company.

The term "personal injury" is quite broad. The types of cases and accidents handled by "personal injury" lawyers are in the hundreds and include assault and battery, wrongful death, emotional distress, defamation, invasion of privacy, malicious prosecution, abuse of process, excessive force, false arrest and false imprisonment, auto accidents, prison assaults, product liability, warranty, debt collection torts, landslides, slip and fall cases, trip and fall cases, auto and motor vehicle accidents, defective products, and malpractice. A review of the various descriptions of each legal area will help you find the right lawyer for the particular type of personal injury case.

Personal Property. Although real property is a distinct legal practice area, personal property as such is not tested as an area of legal practice.

Personnel Law. See **Employment Law.**

Physician and Attorney. Some medical malpractice lawyers are also licensed as physicians, and so advertise to encourage calls from people with potential medical malpractice claims. These lawyers may be well qualified to recognize medical malpractice and hospital malpractice, but they are not necessarily any more qualified to try or settle the cases than a lawyer who is not a physician.

P.I. Slang for personal injury. See also **Personal Injury Law.**

Plastics Materials Problems. See "Finding the Right Lawyer by Using the Advertisements of Experts and Consultants" in Chapter 4 of this book.

Pledges. A pledge is a transfer of possession of personal property for purposes of collateral. Pawnshops take personal property as a pledge. For pledges of property as collateral, see **Chattel Mortgages.**

A pledge can also be a promise to do something or a promise of money or property to be given to charitable organizations. See **Collections Law; Tax Law.**

Police Malpractice. This area includes excessive force, deadly force, lockup management, overcrowding, standards, negligent use of firearms, vehicle pursuits, deaths, standards, promotion, selection, hiring, domestic violence, civil rights, etc. See also **Jail Malpractice** and "Finding the Right Lawyer by Using the Advertisements of Experts and Consultants" in Chapter 4 of this book.

Police Misconduct. See **Police Malpractice.**

Political Law. A narrow area of law practiced by a few lawyers, typically in small firms in capital cities. Political law deals with the laws of politics. A common task performed by political lawyers is advising on how legally to get money or other considerations to the intended destination with no one going to jail. In addition to the laws governing political contributions, these firms often practice administrative law. Sometimes they know election and redistricting laws. They commonly advise PACs (political action committees) on how legally to get and give money to political candidates and campaigns. See also **Administrative Law.**

Pornography. See **Criminal Law.** See also **Constitutional Law; First Amendment and Media Law; Publishing Law.**

Power Lines. This covers distribution and transmission of electric power. See "Finding the Right Lawyer by Using the Advertisements of Experts and Consultants" in Chapter 4 of this book.

Prenuptial Agreements. Agreements between spouses and cohabitees entered into before marriage. The agreements relate to assets and obligations existing before marriage and assets and obligations acquired after the marriage ceremony. If the agreement is entered into after marriage, it is called a nuptial agreement. Each party needs to have his or her own independent lawyer before signing the agreement or agreeing to it orally. These agreements are normally prepared by family lawyers. See also **Marital Settlement Agreements; Nuptial Agreements.**

Price Fixing. See **Antitrust Law.**

Primary Coverage. See **Insurance Coverage.**

Prison Assaults. See **Jail Malpractice.**

Prison Injuries. See **Jail Malpractice.**

Private Criminal Law. Defending or representing accused as private fee-paying clients, rather than being employed by governmental agencies as employees to prosecute criminal cases. Private criminal law is sometimes used to distinguish a private lawyer from a public defender or similar public official who represents persons accused of crime.

In some parts of the United States, private lawyers and firms are hired on a contract basis to defend and/or prosecute cases. These lawyers are in the private practice of criminal law, not government employees. In some cases, prosecutors are also allowed to defend cases that they don't prosecute.

Probate. Probate is technically the process by which a will is offered in court and proven to be genuine and operative and under the terms of which assets of the decedent are collected, valued, administered, debts are paid, and the asset passed on according to the decedent's wishes if there is a will (testate succession) or according to state law if there is no will (intestate succession). As a practical matter, the term is now used very broadly. A probate lawyer may have abilities in a large variety of matters connected with aging and dying people and the care and passing on of their assets.

The probate procedure protects the intended beneficiaries. It should not be avoided unless the individual gets competent advice from a competent lawyer. In large estates there are often tax advantages available to the estate when using a probate. Loss of tax benefits and defalcations (thefts) can be the price paid for avoiding probate. See also **Elder Law; Estate Planning.**

Probate Contests. See **Will Contests.**

Probation. See **Criminal Law.** See also **Bail; Sentencing Alternatives.**

Professional and Business Divorces. An area of law that includes legal rights and/or remedies and enforcement between co-owners of a business or professional practice when one or more of them wants to disassociate from the other(s).

Professional Associations. Many years ago, professionals formed "professional associations" because incorporation was prohibited. Now that professionals are allowed to form professional corporations, the abbreviations "Ltd." or "P.A." (professional association) are used to indicate the professional is incorporated. See also **Professional Corporations.**

Professional Corporations. Professional corporations are normally incorporated service professionals, such as lawyers, practitioners of health sciences (such as physicians and dentists), and others (such as accountants and architects). These professional corporations sometimes have tax or liability advantages. Although professional corporations could be formed and maintained by general business or corporate lawyers, they are normally handled by tax lawyers and sometimes by health care lawyers. See also **Asset Protection Law; Health Care Law; Tax Law.**

Professional Disciplining and Licensing. See **Administrative Law.**

Professional Negligence. See **Malpractice.**

Property Damage. The portion of a negligence claim relating to damage done to property rather than damage done to people. The latter is called personal injury. Accident lawyers, personal injury lawyers, and negligence lawyers can do this type of work.

Prosecution. Prosecution lawyers normally are prosecutors employed by a governmental unit to prosecute accused. See also **Criminal Law; Private Criminal Law.**

Public Defenders. Government employees (sometimes called "P.Ds.") who are paid to defend the accused in a criminal case where the accused does not have the ability to pay for private legal counsel.

Public Housing Injuries. Claims against public housing ownership normally requires both the general ability to handle negligence or personal injury law and the ability to handle claims against government entities. Claims arising in public housing often involve different rules (standards of care), procedures, and time periods (limitations) in which to file and perfect claims than claims for injury against ordinary owners.

Public Utility Law. Most public utility law is practiced by lawyers who are in-house counsel to the public utility. Some public utility law is practiced by lawyers employed by municipalities. When governments and public utilities go to outside counsel, they tend to select the largest firm in town. Accordingly, unless you have a matter of consumer law, you should seek counsel from the largest firms. They are most likely to have the expertise. In some cases, the expertise can be found in the law peculiar to the underlying utility, such as cable television, rubbish collection, or water.

Publishing Law. An area of law that often includes libel and slander (defamation), obscenity, pornography, and First Amendment rights. Publishing law normally deals with the special problems of newspapers, magazines, and other periodicals. While publishing law can also include the commercial problems of authors and book publishers, these areas are usually handled by literary lawyers rather than publishing lawyers. Publishing lawyers are normally found as part of a larger law firm. See also **Media Law.**

Quadriplegia. See **Serious Injuries.**

Quality Control. See "Finding the Right Lawyer by Using the Advertisements of Experts and Consultants" in Chapter 4 of this book.

Railway Accidents. Representation of people injured in railway or subway accidents. If you need a lawyer with that expertise look for a railroad lawyer. These cases are sometimes lumped together with any case against a transit or transportation company. Aircraft cases are normally treated separately. These cases normally are handled by personal injury lawyers. See also **Railway Injuries.**

Railway Bridges. See "Finding the Right Lawyer by Using the Advertisements of Experts and Consultants" in Chapter 4 of this book.

Railway Crossings. This covers the design and safety of railway crossings. See "Finding the Right Lawyer by Using the Advertisements of Experts and Consultants" in Chapter 4 of this book.

Railway Injuries. Railway injuries normally is a specialized area of workers' compensation referring to job-connected injuries of railway employees. See also **FELA; Railway Accidents; Workers' Compensation Law.**

Railway Stations. See "Finding the Right Lawyer by Using the Advertisements of Experts and Consultants" in Chapter 4 of this book.

Ranch Law. See **Farm and Ranch Law.**

Rape. Rape is normally a matter for general criminal lawyers, although some criminal lawyers specialize in rape cases. Typically, rape is a sexual assault that involves penetration of a female's vagina without her consent. Without penetration, the crime might be called attempted rape. If the victim is a child, the crime charged is often called statutory rape or child molestation. The technical definitions differ from state to state.

Some lawyers claim that female defense lawyers do a better job in jury trials in representing men accused of rape. The theory is that some jurors believe no female lawyer would represent a rapist who was guilty. The rape of a male is often referred to as sodomy, although the definitions are changing in some states. See also **Sodomy.**

Real Estate Law. A broad term that can include anything from the purchase and sale of a single-family home or farm to a complex situation involving acquisition, construction, zoning, land-use regulation, syndication, marketing, financing, and a large number of activities related to a large real estate project.

The only way to find out exactly what lawyers mean when they say they handle real estate law is to ask them for more details. Ask them if they can handle the problem(s) you have or expect to have. Real estate law is also called real property law. Commercial real estate law is a board-certified specialty in some jurisdictions. See also **Personal Property Law.**

Real Property Law. See **Real Estate Law.**

Reckless Driving. Reckless driving is normally a much more serious offense than simple speeding, but not as serious as drunk driving or driving under the influence of drugs or alcohol. There are often important differences between reckless driving and drunk driving in terms of jail sentence, future auto insurance problems, and civil liability in the event of an accident. In many jurisdictions, reckless driving is so serious that one must appear for trial and cannot simply forfeit bail (i.e., merely pay the ticket). A skilled lawyer can accomplish a lot in getting a drunk driving charge reduced to a reckless driving charge. What you spend on lawyer's fees you may save many times over in future insurance premiums.

These cases are normally handled by criminal lawyers and lawyers who specialize in traffic offenses. See also **Traffic Offenses.**

Recording Contracts. See **Entertainment and Sports Law.**

Record Sealing. In some instances, people have the right to ask or demand that their records be sealed. Common examples are some criminal convictions after serving of sentence or after a certain length of time. Hospital and birth records can be sealed in some adoption matters. Some medical and psychiatric records can be sealed. Driver's licenses and driving records can sometimes be sealed. Various court and administrative records can be sealed. A court record or administrative hearing record may contain evidence that could be harmful if used in another proceeding. While, technically, "expungement" means removing a record, as a practical matter it means sealing a record. See also **Criminal Law.**

Recreation Accidents. See "Finding the Right Lawyer by Using the Advertisements of Experts and Consultants" in Chapter 4 of this book.

Recreational Vehicle Accidents. See ATV (All-Terrain Vehicle) Accidents.

Redevelopment Law. Redevelopment law deals with the acquisition of property by a government agency and the subsequent development and use of the property for some public benefit. As a practical matter, it deals mainly with a city's taking old houses and buildings from one group of private owners (typically homeowners) and giving the property to another group of private owners to be developed, often into office buildings, hotels, restaurants, parking lots, etc. See also **Condemnation; Municipal Law.**

Refusal to Settle. In some situations, an insurance company has an obligation to settle a case to protect its insured. If the company refuses to settle and the insured suffers damage, the insured may have a claim against its insurance company. See also **Bad Faith Cases; Insurance Law.**

Regulatory Law. See **Administrative Law.**

Reinsurance. Companies sometimes buy insurance from companies which, in turn, reinsure part of the risk with another insurance company, called a reinsurer. The reinsurers, such as Lloyd's of London, are often in Bermuda, England, or other countries outside the United States. Reinsurance work is usually done by insurance lawyers in large law firms. Reinsurance work is sometimes done by international lawyers. See also **Self Insurance.**

Release. The document that in most cases is the end of a claim. A person without a lawyer would usually be well advised to pay a lawyer for a consultation before signing a release. The lawyer chosen would depend on the area of law involved. A general practitioner would be a good starting point.

Religious Law. See **Church Law.** See also **Ecclesiastical Law.**

Rent-a-Judge. Rent-a-judge is a slang term given to private arbitration in some states. It is common for private companies to hire a retired judge to sit as an arbitrator to decide a case when both sides are willing. By hiring retired judges instead of regular lawyers or technical experts, the parties feel they will get a decision that is more or less what it would be if the parties went through the public system and were assigned a judge.

Retired judges are not cheap; in fact, they are very expensive. One common reason for using a private rent-a-judge is to avoid the delay in waiting in turn for a judge and courtroom. Another reason is to keep the case private so business competitors, the media, and others can't find out what the case is all about. See also **Arbitration.**

Rental Cars. See **Loans and Rental Cars.**

Rent Control Law. Local laws limiting changes in rent or occupancy terms. Many cities have a rent control law and an administrative agency, called a rent control board or panel, to administer the law. Some lawyers specialize in representing landlords or tenants before these boards. In most cases, you would want to be represented by a local lawyer who is "well connected" and known to the members of the panel or board. Having a good working relationship with the members of the panel and the community may be much more important than being skilled in the law. In larger communities, you may want a real property or land-use regulation lawyer. In smaller communities, a general practitioner who knows the panel members is more than adequate.

Reorganizations. Reorganizations in a consumer or business listing normally refers to bankruptcy and debtor proceedings. In a tax situation, reorganizations normally refer to corporate mergers, dissolutions, etc., as defined by the Internal Revenue Code. See also **Bankruptcy; Bankruptcy, Insolvency, and Reorganization Law; Tax Law.**

Replevin. See **Claim and Delivery.**

Repossessions. See **Claim and Delivery.**

Representation Before Congress. See **Lobbying.**

Representation Before Federal and State Agencies. See **Lobbying.**

Reservation of Rights. When an insured's insurance company does not want to accept responsibility for defending a claim or paying a claim, it may proceed to defend the claim on a temporary or limited basis "preserving" the right to stop its work and even to sue its insured. When this happens, the company normally sends a "reservation of rights" letter. If you ever receive such a letter, immediately consult with an independent lawyer. See also **Bad Faith Cases; Insurance Coverage.**

Residency and Loss of Residency. See **Immigration Law.** See also **Tax Law.**

Residential Real Estate. This area of law normally refers to the purchase and sale of private homes and farms. It is normally handled by real estate lawyers and general practice lawyers.

Restraining Orders. For general civil disputes, see **Injunctions.** For domestic violence, see **Family Law.**

Restraint of Trade. See **Antitrust Law.**

RICO. An abbreviation for Racketeer Influenced and Corrupt Organizations Act. RICO can be either a criminal matter, a civil matter, or both. RICO can also be started as a civil matter and become a criminal matter, or vice versa. A criminal RICO case can involve heavy prison terms, fines, and forfeitures. A civil RICO case can involve treble damages. This is a new area of law increasingly being used as a tool of business strategy between competitors, as well as being used by criminal prosecutors. When a RICO investigation or allegation is involved, seek a criminal lawyer who specializes either in RICO or in white-collar crime, including RICO. In addition, seek a civil lawyer specializing in RICO.

Rollovers of Vehicles. This covers analysis for tractor-trailers, lift trucks, and mobile equipment. See also **ATV (All-Terrain Vehicle) Accidents** and "Finding the Right Lawyer by Using the Advertisements of Experts and Consultants" in Chapter 4 of this book.

Roofing and Waterproofing. See "Finding the Right Lawyer by Using the Advertisements of Experts and Consultants" in Chapter 4 of this book.

Safety Equipment. Failure to use, provide, or require safety equipment, or properly functioning safety equipment, can have a significant outcome on the results of a case. If the party's injury was possibly job-connected, a workers' compensation lawyer is the right starting point. If the person injured was not an employee, a personal injury lawyer is the right starting point. In general, a workers' compensation lawyer will be more knowledgeable as to whether or not safety equipment was an important factor.

In working with or choosing a lawyer where injury or death was the result, take it upon yourself to ask the lawyer the specific question, "Did you make a determination as to whether or not any legal issues about safety equipment exist?" Frankly, many lawyers overlook this area of responsibility because they don't know current safety equipment or safety procedures.

Safety Procedures. See **Safety Equipment.**

Sale of Business. A "sale of business" or "purchase and sale of business" listing indicates the lawyer knows the law and problems connected with the purchase or sale of a business. This includes such things as buy-sell agreements, competitive business practices, financing, securities laws, employment agreements, etc.

Scuba Accidents. See "Finding the Right Lawyer by Using the Advertisements of Experts and Consultants" in Chapter 4 of this book.

Seamen's Injuries. Seamen's injuries is a specialized area of workers' compensation law. See also **Maritime Law; Workers' Compensation Law.**

Seatbelts and Seatbelt Claims. See "Finding the Right Lawyer by Using the Advertisements of Experts and Consultants" in Chapter 4 of this book.

Secondary Coverage. See **Insurance Coverage.**

Secondary Offerings. See **Securities Law.**

Securities Class Actions. See **Class Actions.** See also **Securities Regulation.**

Securities Fraud. See **White-Collar Crime.** See also **Securities Law** and "Finding the Right Lawyer by Using the Advertisements of Experts and Consultants" in Chapter 4 of this book.

Securities Law. Securities law, also called corporate securities law, deals with the taking of money to put into a business. A security includes anything purchased for investment that can go up or down in value with no effort on the part of the investor. There are both state and federal securities laws, and the laws can apply to stocks, bonds, loans, and just about anything you can call a transfer of money from one person to another. The penalties for violating these laws can be both criminal and civil in addition to having to give the money back. Anytime a person goes to another person for money there is a possible violation of these laws. Most business lawyers (corporate lawyers) should be able to give you simple guidelines as to what you can and cannot legally do in your particular situation. When money is lost in an investment, there may or may not have been an intentional violation of these laws. See also **Churning; Securities Regulation.**

Securities Litigation. See **Securities Law.** See also **Securities Regulation.**

Securities Regulation. Securities regulation deals with compliance with various state and federal laws governing the sale, issuance, and trading of various types of securities. Included in this area are traditional stocks and bonds, as well as nontraditional securities such as certain commodity transactions and certain real estate loans and investments. Gold, silver, coins, and stamps could also be included. A whole universe of items given to investors in exchange for their money can come under the area of securities regulation. Regulation of stockbrokers, stock and commodity exchanges, and investment advisers is sometimes included in this area of law. See also **Securities Law.**

Security Clearance. There are lawyers skilled in the area of security clearance granting and denials as it affects employment law and government contract law. This is a specialty requiring knowledge of the procedures and remedies available. You would most likely find the right lawyer in either a government contracts or an employment law firm, depending on your fact situation.

Security Interests. See **UCC Law.** See also **Chattel Mortgages.**

Se Habla Espanol. Spanish for "Spanish spoken here." These words in an ad mean that the office wants Spanish-speaking clients, and that someone is available to interpret. That person may or may not be a lawyer.

Self-Insurance. Self-insurance refers to companies and governments that put money into reserve funds for self-insurance instead of buying the insurance from a commercial insurance company. This type of work is usually done by insurance lawyers in large law firms. See also **Reinsurance.**

Senior Citizens' Discounts. Reduced prices for clients over some specific age. Some law firms advertise senior citizens' discounts.

Sentencing Alternatives. When a person is guilty of a crime and is eligible to be sent to jail, there can be alternative forms of serving the sentence. Often the form of sentence is a major factor in deciding whether to plead guilty to an accusation or to go to trial. Some of the common alternatives to "straight time" include community service, traffic school, drug or alcohol rehabilitation programs, psychiatric treatment programs, weekend jail time, house arrest (wearing an electronic beeper at all times), minimum-security facilities (complete with golf courses), halfway houses, and probation. Only a criminal lawyer with knowledge of the local calendar and local jail overcrowding situation can advise of the alternatives available on a given day.

Separation Agreements. See **Marital Settlement Agreements.** See also **Family Law.**

Separations. Separations are normally an alternative to divorce, and are often used for religious or technical reasons. See also **Divorce; Legal Separation.**

Serious Injuries. In some states, the law may allow only policyholders to receive money on the uninsured or underinsured motorist provisions of their auto insurance policy if there is "serious injury." In some states, a person may be able to recover money from negligent people in certain kinds of cases only if there is "serious injury."

The words "serious injury" may be placed in a lawyer's ad to alert the injured that the law firm does not want people to call unless there is serious injury. The problem with this limitation is that injuries sometimes begin small but become serious with the passage of time. A person should not, in my opinion, try to determine whether he or she was seriously injured. This decision should be made by a lawyer and a doctor together.

The words "serious injuries" by themselves tell you absolutely nothing about the kinds of legal matters the law firm can competently handle and the kinds it cannot competently handle. The law firm is, however, stating that it has the skilled lawyers and financial resources to handle a case that requires huge amounts of legal time and money for experts, laboratories, and the like. There is an inference that it does contingent injury work. The words "serious injuries" would include brain damage, paraplegia, quadriplegia, amputations, paralysis, disfigurement, spinal injuries, fractures, etc.

Settlement of Estates. See **Probate.** See also **Estate Planning.**

Settlements. In theory any case can involve a settlement, which is an agreement to end a dispute. In common usage in many states, the word "settlements" refers to the transfer of money and title when real estate is bought and sold. Typically, the real estate involved is a private house or farm. In some states, settlements are called "closings." Settlements usually are done by real estate lawyers or general practitioners. In some states, "settlements" refers to settlement of decedents' estates. See also **Closings; Probate.**

Sex Arrests. See **Sex Cases.**

Sex Cases. A term that refers to defense of criminal prosecutions involving conduct that has some sexual connotation. Rape and child molestation are common examples. Sex cases normally do not include civil sex discrimination or harassment cases. Sex cases are normally handled by criminal lawyers.

Sexual Discrimination. See **Employment Law.** See also **Civil Rights Law.**

Sexual Harassment. See **Employment Law. See also Civil Rights Law.**

Sexuality and Sexual Behavior. See "Finding the Right Lawyer by Using the Advertisements of Experts and Consultants" in Chapter 4 of this book.

Shipping Law. See **Maritime Law.**

Shoplifting. Stealing items from a store. Depending on the value of the items claimed to be stolen, shoplifting can result in a felony or misdemeanor prosecution. This area of law is normally handled by criminal lawyers.

Shopping Center Laws and Rules. See **Land-Use Regulation.** See also **Association Law; Real Estate Law.**

Sidewalks. Some personal injury lawyers claim to have expertise in cases involving sidewalks. Sidewalk cases are sometimes included within slip and fall cases. (In England a sidewalk is called a "footpath.") See also **Slip and Fall.**

Silicosis. See **Asbestos Cases.**

Ski Injuries. See "Finding the Right Lawyer by Using the Advertisements of Experts and Consultants" in Chapter 4 of this book. Also check with personal injury lawyers practicing near ski resort areas.

Slip and Fall. Slip and fall cases are normally handled by personal injury lawyers. Many personal injury lawyers do not like to handle these cases, especially where they involve elderly people. In a slip and fall case, a person slips on a floor or other surface and falls. Often no other person is involved, and it is difficult to find witnesses as to the condition of the floor or other surface at the time of the slip. Typically, the same surface was trod upon by many others before and after the slip without incident.

It is possible for a lawyer to earn a good recovery and fee if it can be proven that the cause of the fall was a foreign substance or negligent design or maintenance. However, these cases are difficult to win, and lawyers who do handle them often have the investigators, laboratories, and testing facilities necessary to prove a case. Many lawyers who say they want slip and fall cases are really only fishing for the rare case where there is substantial injury, good witnesses, or, possibly, a connected workers' compensation case. Be sure the lawyer who says he or she wants the case really does want it or the case can languish from lack of attention.

Slip and fall cases should be distinguished from trip and fall cases, where a foreign object or substance more likely can be proven to be the cause of the fall.

If you can find a personal injury lawyer who claims to want slip-falls and trip-falls, then you should contact that lawyer first. Some lawyers claim to specialize in slip-falls in stores and malls and others in slip-falls on sidewalks and stairs. See also **Dangerous Premises; Unsafe Premises.**

Small Claims. Claims heard in the court where smaller cases can be tried by a judge without a lawyer representing either side. See "Using a Small-Claims Court as an Alternative to Finding and Using a Lawyer" in Chapter 3 of this book.

Snow and Ice Control. See "Finding the Right Lawyer by Using the Advertisements of Experts and Consultants" in Chapter 4 of this book.

Social Security Appeals. See **Social Security Law.**

Social Security Law. A newly developing legal specialty. In the past, Social Security amounts and bureaucracy made it economically impossible for a lawyer to help an applicant effectively. With the increases in types and amounts of benefits, this area is now coming into its own. Lawyers who specialize in Social Security law cover many areas for the participant, survivors, and dependents, including establishing eligibility, back benefits awards, disability appeals, termination of benefits, overpayments, Medicare, integrating various state and federal programs, appeals, etc. Most of the services done by lawyers in Social Security matters are done on a contingent basis.

Sodomy. Sodomy is normally the penetration of an anus, male or female, without consent. It is sometimes referred to as male rape. In some states, it is a crime with or without consent. Criminal lawyers are the proper lawyers to consult.

Solicitors. See **Barristers.**

Songs. See **Entertainment and Music Litigation.** See also **Literary Property.**

Space and Aviation Law. Space law is often listed with aviation law for lack of another place to put it when the Space Age began. Space law is new and is not yet well defined. It includes just about anything remotely connected to the exploration of outer space. Space law can include negotiation and interpretation of international treaties concerning the use of space. It can also include the various problems connected with the design, manufacture, and defects of items and services made for space vehicles. Telecommunications law, dealing with satellite communication, is sometimes included within the description of space law. I personally have been designated a Visiting Lecturer in Space Law at International Space University for work which I did in the design of a political and financial structure for a spaceport to be located in Latin America and owned by a multinational consortium of nations and private companies within the ambit of the United Nations. I've presented the design to a special United Nations Conference on Space. Space law can even include selling advertising space on rockets.

Special Education. The rights of handicapped children and others with respect to their education.

Speeding. See **Driving Offenses.** See also **Traffic Cases.**

Spinal Cord Injuries. See **Serious Injuries.**

Spinal Injuries. See **Serious Injuries.**

Sports Accidents. See **Sports Injuries.**

Sports Injuries. An area of law that typically involves legal actions taken as a result of physical injury suffered while playing a team sport. The action may be against the other team, the promoters, the school, or others. The claim may be for personal injury, workers' compensation, defective equipment, or defective protective equipment. A personal injury lawyer would be the appropriate lawyer to begin with. See also "Finding the Right Lawyer by Using the Advertisements of Experts and Consultants" in Chapter 4 of this book.

Sports Law. See **Entertainment and Sports Law.**

Spots Before the Eyes. Spots and flashes before the eyes can be caused by injury. A personal injury lawyer knowledgeable in eye injury can be of great help in determining whether there is or could be a relationship between the eye problem and the injury.

Spousal Support. See **Alimony.**

Spy Law. See **Espionage.**

Squatters. See **Adverse Possession.**

State-of-Mind Testimony. See "Finding the Right Lawyer by Using the Advertisements of Experts and Consultants" in Chapter 4 of this book for experts to help in state-of-mind cases for will contests, competency, and homicide.

Station Crossings. See **Railway Crossings.**

Statute of Limitations. A law that lists the time periods within which a case must be started or forever barred. In some cases, the period of limitations is only a few days (claims against decedents and government agencies). In some cases, the period can be years or indefinite. In most cases, only a lawyer can properly advise you whether you have waited too long to do something. Delay in getting to a lawyer can cost you your legal rights. In some cases, you run the risk of being barred by laches, a technical doctrine involving delay that can also cost you your legal rights. In bankruptcy proceedings, the last date to file a paper or to something is sometimes called a "bar date." In lawyer's slang, when one has not acted before a deadline, it is said that the statute has been "blown."

Statutory Rape. See **Rape.**

Stays. For stays in bankruptcy situations, see **Lift Stay Motions.** For stays pending appeal, see **Appeals.**

Stepparent Adoptions. For various reasons, including employee benefits, taxes, and inheritance rights, a stepparent may wish to legally adopt a stepchild. In some cases a child can be adopted after becoming an adult. See also **Family Law.**

Stepparenting. See Family Law.

Stock Option Plan (SOP). See Employee Stock Options.

Straight Bankruptcy. See Bankruptcy; Chapter 7.

Structured Settlements. When injuries are catastrophic, lasting over an uncertain lifetime or uncertain life expectancy, it is common to structure settlements to the needs and lifetime of the injured party. This assures funds for ongoing future care and prevents windfalls to heirs if the person does not live long. Structured settlement skills are a subspecialty within personal injury law and workers' compensation law. See also **Lump-Sum Settlements.**

Student Loans Defaults. Failure to make payments on a student loan. Student loan default cases are often handled by bankruptcy lawyers.

Student Visas. See Immigration Law.

Subrogation Law. When an insurance company pays its insured pursuant to a claim, the company may seek to recover what it paid from a third party or the insurance company of the third party. It attempts this through a process called "subrogation," where it attempts to succeed or subrogate to the rights of its insured. (This is the common type of subrogation. There are situations wherein no insurance carrier is involved or where there really is no third-party negligence.) Common examples are payments by insurance companies for moneys paid for fire losses, property damage, or uninsured motorist payments. The lawyers who prosecute these cases for the insurance companies are called subrogation lawyers. They sometimes work on a contingent fee basis. The cases are defended by the lawyer who knows the area of law involved.

Another form of subrogation is called "bad faith." Here, the insurance company allegedly has treated its insured with bad faith and a third party accepts an assignment or subrogation of rights from the insured. See also **Bad Faith Cases; Insurance Law.**

Substance Abuse. See Drug Cases.

Subway and Bus Accidents. Some lawyers claim to have special expertise in bringing claims against subway systems, bus systems, and other municipal transit systems. See also **Railway Accidents.**

Succession. The rules for who inherits when there is no will. Technically, this situation is called intestate succession. This area of law is normally handled by probate lawyers and estate planners.

Superfund. See Environmental Law.

Surety Law. See Construction Law. See also **Insurance Law.**

Surrogate Parenting. A newly developing area of law. Typically, a sperm from the husband is used to fertilize an egg from the wife. The fertilized egg (embryo) is placed in the body of another woman who carries the child until it is born. The woman who carries the fertilized egg is called the surrogate mother. The surrogate mother may be a relative of the husband or wife, or she may be a total stranger. She may carry the embryo for monetary or nonmonetary compensation. This area of law is handled by family lawyers, lawyers who specialize in adoptions, and lawyers who use a variety of descriptions such as bio-reproductive lawyers. See also **Adoptions; Family Law.**

Suspended License. Defending the charge of driving with a suspended or revoked driver's license is normally handled by criminal lawyers and by lawyers who specialize in traffic offenses. These lawyers as well as lawyers who practice administrative law are the ones to contact to try to get a driver's license reinstated or prevent a driver's license from being suspended or revoked. Suspension of licenses other than drivers' licenses is normally a matter of administrative law.

Swimming Pool Accidents. See **Swimming Pool Cases.**

Swimming Pool Cases. Cases that involve the injury (normally an adult) or death (normally a child) of a person in or near a swimming pool. Construction claims and contractor disputes normally are not included in this category, although certainly they could be included. These cases are normally handled by general practitioners and personal injury lawyers. Lawyers who handle swimming pool cases also list themselves as handling cases of unsafe premises, attractive nuisance, or lack of security.

Swimming Pools. This involves construction and safety cases. See "Finding the Right Lawyer by Using the Advertisements of Experts and Consultants" in Chapter 4 of this book.

Swiss Corporations. See **Blue-Sky Laws.** See also **Asset Protection Law.**

Syndications. Most real estate syndications are normally handled by securities lawyers and by real estate lawyers if real property is involved. The opinion of a securities lawyer is normally sought if there are any questions of complying with, or violating, any state or federal securities laws. Syndications of horses are handled by equine lawyers. TV syndication is handled by entertainment lawyers.

Takeovers. Mergers can be "friendly" in that everyone wants the takeover to occur, or they can be "hostile" in that there is opposition to the merger. See **Mergers and Acquisitions.** See also **Chancery Law.**

Taxation. An area of law that breaks down into hundreds of sub-areas. No one lawyer or firm could possibly know all there is to know about local, state, and federal tax laws. I have met lawyers who specialize in the property taxation of telephone poles. That's all they do.

In some jurisdictions, taxation is a board-certified specialty. Tax lawyers generally know how to find other tax lawyers. CPAs sometimes can be of help in finding the right lawyer. There is even an organization of lawyers who are also CPAs, and they generally are excellent at locating the right lawyer for the matter (The American Association of Attorney-CPAs). The help you need might involve one of the following subareas: corporate, criminal, personal, estate, gift, employment, sales and use, property, income, excise, personal, exempt organizations and nonprofits, pension and profit sharing, franchise, real property, personal property, gross receipts, state and local, international, etc.

Tax Court. Tax courts normally determine only tax cases. There normally are no juries and the courts may tend to be pro-government. There are both state and federal tax courts. Often, one does not have to be a lawyer to represent a taxpayer in a tax court. CPAs and others can represent taxpayers. The U.S. Tax Court has a small-claims division.

Tax-Deferred Exchanges. See **Tax-Free Exchanges.**

Tax Fraud. See **Criminal Tax Law.** See also **White-Collar Crimes.**

Tax-Free Exchanges. What are commonly called tax-free exchanges are actually tax-deferred exchanges. Real property can sometimes be exchanged for other real property with no current payment of taxes, if it is handled properly. If a person intends to sell one piece of property and buy another, that person should get help before signing anything. Tax-free exchanges are normally handled by tax lawyers or by real property lawyers with tax lawyer advice. Even the most knowledgeable real estate brokers will not normally claim to know the current tax law as applied to real estate exchanges. Special care must be taken when more than two parties are involved.

Tax Law. See **Taxation.**

Tax Litigation and Controversy. See **Taxation.** See also **Criminal Tax Law; White-Collar Crimes.**

Technology Business Startups. See **Venture Capital.**

Theft. Intentionally taking or keeping something without the permission of the owner. Theft is normally a matter for general criminal lawyers, although there sometimes can be civil consequences of significance. There can be dozens or even hundreds of definitions of various kinds of theft, depending on the value or nature of the object alleged to have been taken. The civil equivalent to theft is usually called "conversion."

Thrift Institutions' Law. Thrift institutions' law includes just about any aspect of law dealing with a thrift institution. Typical ones are banks, credit unions, savings and loan associations (or whatever the local equivalent is), factors, pawnbrokers, industrial moneylenders and other moneylenders who are regulated by state or federal laws.

Timeshare Law. The lawyers who specialize in timeshare law are sometimes in the real estate or franchising departments of law firms. See also **Land-Use Regulation.**

Tires. Among the areas covered are defective tires, rims, and wheels which explode or fail. See also "Finding the Right Lawyer by Using the Advertisements of Experts and Consultants" in Chapter 4 of this book.

Title Insurance. When listed in the Yellow Pages, this normally refers to title insurance in connection with the purchase and sale of a house where the lawyer represents one of the parties. In a few situations, title insurance refers to claims against title insurance companies. In the former situation, begin with general practitioners and real estate lawyers. In the latter, real estate lawyers and litigation lawyers are more appropriate.

Title Searches. A process that is normally part of the title checking done by a lawyer in connection with a sale and purchase of real property. The title search is done to assure that the buyer is getting a clean title before giving money to the seller. Title searches are normally done by real estate lawyers or general practitioners.

Tobopum No Pyccku. A Latin letter approximation of "Russian spoken." This means that the law firm has someone (not necessarily a lawyer) available to interpret for Russian- speaking clients. This means that the firm wants Russian-speaking clients.

Toxic Chemicals. See "Finding the Right Lawyer by Using the Advertisements of Experts and Consultants" in Chapter 4 of this book.

Toxic Waste. See **Environmental Law.**

Trade Associations. Trade association law is normally done by lawyers who know tax law because of the nonprofit or tax-exempt character of most trade associations. I personally have done trade association work for more than a quarter century. The problems of a specific trade association may be handled by a subspecialist in antitrust, trade regulation, political law, or lobbying.

Trademarks and Trade Names. See **Intellectual Property Law.**

Trademark Searches. See **Intellectual Property Law.** See also "Finding the Right Lawyer by Using the Advertisements of Experts and Consultants" in Chapter 4 of this book.

Trade Names and Trade Name Protection. See **Intellectual Property Law.** See also **Deceptive Trade Practices; Lanham Act Law; Unfair Competition Law.**

Trade Regulation Law. Trade regulation law deals with unfair competition, antitrust, deceptive trade practices, etc., and is normally handled by lawyers with subspecialties in those fields. See also **Antitrust Law.**

Trade Secrets Protection. See **Intellectual Property Law.** See also **Unfair Competition Law.**

Traffic Accidents. A broad general term covering accidents where a vehicle is involved and someone is injured. Traffic accidents is normally used only for civil cases for money damages. Traffic cases or traffic offenses usually refers to criminal cases. Traffic accidents are normally handled by personal injury lawyers and general practice lawyers.

Traffic Cases. Cases that normally involve alleged criminal conduct of the driver of a car, although they could also involve conduct of a pedestrian or a passenger. Common situations are speeding and reckless driving. Traffic cases are normally handled by general practice lawyers and criminal lawyers. See also **Driving Offenses; Drunk Driving; DUI.**

Traffic Law. See **Traffic Offenses.**

Traffic Offenses. Traffic tickets or citations. This area of criminal law is normally handled by criminal lawyers for the more serious offenses and by general practice lawyers for the lesser offenses not likely to result in jail time. Drunk driving and driving under the influence cases are often handled by specialists. See also **Drunk Driving; DUI; DWI; Reckless Driving.**

Traffic Tickets. See **Traffic Offenses.**

Transactional Law. A phrase meaning the lawyer drafts and sometimes helps negotiate contracts, as opposed to litigating in court. Years ago, a transactional lawyer might have been called an "office lawyer," that is, a lawyer who does all the work without leaving the office.

Transfer Visas. Depending on the circumstances, a company may be able to transfer into the United States a manager or technician who, once inside the United States, may seek permanent residency status.

See also **Immigration Law.**

Transfusions. See Medical Malpractice.

Transnational Investments and Acquisitions. See International Law.

Transplants. See Organ Donation.

Transportation Law. Transportation law refers to the laws affecting transportation companies, particularly trucking companies. Much of the work is related to the setting of rates (tariffs) and in obtaining licenses to haul specific goods over specific routes (authorities). Deregulation has greatly affected this field of law. Transportation law can also apply to railroads, airlines, shipping lines, etc., but normally emphasizes trucking companies. Transportation law is a specialty.

Travel Law. Travel law normally deals with the relationships, responsibilities, and liabilities among travel agencies, hotels, tour operators, tour wholesalers, common carriers such as cruise companies and airlines, and the customer or passenger. Travel law is usually an adjunct to a general practice or a business practice. Often, a personal injury lawyer should consult with a travel lawyer to determine whom to sue.

Treaty Investors. By treaty, the nationals of certain countries have gotten an immigration status priority if they invested a certain amount of money in the United States. See also **Immigration Law.**

Trees. This covers line break and power-line contact. See "Finding the Right Lawyer by Using the Advertisements of Experts and Consultants" in Chapter 4 of this book. See also **Neighbor Law.**

Trial Advocacy. See **Litigation.**

Trial Practice. In some states, litigation is referred to as "trial practice." Trial practice is sometimes broken down into commercial, general, personal injury, wrongful death, etc. See also **Litigation.**

Trials. See **Litigation.**

Tribal Law. See **Native American Law.**

Trip and Fall. Cases in which a person usually has tripped over a foreign object and fallen. A foreign object is an object that should not be where it was, not something imported. These cases are normally handled by personal injury lawyers, who may also handle slip and falls. See also **Slip and Fall.**

Trucks. Defective loading or packaging procedures. See "Finding the Right Lawyer by Using the Advertisements of Experts and Consultants" in Chapter 4 of this book.

Trust Deed Law. See **Mortgages; Real Property Law.**

Trust Law. Trusts are usually created by firms that do probate law. Do not confuse trusts with trust deeds. See also **Asset Protection Trusts; Living Trusts.**

Tying. See **Antitrust Law.**

UCC Law. UCC stands for the Uniform Commercial Code. UCC lawyers typically create what used to be called chattel mortgages on personal property. In modern practice in most states, what used to be called chattel mortgages are now called "security interests." UCC lawyers normally protect the interests of creditors, such as banks and insurance companies, which lend money and take security. UCC lawyers also attack the work done by other UCC lawyers when a client wants to invalidate someone else's security interest.

U.M. Abbreviation for uninsured motorist or underinsured motorist. See **Uninsured Motorist Cases.**

Unclaimed Credits. See **Escheats.**

Uncontested Custody. Cases in which there is no dispute or disagreement between the parents as to child custody. The lawyer gets a court order just to keep the record straight.

Uncontested Divorce. A divorce case where at the beginning there is no dispute as to asset division, payment of outstanding bills, or support payments. Typically there are no children in this type of case. These cases usually start out uncontested and end up bitterly contested as the parties talk to their friends and get new ideas about their legal rights. This type of case should be taken to a general practitioner or a family lawyer. See also **Divorce; Family Law.**

Underground Storage Tanks. Leaking underground storage tanks are often called LUSTS. This is an area of environmental law or toxic waste. See also "Finding the Right Lawyer by Using the Advertisements of Experts and Consultants" in Chapter 4 of this book.

Underinsured Motorists. See **Uninsured Motorist Cases.**

Unemployment Compensation. See **Unemployment Law.**

Unemployment Law. Large unemployment law cases are usually handled by labor lawyers when it is an employer problem that, although small, could have great negative effect as precedent. As a practical matter, when a hearing is held the hearing officer (or administrative law judge) normally takes the side of the employee and tries to help the employee as much as possible. If a significant general principle of law is involved, legal aid may help the employee.

In many cases, there is an interplay of unemployment law and workers' compensation law. Accordingly, workers' compensation lawyers are often very knowledgeable about such unemployment claims and law, even though they may not actively seek such cases.

When unemployment taxes are involved, a tax lawyer may be appropriate.

Unfair Business Practices. See **Unfair Competition Law.**

Unfair Competition Law. Unfair competition is sometimes called unfair business practices. This area generally involves conduct that is prohibited or regulated by state or federal law, or conduct between two businesses that is considered "dirty." A common example is the hiring away of key people to take trade secrets, customer lists, and information with them. Business defamation or selling at or below cost (or in violation of certain laws) can be included. False advertising may be involved. Some of the conduct involved in unfair competition can also involve antitrust law. Litigation lawyers, business lawyers, and general practitioners may be able to help, depending on their experience level in this field. See also **Consumer Protection Laws; Deceptive Trade Practices.**

Uninsured Motorist Cases. Cases in which there has been an automobile accident, and the other side has either no insurance or not enough insurance. In some states, you may buy uninsured or underinsured motorist coverage under your own policy. Some insurance companies, however, do not like to write this type of coverage. It is possible you think you have the coverage but don't know you may not have it if the insurance company didn't sell it to you. Buying "full coverage" may or may not include uninsured or underinsured motorist coverage, depending on your state. If you thought you had the coverage, but don't, check to see whether you can hold either the carrier or the agent for the U.M. coverage with an action to reform (rewrite) the policy. You may have to sue the agent for not providing "full coverage" under the agent's own errors and omissions (malpractice) policy.

In some states, one may not be able to pursue a claim under one's own uninsured or underinsured policy provisions unless there is "serious injury," or other words to that effect.

University Law. See **College and University Law.**

Unsafe Premises. Unsafe premises is a rather vague classification. As the name implies, there is a claim that in some manner a place was unsafe. The most common reasons are failure to light, failure to post warnings, failure to guard, failure to erect barriers, or failure to maintain the premises properly. Depending on the exact facts, the case should be brought to the attention of a lawyer who does landlord and tenant law, workers' compensation law, or personal injury law. A general practice lawyer is a good place to start. See also **Attractive Nuisance; Dangerous Premises; Lack of Security; Slip and Fall; Trip and Fall.**

Use Tax. A tax, normally equivalent to the corresponding sales tax, applied when property is purchased or used without payment of the correct sales tax. This is a very technical area of taxation and is normally handled by tax lawyers with a subspecialty in sales and use taxes.

Utah Corporations. See **Blue-Sky Laws.**

Utility Law. Utility law normally covers the administrative and regulatory problems of utilities, including rates and appearing before various governmental agencies on behalf of the utility. In some firms, utility law covers any problem a public or private utility could have, including defending or prosecuting negligence claims.

Utility Poles. This involves hazards and safety of poles. It also involves cars hitting poles and electrocutions. See "Finding the Right Lawyer by Using the Advertisements of Experts and Consultants" in Chapter 4 of this book.

Vehicular Manslaughter. See **Traffic Offenses.** See also **Criminal Law.**

Venture Capital. When the stock market is hot, many law firms claim to be specialists in venture capital. They sometimes lead clients to believe the law firm can also get venture capital money for the client (after payment of an up-front fee with no guarantee of any results). Some of these firms can and do get capital for the client; others get no results after receiving a lot of up-front money.

Never look to a law firm to get you money without checking its record and without getting independent legal advice from another lawyer about the deal the venture capital lawyer wants you to sign. When a lawyer is getting you money, the lawyer is not acting as a lawyer. Venture capital firms that give legal advice can help you structure a deal designed to help you attract investors on a fair basis. Venture capital work is commonly done by business lawyers, corporate lawyers, mergers and acquisitions lawyers, and sometimes by general practitioners.

Veterans' Benefits. A specialty area of law that is sometimes lumped together with military law. Veterans' benefits law, as the name implies, deals with the rights and benefits to which a person is entitled arising out of that person's military service. The area also deals with the rights of veterans' survivors and family members, as well as others who have some legal relation to one who serves or served in the military. The definition of "veteran" or "military service" can vary, depending upon the particular benefit involved. The benefits also can vary, depending on when, where, and for how long a person served in the military. Lawyers who practice veterans' benefits law are usually located near a large military installation or near the homes of a large number of retired military persons. See also **Military Law.**

Veterans' Rights. See **Veterans' Benefits.**

Vicious Animals. See **Dog Bite Cases.**

Victims of Crimes. Many states have a procedure to offer compensation to people who were victims of crimes, especially crimes of violence. These programs are not widely known, and most lawyers are unaware of their existence. Many of these programs will also pay the legal fees of the lawyer who helps you prepare and file and prove the claim. It may be necessary for you or the lawyer to ask questions of state officials to get the information and the forms. The office of the state attorney general is a good starting point. A general practitioner can usually help you. See also **Hate Crimes; Victims' Rights.**

Victims of Drunk Drivers. The lawyer with this ad was obviously seeking to represent injured people against drunk drivers. See also **Personal Injury Law.**

Victims' Rights. The rights of victims of crime to be compensated. The term can also refer to the rights of victims of crime to be present and participate in criminal prosecutions, and to be heard in connection with sentencing of a guilty person. See also **Victims of Crimes.**

Visas. If someone routinely wants or needs an incoming U.S. visa or visa renewal, an immigration lawyer is the proper lawyer to contact. If, on the other hand, a visa to a foreign country is needed, see Chapter 11 of this book on "Finding the Right Lawyer in a Foreign Country." Some immigration lawyers network with embassies and consulates in the United States and can help with getting visas from these countries. See also **Immigration Law.**

Visitation Modification. Changes in court orders concerning custody of children or grandchildren, and the right of a parent or grandparent to visit a child. This type of work is usually done by a divorce or family lawyer.

Visitation Rights. See **Family Law; Grandparent Visitation Rights.**

Wage and Hour Laws. Laws that usually refer to overtime rights and responsibilities. Many of these laws have been found to be partially invalid due to sex discrimination in the law. (Men and women had different rights.) There can be an overlap or a difference between federal and state law and enforcement in this area. See also **Employment Law.**

Wage Earner Plans. Employees on jobs who want to be protected from civil collection procedures can sometimes get protection under Chapter 13 of the bankruptcy law. See a bankruptcy lawyer.

Wage Garnishments, Wage Levys, Wage Attachments. See **Bankruptcy.** See also **Wage Earner Plans; Workouts.**

Walk-in Consultations. A phrase meaning the lawyer will accept, and even wants, walk-ins without appointments. Most lawyers do not want walk-in cases because they cause interruptions in the lawyer's workday and because the lawyer has no chance to prepare for the meeting. Walk-ins are reportedly common in resort areas.

Warning Labels. This involves readability and effectiveness of labels. See "Finding the Right Lawyer by Using the Advertisements of Experts and Consultants" in Chapter 4 of this book.

War of the Roses. I imagine that this reference to the movie in a divorce lawyer's ad means the firm wants bitter, vicious divorce cases. See **Family Law.**

Warrants. Warrants normally refers to arrest warrants rather than stock warrants. When an arrest warrant is issued, the person named might be in serious trouble and certainly is subject to arrest. A criminal lawyer should be sought.

Warranty Law. When a product is believed defective and causes injury, a "warranty" suit may be brought against the dealer and manufacturer. Personal injury lawyers prosecute those cases and defense lawyers defend them.

Water Law. Sometimes known as riparian rights law, this area of law can include several different subspecialties, including the shifting of real estate boundary lines when rivers change course or shorelines change, rights to extract water, and the responsibility for polluting or interfering with the water of another. In some parts of the United states, water law is listed as a specialty area in the Yellow Pages. This area of law is sometimes included with natural resources law, mining law, or oil and gas law.

Water Leakage. This involves water leakage from doors, windows, and glass. See "Finding the Right Lawyer by Using the Advertisements of Experts and Consultants" in Chapter 4 of this book.

Waterskiing Accidents. See "Finding the Right Lawyer by Using the Advertisements of Experts and Consultants" in Chapter 4 of this book.

Weather Experts. This involves weather records and testimony. See "Finding the Right Lawyer by Using the Advertisements of Experts and Consultants" in Chapter 4 of this book.

Welfare Law. Matters of law related to welfare problems. Private firms rarely handle welfare law, except on a charitable or pro bono basis.

A person with a welfare problem probably would be wise to more narrowly define the problem in terms of the specific law and problem and then visit legal aid. Its lawyers would indicate whether the person's case should be processed by legal aid, a private law firm, or some other government agency.

Wheels. See Tires.

Whiplash. A term intended to describe that in an accident, especially a rear-end accident, the spinal cord goes forward and backward like a whip, and the human head snaps forward and backward as though at the end of a whip. Often, no injuries can be seen on an X-ray, reinforcing the belief that the injury is staged, even though such an injury often would not be expected to show up on an X-ray. Whiplash is almost an obsolete term in many communities because of a connotation that a person who complains of a whiplash injury is faking the injury. Whiplash cases are handled by personal injury lawyers and general practitioners.

Whistle Blowing. See Employment Law.

White-Collar Crimes. A broad range of crimes not based on violence, such as filing false income tax returns or violating laws of the Securities and Exchange Commission. This area of law is sometimes called business crimes law. Some lawyers and firms include white-collar defense as part of their general criminal practice. Some lawyers specialize in defending white-collar crimes. Some civil law firms and lawyers that will not represent people charged with crimes of violence will represent persons charged with white-collar crimes. Some lawyers and firms treat white-collar crimes as being more serious than traffic offenses but less serious than crimes of violence. It is a mistake not to treat accusations of white-collar crime seriously. Conviction can result in long prison sentences in which one shares a cell with murderers, drug dealers, and others you wouldn't want as house guests. The fines and penalties that follow conviction often bankrupt the defendant and family. See also **Blue-Sky Laws; Criminal Tax Law; RICO; Securities Regulation.**

Will Contests. A situation where someone objects to the terms of, or contests the admission of, a will. The term is loosely applied to any situation where someone is unhappy with the terms of a proposed inheritance. If this happens, you will need a lawyer who knows the law of wills, the rules and procedures of probate court, and the rules of evidence in probate cases and will contests. There are lawyers who specialize in or concentrate on will contests. Some general practitioners, some probate lawyers, some litigation lawyers, and some elder law lawyers can do this type of work. You will have to ask around to find the right lawyer. In this area of law, it is urgent that you do not delay in getting legal help. This type of case often has special time limitations. See also "Finding the Right Lawyer by Using the Advertisements of Experts and Consultants" in Chapter 4 of this book.

Wills. Wills are often grouped with estates and trusts. See **Estate Planning.** See also **Elder Law; Living Trusts.**

Windows. See "Finding the Right Lawyer by Using the Advertisements of Experts and Consultants" in Chapter 4 of this book.

Wineries. See **Farm and Ranch Law.** See also **Alcoholic Beverage Law; Real Estate Law.**

Withholding Taxes. See **Taxation.** See also **One Hundred Percent Penalty Cases.**

Women's Rights. See **Employment Law.** See also **Civil Rights Law.**

Wood Products and Preservatives. See "Finding the Right Lawyer by Using the Advertisements of Experts and Consultants" in Chapter 4 of this book.

Workers' Compensation Law. A very broad area of law that covers injuries or other problems caused by, or connected to, a person's past or present employment. The injuries can be physical, mental, or psychiatric. Workers' compensation lawyers and the medical experts they work with are very creative in finding a relationship between injuries and the job. Workers' compensation lawyers are sometimes also called workmen's compensation lawyers.

Sometimes an on-the-job injury or work-connected injury has ramifications beyond workers' compensation law and into areas of personal injury, administrative, and even criminal law. For example, if a truck driver were rear-ended while stopped for a red light by a new automobile driven by a city employee on city business, due to faulty manufacture of the city vehicle's brakes, then the claimant might need a workers' compensation lawyer, a negligence lawyer, or a personal injury lawyer to handle the cases against the city and its driver (called third-party cases). The claimant might need a defective products or warranty lawyer to handle the claim against the manufacturer and distributor of the city trucks and their brake manufacturer.

Some workers' compensation lawyers refer out the third-party negligence cases to experts in those areas of law. Others try to handle such cases in-house. You should ask the workers' compensation lawyer how third-party cases will be handled. In addition, ask what the fees will be if the workers' compensation is also a third-party case. Workers' compensation lawyers often are also knowledgeable in unemployment law and disability claims.

Workers' Rights. See **ADA; Employment Law.** See also **Civil Rights Law; Discrimination Law.**

Work Injuries. See **Workers' Compensation Law.**

Workouts. A term applied to the negotiations and resulting deal made between creditors and debtors and owners of businesses. Workouts normally occur in bankruptcy court, in state court receiverships, and in nonjudicial assignments for the benefit of creditors. Workouts are normally done by bankruptcy lawyers, whether or not there is in fact a bankruptcy. A knowledge of bankruptcy law is required because any workout situation can ultimately end up in bankruptcy court. The negotiating position of the parties may be influenced by what may or may not happen if the case is litigated in the bankruptcy court. See also **Assignments for the Benefit of Creditors; Bankruptcy Law.**

Work-Related Injuries. Injuries that occur on the job, or in some manner are connected with a person's present or past employment. These cases are normally handled by workers' compensation lawyers, working alone or as part of a team with personal injury lawyers. See also **Workers' Compensation Law.**

Work Visas. See **Visas.** See also **Immigration Law.**

Wrongful Death Cases. The words "wrongful death" simply mean that someone is dead and that the deceased person did not die of old age. The lawyers who handle wrongful death cases are usually personal injury lawyers or workers' compensation lawyers. They try to find a source of money to compensate someone who has suffered loss when the death was caused by a third party. Lawyers who seek wrongful death cases are looking for big cases.

To find the right lawyer, you'll have to go beyond the fact that someone has died. You have to go into how the person died to determine the type of lawyer or lawyers needed to do the best job. Good places to start include personal injury lawyers, workers' compensation lawyers, and general practice lawyers.

Wrongful Discharge. See **Wrongful Termination.** See also **Civil Rights Law; Discrimination Law; Employment Law.**

Wrongful Life. A term applied to cases against physicians or drug companies. Usually, contraceptive drugs or devices were not effective and there is a conception with resulting damage to the mother, father, or child. (Bad vasectomies or tubal ligations are common cases.) This area of law is also called "wrongful birth." Lawyers who handle these cases are typically medical malpractice or hospital malpractice lawyers.

Wrongful Termination. An employer's termination of an employee under circumstances the employee believes to be wrongful. This is an area of employment law. Some lawyers specialize in the handling of wrongful termination cases without practicing general labor law. Some personal injury lawyers handle wrongful termination cases. See also **Civil Rights Law; Discrimination Law; Employment Law.**

Zoning. An area of law that deals with the use of real estate as regulated by local governments. This area of law is normally practiced by local real estate lawyers as part of land-use regulation. See also **Land-Use Regulation.**

List of Bar Association-Sponsored Lawyer Referral Services

ALABAMA

Birmingham Bar Lawyer
Referral Service
Birmingham, AL
(205) 251-8006

Lawyer Referral &
Information Service of
Madison County
Huntsville, AL
(205) 539-2275

Mobile Bar Association
Lawyer Referral Service
Mobile, AL
(205) 433-1032

Alabama State Bar Lawyer
Referral Service
Montgomery, AL
(205) 269-1515

ALASKA

Alaska Bar Association Lawyer
Referral Service
Anchorage, AK
(907) 272-7469

ARKANSAS

Arkansas Bar Association
Lawyer Referral Service
Little Rock, AR
(501) 375-4605

ARIZONA

Maricopa Bar Association
Lawyer Referral Service
Phoenix, AZ
(602) 257-4434

Pima County Bar Association
Lawyer Referral Service
Tucson, AZ
(602) 623-6159

CALIFORNIA

Lawyer Referral Service of
Placer County
Auburn, CA
(916) 823-1094

Lawyer Referral Service of
Kern County Inc.
Bakersfield, CA
(805) 327-3663

Disability Rights, Education
And Defense Fund LRS
Berkeley, CA
(510) 644-2555

Lawyer Referral Service &
Legal Aid of the Burbank
Bar Association
Burbank, CA
(818) 843-0931

Butte County Bar Association
Lawyer Referral Service
Chico, CA
(916) 891-6808

South Bay Lawyer Referral
Service
Chula Vista, CA
(619) 422-5377

South Central District Bar
Lawyer Referral Service
Compton, CA
(213) 632-0700

Attorneys' Reference Panel
Concord, CA
(510) 825-5700

East San Diego County Lawyer
Referral Service
El Cajon, CA
(619) 588-1936

Experienced Attorneys Referral
Service
Encinitas, CA
(619) 943-2333

San Fernando Valley Bar
Association Lawyers Referral
& Information Service
Encino, CA
(818) 906-3200

Humboldt County Bar
Association
Eureka, CA
(707) 445-2652

Washington Township Bar
Association Lawyer
Reference Service
Fremont, CA
(415) 797-0244

Attorney Referral &
Information Service of the
Fresno County Bar Assoc.
Fresno, CA
(209) 264-0137

College Legal Clinic
Fullerton, CA
(714) 870-5757

Glendale Bar Association
Lawyer Referral Service
Glendale, CA
(818) 956-1633

Nevada County Lawyer
Referral Service
Grass Valley, CA
(916) 272-6064

Southern Alameda County Bar
Association Attorneys
Referral Service
Hayward, CA
(415) 582-0091

Asian American Lawyer
Referral And Information
Service, Inc.
Los Angeles, CA
(213) 384-8072

East Los Angeles/Montebello
Bar Association LRS
Los Angeles, CA
(213) 722-3822

Los Angeles County Bar
Association LRIS
Los Angeles, CA
(213) 243-1525
(213) 896-6449

Primex Talking Yellow Pages
Lawyer Referral Service
Los Angeles, CA
1-800-777-7776

Universal Lawyer Referral
Service
Los Angeles, CA
(213) 626-0011

Lawyer Referral Service of
Merced County, Inc.
Merced, CA
(209) 383-3886

Stanislaus County Bar
Association
Modesto, CA
(209) 571-5727

Lawyer Referral Service of
Monterey County Bar
Association
Monterey, CA
(408) 375-9889

Lawyers Reference Service /
Southeast District Bar
Association
Norwalk, CA
(310) 868-6787

Alameda County Bar
Association Lawyer Referral
Service
Oakland, CA
(510) 893-8683

Law Liens - Lawyer Referral
And Information Service
Orange, CA
(714) 639-1317

Certified Legal Services
Pacoima, CA
(818) 899-1938

Palo Alto Area Bar Association
Lawyer Referral Service
Palo Alto, CA
(415) 324-9811

Project Sentinel
Palo Alto, CA
(415) 321-6291

Centro De Proteccion Referral
Service
Pasadena, CA
(818) 441-7576

Pasadena Lawyer Referral And
Information Service
Pasadena, CA
(818) 793-1422

Professional Referrals, Inc.
Pleasanton, CA
(510) 416-0808

Profiles
Pleasanton, CA
(510) 416-0808

Western San Bernardino
County Bar Association
Lawyer Referral Service
Rancho Cucamonga, CA
(919) 945-2980

Shasta-Trinity Counties Bar
Association Lawyer
Reference Service
Redding, CA
(916) 241-4490

Lawyer Referral Service of the
San Mateo County Bar
Association
Redwood City, CA
(415) 369-4149

Riverside County Bar Association
Lawyer Referral Service
Riverside, CA
(909) 682-7520

Sacramento Area Feminist
Legal Services
Sacramento, CA
(916) 446-7244

Sacramento County Bar
Association Lawyer Referral
& Info Service
Sacramento, CA
(916) 446-7125

San Bernardino County Bar
Assn. Lawyer Referral
Service
San Bernardino, CA
(909) 888-6791

Attorney Referral Service of
San Diego Trial Lawyers
Association
San Diego, CA
(619) 696-6200

Attorney Referral Service of
Southern California
San Diego, CA
(619) 294-4000

Cannon Lawyer Referral
Service
San Diego, CA
(619) 544-1455

Lawyer Referral Service of the
Legal Aid Society of San
Diego, Inc.
San Diego, CA
(619) 263-3835

National Lawyers Guild
Military Law Panel
San Diego, CA
(714) 233-1701

Pacifica Attorney Referrals
San Diego, CA
(619) 698-7777

Bar Association of San
Francisco Lawyer Referral
Service
San Francisco, CA
(415) 764-1616

California Advocates for
Nursing Home Reform
(CANHR)
San Francisco, CA
(415) 474-5171

California Lawyers for the Arts
Lawyer Referral Service
San Francisco, CA
(415) 775-7200

Gay Legal Referral Service
San Francisco, CA
(415) 621-3900

La Raza Lawyer Referral Service
San Francisco, CA
(415) 575-3500

Santa Clara County Bar Association/ Lawyer Referral Service
San Jose, CA
(408) 971-6822

San Luis Obispo County Bar Lawyer Referral Service
San Louis Obispo, CA
(805) 544-9334

Los Defensores, Inc. Lawyer Referral Service
San Pedro, CA
(213) 519-4060

Lawyer Referral Service of the Marin County Bar Association
San Rafael, CA
(415) 453-5501

Eastern Alameda County Bar Association Lawyer Referral
San Ramon, CA
(510) 462-2714

Orange County Bar Association Lawyer Referral Service
Santa Ana, CA
(714) 541-6222

Sunnyvale Cuppertino Attorney Referral Service
Santa Clara, CA
(408) 736-2520

Santa Cruz County Bar Association Lawyer Referral Service
Santa Cruz, CA
(408) 425-4755

California Lawyers for the Arts (Los Angeles Branch)
Santa Monica, CA
(310) 395-8993

Justice Attorney Referral Service
Santa Monica, CA
(818) 344-7700

Santa Monica Lawyer Referral Service And Information Service
Santa Monica, CA
(213) 451-5633

Sonoma County Legal Services Foundation
Santa Rosa, CA
(707) 546-2924

Lawyer Referral Service of the Legal Aid Society of Orange County
Santa Ana, CA
(714) 547-0763

Lawyer Referral Service of the San Joaquin County Bar Association
Stockton, CA
(209) 948-4620

Attorney Referral Service San Diego/Orange Counties And Inland Empire
Temecula, CA
(909) 695-2501
(714) 772-8244

M C O A Legal Network, Inc.
Torrance, CA
(310) 320-3280

South Bay Bar Association of
L A County LRS
Torrance, CA
(213) 320-9350

Personal Injury Hotline
Tustin, CA
(714) 834-0133

Mendocino & Lake Counties
Bar Association Lawyer
Referral Service
Ukiah, CA
(707) 463-0131

Lawyer Referral Service of
Napa And Solano County
Vallejo, CA
(707) 552-7530

Ventura County Bar
Association Lawyer Referral
Service
Ventura, CA
(805) 650-7599

Tulare County Lawyers
Reference Service
Visalia, CA
(209) 732-2513

LRS of Bar Association of
Northern San Diego County
Vista, CA
(619) 758-4755

Lawyer Referral Service of
Yolo County
Woodland, CA
(916) 662-0219

The Legal Rights Defenders,
Inc. Lawyer Referral Service
San Pedro, CA
(213) 519-4060

COLORADO

Metropolitan Lawyer Referral
Service, Inc.
Denver, CO
(303) 831-8000

El Paso County Bar Association
Lawyer Referral Service
El Paso, CO
(719) 636-1532

Larimer County Lawyer
Referral Service
Fort Collins, CO
(303) 226-4343

CONNECTICUT

Fairfield County Lawyer
Referral Service, Inc.
Bridgeport, CT
(203) 335-4116

Hartford County Bar
Association Lawyer Referral
Service
Hartford, CT
(203) 525-6052

New Haven County Bar
Association Lawyer Referral
Service
New Haven, CT
(203) 562-5750

Waterbury Lawyer Referral
Service
Waterbury, CT
(203) 753-1938

New London County Bar
Association, Inc. Lawyer
Referral Service
Yantic, CT
(203) 889-9384

DELAWARE

Delaware State Bar Association
Wilmington, DE
(302) 658-5278

DISTRICT OF COLUMBIA

National Veterans Legal
Services
Washington, DC
(202) 265-8305

FLORIDA

Seminole County Bar
Association Lawyer Referral
Service
Altamonte Springs, FL
(407) 834-0530

Clearwater Bar Association
Lawyer Referral Service
Clearwater, FL
(813) 461-4880

Broward County Bar
Association Lawyer Referral
Service
Ft. Lauderdale, FL
(305) 764-8040

Volusia County Bar
Association Lawyer Referral
Service
Holly Hill, FL
(904) 255-3434

The Jacksonville Bar
Association Lawyer Referral
Service
Jacksonville, FL
(904) 399-5780

Polk County Lawyer Referral
Service Bar Association
Lakeland, FL
(813) 686-8215

Brevard County Bar
Association, Inc. Lawyer
Referral Service
Melbourne, FL
(407) 242-1551

Collier County Bar Association
Lawyer Referral Service
Naples, FL
(813) 775-8566

West Pasco Bar Association
Lawyer Referral Service
New Port Richey, FL
(813) 848-7433

Orange County Bar
Association LRS
Orlando, FL
(407) 422-4537

Escambia-Santa Rosa Lawyer
Referral
Pensacola, FL
(904) 434-8135

Brevard County Bar
Association, Inc. Lawyer
Referral Service
Rockledge, FL
(407) 636-5344

Brevard County Bar
Association Lawyer Referral
Service (Rockledge)
Rockledge, FL
(407) 636-5344

Lawyer Referral Service of the
St. Petersburg Bar
Association
St. Petersburg, FL
(813) 821-5450

St. Petersburg Bar Association
St. Petersburg, FL
(813) 821-5450

The Florida Bar Lawyer
Referral Service
Tallahassee, FL
1-800-342-8011
(904) 561-5600

Lawyer Referral Service of the
Palm Beach County Bar
Association
West Palm Beach, FL
(407) 687-3266

Palm Beach County Bar
Association Lawyer Referral
Service
West Palm Beach, FL
(407) 687-3266

GEORGIA

Lawyer Referral Service of the
Atlanta Bar Association Inc.
Atlanta, GA
(404) 521-0777

Dekalb Bar Association
Attorney Referral Service
Decatur, GA
(404) 373-2580

Lawyer Referral Service of
Cobb County Cobb
Superior Courthouse
Marietta, GA
(404) 424-7149

Lawyer Referral Service of the
Savanna Bar Association
Savannah, GA
(912) 236-9344

HAWAII

Hawaii State Bar Association,
LRIS
Honolulu, HI
(808) 537-9140

IDAHO

Idaho State Bar Lawyer
Referral Service
Boise, ID
(208) 342-8958

ILLINOIS

Northwest Suburban Bar
Association Attorney
Referral Plan
Arlington Heights, IL
(708) 290-8070

National Lawyers Guild
Referral Service
Chicago, IL
(312) 939-2492

The Chicago Bar Association
Lawyer Referral Service
Chicago, IL
(312) 554-2001

Women's Bar Association
Chicago, IL
(312) 541-0048

West Suburban Bar
   Association
Forest Park, IL
(708) 366-1122

Kane County Bar Association
Geneva, IL
(708) 232-6416

Will County Bar Association
Joliet, IL
(815) 726-0383

North Suburban Bar Assoc.
   LRS Cook, Lake & DuPage
   Counties
Northbrook, IL
(312) 564-4800

Lawyer Referral Service, Peoria
   County Bar Association
Peoria, IL
(309) 674-1224

Winnebago County Lawyer
   Referral
Rockford, IL
(185) 964-5152

Illinois State Bar Association
   Lawyer Referral Service
Springfield, IL
1-800-252-8916

Lake County Bar Association
   Lawyer Referral Service
Waukegan, IL
(708) 244-3140

DuPage County Lawyer
   Referral Service
Wheaton, IL
(708) 653-9109

INDIANA

Madison County Lawyer
   Referral Service Madison
   County Bar Association
Anderson, IN
(317) 642-6888

Lake County Bar Association
   Lawyer Referral
Crown Point, IN
(219) 738-1905

Evansville Bar Association
   Lawyer Referral Service
Evansville, IN
(812) 426-1712

Allen County Bar Association,
   Inc. Lawyer Referral Service
Fort Wayne, IN
(219) 432-2358

Legal Aid Society of Greater
   Hammond, Inc. Hammond
   Bar Association
Hammond, IN
(219) 932-2787

Indiana State Bar Association
Indianapolis, IN
(317) 269-2222

Indianapolis Bar Association
   Lawyer Referral Service
Indianapolis, IN
(317) 269-2000

St. Joseph County Bar
   Association Lawyer Referral
   Service
South Bend, IN
(219) 284-9657

IOWA

Iowa State Bar Association
Statewide Lawyer Referral
Service
Des Moines, IA
1-800-532-1108

KANSAS

Topeka Bar Association
Kansas, KS
(913) 233-3945

Kansas Bar Association
Lawyer Referral Service
Topeka, KS
(913) 233-9693

KENTUCKY

Northern Kentucky University
Northern Kentucky Bar
Association LRS
Highland Heights, KY
(606) 781-1300

Fayette County Bar
Association Lawyer Referral
Service
Lexington, KY
(606) 255-7251

Kentucky Lawyer Referral
Service Louisville Bar
Association
Louisville, KY
1-800-372-2999
1-800-899-4529

LOUISIANA

Baton Rouge Bar Association
Lawyer Referral Service
Baton Rouge, LA
(504) 344-9926

Lafayette Parish - Lawyer
Referral Service
Lafayette, LA
(318) 237-4700

Southwest Louisiana Lawyer
Referral Service
Lake Charles, LA
(318) 436-3308

New Orleans Bar Association
Lawyer Referral Service
New Orleans, LA
(504) 561-8828

Shreveport Lawyer Referral
Service
Shreveport, LA
(318) 222-0720

MAINE

Maine Lawyer Referral And
Information Service
Augusta, ME
(207) 622-1460

Maine Volunteer Lawyers Pro
Bono Program
Portland, ME
1-800-442-4293

MASSACHUSETTS

Boston Bar Association
Lawyer Reference Service
Boston, MA
(617) 742-0625

Massachusetts Bar
Association's Lawyer
Referral Service
Boston, MA
(617) 542-9103

National Lawyers Guild
Lawyer Referral Service
Boston, MA
(617) 227-7008

Middlesex County Bar
Association Lawyer Referral
Service
Cambridge, MA
(617) 494-4150

Briston County Bar
Association Lawyer Referral
Service
New Bedford, MA
(508) 990-1303

Hampshire County Bar
Northampton, MA
(413) 586-8729

Essex County Bar Association
Lawyer Referral Service
Salem, MA
(508) 741-7888

Hampden County Bar
Association Lawyer Referral
Service
Springfield, MA
(413) 732-4648

Lawyer Referral Service of the
Worcester County Bar
Association
Worcester, MA
(508) 752-1311

MARYLAND

Lawyer Referral Service, Anne
Arundel Bar Association
Annapolis, MD
(410) 280-6961

Bar Association of Baltimore
City Lawyer Referral &
Information Service
Baltimore, MD
(410) 539-3112

Howard County Bar Association
Lawyer Referral Service
Elliott City, MD
(410) 465-2721

Baltimore County Bar
Association Lawyer Referral
Service
Towson, MD
(301) 337-9100

Lawyer Referral Service of the
Prince George's County Bar
Association
Upper Marlboro, MD
(301) 952-1442

Lawyer Referral Service of
Carroll County
Westminster, MD
(410) 848-1451

MICHIGAN

Washtenaw County Bar
Association Lawyer Referral
& Information Service
Ann Arbor, MI
(313) 996-3229

Oakland County Bar Association
Lawyer Referral Service
Bloomfield Hills, MI
(810) 334-3400

Dearborn Bar Association
Lawyer Referral Service
Dearborn, MI
(313) 565-6711

Detroit Bar Association
Lawyer Referral Service
Detroit, MI
(313) 961-6120

National Lawyers Guild
Referral Service (Detroit)
Detroit, MI
(313) 963-0843

Genesee County Bar Association
Lawyer Referral Service
Flint, MI
(313) 232-6000

Lawyer Referral &
Information Service
Grand Rapids, MI
(616) 454-9493

Kalamazoo Attorney Referral
Service
Kalamazoo, MI
(616) 384-8242

Ingham County Bar
Association Lawyer Referral
And Information Service
Lansing, MI
(517) 482-8816

State Bar of Michigan Lawyer
Referral Service
Lansing, MI
1-800-968-0738

Livonia Lawyer Referral
Service
Livonia, MI
(313) 427-8900

Macomb County Bar
Association Lawyers Referral
& Information Service
Mt. Clemens, MI
(313) 468-8300

Lawyer Referral Service
Saginaw County Bar
Association
Saginaw, MI
(517) 790-4737

Berrien County Bar Lawyer
Referral Service
St. Joseph, MI
(616) 983-6363

Lawyer Referral Service (Iosco
County)
Tawas City, MI
(517) 362-3441

Traverse Attorney Referral
Service
Traverse City, MI
(616) 922-4713

MINNESOTA

Dakota County LRS
Burnsville, MN
(612) 431-3200

Washington County Lawyer
Referral Service
Lake Elmo, MN
(612) 777-6355

Lawyer Referral & Information
Service of the Hennepin
County Bar Assoc.
Minneapolis, MN
(612) 340-0022

Minnesota State Bar
Association Attorney
Referral Service
Minneapolis, MN
1-800-292-4152

Minnesota Women Lawyers
  Referral Service
Minneapolis, MN
(612) 338-3205

Attorney Referral Service of
  Ramsey County
St. Paul, MN
(612) 224-1775

MISSISSIPPI

The Mississippi State Bar
  Lawyer Referral Service
Jackson, MS
1-800-682-0046

MISSOURI

Missouri Bar Lawyer Referral
  Service
Jefferson City, MO
(314) 635-4128

Kansas City Bar Association
  Lawyer Referral Service
Kansas City, MO
(816) 221-9446

The Kansas City Metropolitan
  Bar Association
Kansas City, MO
(816) 221-9473

Greene County Bar
  Association Lawyer Referral
  Service
Springfield, MO
(417) 831-2783

Springfield Metropolitan Bar
  Association
Springfield, MO
(417) 831-2783

Bar Assoc. of Metro St. Louis
  Lawyers Referral &
  Information Service
St. Louis, MO
(314) 621-6681

MONTANA

State Bar of Montana Lawyer
  Referral Service
Helena, MT
(406) 449-6577

NEBRASKA

Lincoln Bar Association LRS
  Legal Services of Southeast
  Nebraska
Lincoln, NE
(402) 435-2161

Omaha Bar Association
  Lawyer Referral Service
Omaha, NE
(402) 341-4104

NEVADA

State Bar of Nevada Lawyer
  Referral Service
Las Vegas, NV
(702) 382-0504

NEW HAMPSHIRE

LRS of the New Hampshire
  Bar Association
Concord, NH
1-800-639-5290

Lawyer Referral Services of the
  New Hampshire Bar
  Association
Concord, NH
1-800-639-5290

295

NEW JERSEY

Atlantic County Bar
  Association LRS
Atlantic City, NJ
(609) 345-3444

Camden County Bar
  Association Lawyer Referral
  Service
Camden, NJ
(609) 964-4520

Cape May County Bar
  Association Lawyer Referral
  Service
Cape May Court House, NJ
(609) 463-0313

Salem County Bar Lawyer
  Referral Service
Carneys Point, NJ
(609) 678-8363

ATLA New Jersey Lawyer
  Referral Service
Edison, NJ
1-800-367-0089

Bar Association of Union
  County Lawyer Referral
  Service
Elizabeth, NJ
(201) 353-4715

Hunterdon County Bar
  Association Lawyer Referral
  Service
Flemington, NJ
(908) 788-5112

Monmouth Bar Association
  Lawyer Referral Service
Freehold, NJ
(908) 431-5544

Bergen County Bar Association
  Lawyer's Referral Service
Hackensack, NJ
(201) 488-0044

Hudson County Bar Assoc.
  Lawyer Referral Service
Jersey City, NJ
(201) 798-2727

Mercer County Bar
  Association Lawyer Referral
  Service
Mercerville, NJ
(609) 585-6200

Morris County Bar Association
  Lawyer Referral Service
Morristown, NJ
(201) 267-5882

Sussex Lawyer Referral Service
Morristown, NJ
(201) 267-5882

Warren Lawyer Referral
  Service
Morristown, NJ
(201) 267-5882

Burlington County Lawyer
  Referral Service
Mount Holly, NJ
(609) 261-4862

Middlesex County Bar
  Association
New Brunswick, NJ
(908) 828-0053

Essex County Bar Association
  LRS
Newark, NJ
(201) 622-6207

Passaic County Bar
Association Lawyer Referral
Service
Paterson, NJ
(201) 278-9223

Somerset County Bar Lawyers
Referral Service
Somerville, NJ
(201) 685-2323

Ocean County Bar Association
Lawyers Referral Service
Toms River, NJ
(201) 240-3666

Cumberland County Bar
Association LRS
Vineland, NJ
(609) 692-6207

Gloucester County Bar
Association LRS
Woodbury, NJ
(609) 848-4589

NEW MEXICO

Albuquerque Bar Association
Lawyer Referral Service
Albuquerque, NM
(505) 243-2615

State Bar of NM Special
Projects Inc. Lawyer
Referral
Albuquerque, NM
(505) 842-6252

State Bar of New Mexico
Lawyer Referral Program
for the Elderly
Albuquerque, NM
(505) 842-6252

State Bar of New Mexico
Lawyer Referral Service
Albuquerque, NM
1-800-876-6227

NEW YORK

Albany County Bar Association
Albany, NY
(518) 445-7691

Capital Chapter Women's Bar
Lawyer Referral Service
Albany, NY
(518) 438-5511

Capital District Women's Bar
Association Referral Service
Albany, NY
(518) 438-5511

New York State Bar
Association LRIS
Albany, NY
1-800-342-3661

Cattaraugus County Bar
Association Lawyer Referral
Service
Allegany, NY
(716) 373-1350

Broome County Bar Association
Binghamton, NY
(607) 723-6331

Bronx County Bar Association
Legal Referral Service
Bronx, NY
(718) 293-5600

Brooklyn Bar Association
Lawyer's Referral Service
Brooklyn, NY
(718) 624-0843

Bar Association of Erie County
Buffalo, NY
(716) 852-3100

Putnam County Bar
Association Lawyer Referral
Service
Carmel, NY
(914) 225-4904

Suffolk County Bar
Association Lawyer Referral
Service
Commack, NY
(516) 864-2100

Chemung County Lawyer
Referral Service
Elmira, NY
(607) 732-6613

Warren County Bar
Association Lawyer Referral
Service
Glens Falls, NY
(518) 792-9239

Orange County Bar
Association
Goshen, NY
(914) 294-8222

Queens County Bar
Association Legal Aid &
Referral Service
Jamaica, NY
(718) 291-4500

Sullivan County Bar
Association Lawyer Referral
Service
Liberty, NY
(914) 794-2426

Nassau County Bar
Association Lawyer Referral
& Information Service
Mineola, NY
(516) 747-4832

Rockland County Bar
Association
New City, NY
(914) 634-2149

Association of the Bar of the
City of NY & NY County
Lawyers Assn. LRS
New York, NY
(212) 626-7373

Niagara Falls Bar Association
Lawyer Referral Service
Niagara Falls, NY
(716) 282-1242

Dutchess County Bar
Association Lawyer
Poughkeepsie, NY
(914) 473-2488

Monroe County Bar
Association LRS
Rochester, NY
(716) 546-2170

Richmond County Bar
Association Lawyer Referral
Service
Staten Island, NY
(718) 442-4500

Lawyer Referral Service,
Onondaga County Bar
Association
Syracuse, NY
(315) 471-2690

298

Rensselaer County Bar
　　Association Lawyer Referral
　　Service
Troy, NY
(518) 272-7220

Jefferson County Bar
　　Association Lawyer Referral
　　Service
Watertown, NY
(315) 782-3520

Westchester County Bar
　　Association Lawyer Referral
　　Service
White Plains, NY
(914) 761-5151

NORTH CAROLINA

Mecklenburg County Bar LRS
Charlotte, NC
(704) 375-0120

North Carolina Bar
　　Association Lawyer Referral
　　Service
Raleigh, NC
1-800-662-7660

North Carolina Lawyer
　　Referral Service
Raleigh, NC
(919) 828-1054

NORTH DAKOTA

Lawyer Referral &
　　Information Service of
　　North Dakota
Bismarck, ND
1-800-932-8880

OHIO

Clermont County Bar
　　Association Lawyer Referral
　　Service
Batavia, OH
(513) 732-2050

Stark County Bar Association
　　Lawyer's Referral Service
Canton, OH
(216) 453-0686

Lawyer Referral Service of the
　　Cincinnati Bar Association
Cincinnati, OH
(513) 381-8359

PRO SENIORS the Legal
　　Hotline for Older Ohioans
Cincinnati, OH
(513) 621-8721

Cleveland Bar Association
　　Lawyer Referral Service
Cleveland, OH
(216) 696-3525

Cleveland Lawyer Referral
　　Service
Cleveland, OH
(216) 696-3525

Cuyahoga County Bar
　　Association Lawyer Referral
　　Service
Cleveland, OH
(216) 621-2414

Columbus Bar Association
　　Attorney Referral &
　　Information Service
Columbus, OH
(614) 221-0754

Coshocton County Bar
Association Lawyer Referral
Service
Coshocton, OH
(614) 622-2011

Dayton Bar Association
Lawyer Referral Service
Dayton, OH
(513) 222-6102

Lorain County Bar Association
Referral Program
Elyria, OH
(216) 323-8416

Butler County Bar Association
Hamilton, OH
1-800-543-0846

Lawrence County Law Library
And Bar Association
Ironton, OH
(614) 533-0582

Hocking County Bar
Association
Logan, OH
(614) 385-4456

Washington County Bar
Association
Marietta, OH
(614) 374-2629

Holmes County Bar
Association Lawyer Referral
Service
Millersburg, OH
(216) 674-0457

Tuscarawas County Bar
Association
New Philadelphia, OH
(216) 364-3004

Lake County Bar Association
LRS
Painesville, OH
(216) 352-4460

Lake County Bar Association
Lawyer's Referral Service
Painesville, OH
(216) 352-6044

Portage County Bar Association
Lawyer's Referral Service
Ravenna, OH
(216) 296-6357

Springfield Bar Association
Lawyer Referral Service
Springfield, OH
(513) 322-7427

Belmont County Bar Association
St. Clairsville, OH
(614) 695-9202

Lawyer Referral &
Information Service of the
Toledo Bar Association
Toledo, OH
(419) 242-9363

Trumbull County Bar
Association
Warren, OH
(216) 675-2415

Wayne County Bar Association
Lawyer Referral Service
Wooster, OH
(216) 262-6198

Mahoning County Bar
Association Lawyer Referral
Service
Youngstown, OH
(216) 746-2933

OKLAHOMA

Cleveland County Bar
   Association Lawyer Referral
   Service
Norman, OK
(405) 360-0912

Tulsa County Bar Association
   Lawyer Referral Service
Tulsa, OK
(918) 584-5243

OREGON

Oregon State Bar LRS
Lake Oswego, OR
(503) 684-3763

National Lawyers Guild LRS
   Portland Chapter
Portland, OR
(503) 228-5222

PENNSYLVANIA

Lawyer Referral Service of the
   Bar Association of Lehigh
   County
Allentown, PA
(215) 433-7094

Bar Assns of Franklin &
   Fulton Counties Legal
   Reference Service
Chambersburg, PA
(717) 261-3848

Lawyer Referral Service Bucks
   County Bar Association
Doylestown, PA
(215) 348-9413

Attorney LRIS Northampton
   County Bar
Easton, PA
(610) 258-6333

Erie County Bar Association
   Lawyer Referral Service
Erie, PA
(814) 459-4411

Lawyer Referral Service of the
   Westmoreland Bar
   Association
Greensburg, PA
(412) 834-8490

Dauphin County Bar
   Association Lawyer Referral
   Service
Harrisburg, PA
(717) 232-7536

Pennsylvania Lawyer Referral
   Service Pennsylvania Bar
   Association
Harrisburg, PA
(717) 238-6715

Blair County Lawyers Referral
   Blair County Bar
   Association
Hollidaysburg, PA
(814) 695-5541

Lancaster Bar Association
   Lawyer Referral Service
Lancaster, PA
(717) 393-0737

Delaware County Bar
   Association Lawyers
   Referral Service
Media, PA
(215) 566-6625

Montgomery Bar Association
Lawyer Referral Service
Norristown, PA
(215) 279-9660

Lawyer Referral &
Information Service of the
Philadelphia Bar Assoc.
Philadelphia, PA
(215) 238-6300

Allegheny County Bar Lawyer
Referral Service
Pittsburgh, PA
(412) 261-0518

Berks County Lawyer Referral
Service
Reading, PA
(610) 375-4591

Lawyer Referral Service
Fayette County Bar
Association
Uniontown, PA
(412) 430-1227

Washington County Bar
Association Lawyer Referral
Service
Washington, PA
(412) 225-6710

Chester County Bar
Association Lawyer Referral
Service
West Chester, PA
(610) 429-1500

Wilkes-Barre Law & Library
Association LRS Luzerne
County Bar
Wilkes-Barre, PA
(717) 822-6712

York County Bar Association
Lawyer Referral Service
York, PA
(717) 771-9361

RHODE ISLAND

Rhode Island Bar Assn. Legal
Info & Referral Service for
the Elderly
Providence, RI
(401) 552-1504

Rhode Island Bar Association
Lawyer Referral Service
Providence, RI
(401) 421-7799

SOUTH CAROLINA

South Carolina Bar Lawyer
Referral Service
Columbia, SC
1-800-868-2284

SOUTH DAKOTA

Brown County Bar Association
Lawyer Referral Service
Aberdeen, SD
(605) 225-1354

South Dakota Lawyer Referral
Service State Bar of South
Dakota
Pierre, SD
1-800-952-2333

TENNESSEE

Chattanooga Bar Association
Lawyer Referral Service
Chattanooga, TN
(615) 266-5950

Knoxville Bar Association
 Lawyer Referral Service
Knoxville, TN
(615) 522-7501

Memphis Bar Association Inc.
 Lawyer Referral Service
Memphis, TN
(901) 529-8800

Nashville Bar Association
 Lawyer Referral Service
Nashville, TN
(615) 242-6546

TEXAS

Lawyer Referral Service of the
 Travis County Bar
 Association, Inc.
Austin, TX
(512) 472-8303

State Bar of Texas Lawyer
 Referral & Information
 Service
Austin, TX
1-800-252-9690

Jefferson County Bar
 Association Lawyer Referral
 Service
Beaumont, TX
(409) 835-8438

Corpus Christi Bar Association
 Lawyer Referral Service
Corpus Christi, TX
(512) 883-3971

Dallas Bar Association Lawyer
 Referral Service
Dallas, TX
(214) 979-9090

El Paso Bar Association
 Lawyer Referral Service
El Paso, TX
(915) 327-7052

Lawyer Referral Service of
 Tarrant County Bar
 Association
Fort Worth, TX
(817) 336-4101

Harris County Criminal
 Lawyers Association LRS
Houston, TX
(713) 227-2404

Houston Lawyer Referral
 Service, Inc.
Houston, TX
(713) 237-9429

San Antonio Bar Association
 Lawyer Referral Service
San Antonio, TX
(512) 227-1853

UTAH

Utah State Bar Lawyer
 Referral Service
Salt Lake City, UT
(801) 531-9075

VIRGINIA

Alexandria Lawyer Referral
 Service
Alexandria, VA
(703) 548-1105

Arlington County Bar
 Association Lawyer Referral
 Service
Arlington, VA
(703) 358-3390

303

Charlottesville-Albemarle Legal
Aid Society
Charlottesville, VA
(804) 977-0553

Fairfax Bar Association
Lawyer Referral Service
Fairfax, VA
(703) 246-3780

Lawyer Referral Service of the
Norfolk - Portsmouth Bar
Association
Norfolk, VA
(804) 622-3152

Virginia Lawyer Referral
Service
Richmond, VA
1-800-552-7977

Roanoke Bar Association
Lawyer Referral Service
Roanoke, VA
(703) 982-2345

VERMONT

Vermont Bar Association
Lawyer Referral Service
Montpelier, VT
1-800-639-7036

WASHINGTON

Lewis County Lawyer Referral
Service Lewis County Clerk
Chehalis, WA
(206) 748-0430

King County Bar Lawyer
Referral Service
Seattle, WA
(206) 623-2551

National Lawyers Guild
Seattle, WA
(206) 622-5144

Spokane County Bar Association
Lawyer Referral Service
Spokane, WA
(509) 623-2665

Puget Sound Legal Assistance
Foundation
Tacoma, WA
(206) 572-4343

Tacoma - Pierce County Bar
Association LRS
Tacoma, WA
(206) 383-3432

WEST VIRGINIA

The West Virginia State Bar
Lawyer Referral Service
Charleston, WV
(304) 558-7991

WISCONSIN

State Bar of Wisconsin Lawyer
Referral & Information
Service
Madison, WI
1-800-362-9082

Milwaukee Bar Association
Lawyer Referral &
Information Service
Milwaukee, WI
(414) 274-6768

WYOMING

Wyoming State Bar
Cheyenne, WY
(307) 632-9061

CANADA

Law Society of Upper Canada
  LRS
Toronto
Ontario
(416) 947-3465

Law Phone-in & Lawyer
  Referral Program
Winnipeg
Manitoba
1-800-262-8800

Nova Scotia Barristers' Society
  Lawyer Referral Service
Halifax
Nova Scotia
(902) 422-1491

Index

Confidentiality of lawyer, 131–32
Conflicts of interest, 133–34
Consulates, local, of foreign governments, 165
Consultants
  finding the right lawyer with advertisements of, 46–48
  listing of, 48–50
  as source of recommendation, 140
Consultation, 9–10
  fees for first, 65–66
  and goal setting, 15–16
Contingent fees, 76–77
Conversation, addressing lawyer in, 100–101
Cost estimate forms in controlling legal costs, 143–47
Country desk, 159–60
Court, 103–4
Courtesy of lawyer, 125–26
Credit card, payment of legal fees with, 68–69
Criminal defense, 13–14

D

Defendant, 21
Diplomatic pouch, 162–63
Directories as source of recommendation, 46, 140
Direct solicitation, 141–42
Due diligence, 3

E

Education
  for American lawyers, 111–14
  importance of class standing of lawyer, 115–16
  number of years required, 116
  and practical experience in law school, 117–18
Embassies, local, of foreign governments, 165
Emergency Services for U.S. Citizens Overseas, Office of,
    158–59

getting a visit to jails in, 160

local embassies and consulates and, 165

Forms

cost estimate, 144–47

need for lawyer in filling out legal or official, 25–26

using preprinted, 26

Friends as source of recommendation, 140

G

Gender of lawyer, 132–33

Geographic area, reducing legal fees by selecting, 80–81

H

Hurt feelings cases, 106

I

Information, consultation for, 9–10

In propria persona, 102

versus representing oneself, 17–19

Insurance companies

methods used in finding the right lawyer, 137–55

payment of legal fees through, 71–74

questions asked by, in selecting or keeping their law firms, 150–53

use of fee agreements to control billing abuses, 147–50

Insurance for legal fees, 87

Internet, 63

J

Judges, 103–4

as source of recommendation, 139

Juris Doctor (J.D.), 112

Jury, 23

L

Landlord-tenant cases, 105–6

Large firms, 97–98

P

Payments. *See* Legal fees

Personality of lawyer, 126–28

Philosophy and beliefs of lawyer, 128–29

Piety, finding the right lawyer through, 62–63

Pit, 23

Plaintiff, 21

Practice areas, listing of, 39–42. *See also Foonberg's Glossary of Legal Specialties*

Prejudice, 67

Pre-law, 112

Prepaid legal plans, 73–74

  finding the right lawyer through, 60–61

Privilege, 5–6

Pro bono legal work, 66–67, 82–84

Prodigy, 63

Pro per, 102

Pro se, 102

PSI Com, 63

Public defenders, 14

R

Recommendations

  finding the right lawyer by getting, 3–7

  questions to ask before seeking, 4–6

  sources of, 6–7, 138–41

Referral services as source of recommendation, 51–54, 140, 283–305

Relatives as source of recommendation, 140

Religious fanatics, 108

Request for proposal procedure (RFP), 141

Retainer, definition of, in fee agreement, 90

Return-of-service, 22

Rules of evidence, 18

S

Schedule for payment, 87–88
Security, acceptance of monthly payments without, 70
Self-representation, 17–19, 102–3
Service fee, 21
Serving officer, 21–22
Settlement versus litigation, 142–43
Sheriff, 21
Small-claims court, as alternative to finding and using
 lawyers, 19–25
Small firms, 97
Solo practitioner, 97
Specialists, loyalties of, 95–96
Specialization, 93–96, 118. *See also Foonberg's Glossary of*
 Legal Specialties
Spouse, legal representation by, 102
State, U.S. Department of, 158–60
State restrictions on practice, 101–2
Straight hourly fees, 77–78

T

Third party, acceptance of payment of legal fees from,
 70–71
Trade associations, as source of recommendation, 139–40
Trial, 22–24

U

United States Consulates and Embassies, accessing, 161–63
UU Net, 63–64

V

Vengeance cases, 106–7
Vercammen, Ken, 6

W

Walton, Sam, 92
Well, 23
West Publishing, 63
Work habits of lawyer, 126

Y

Yellow Pages
    finding the right lawyer by using, 29–38
    practice area listings in, 39–42

Selected Books From . . .
THE SECTION OF LAW PRACTICE MANAGEMENT

ABA Guide to International Business Negotiations. A guide to the general, legal, and cultural issues that arise during international negotiations.

ABA Guide to Legal Marketing. A collection of new and innovative marketing ideas and strategies for lawyers and firms.

ACCESS 1994. An updated guidebook to technology resources. Includes practical hints, practical tips, commonly used terms, and resource information.

Becoming Computer Literate. A guide to computer basics for lawyers and other legal professionals.

Beyond the Billable Hour. A collection of 26 articles discussing issues related to alternative billing methods.

Breaking Traditions. A guide to progressive, flexible, and sensible work alternatives for lawyers who want to balance the demand of the legal profession with other commitments. Model policy for childbirth and parenting leave is included.

Changing Jobs, 2nd Ed. A handbook designed to help lawyers make changes in their professional careers. Includes career planning advice from nearly 50 experts.

Flying Solo: A Survival Guide for the Solo Lawyer, 2nd Ed. An updated and expanded guide to the problems and issues unique to the solo practitioner.

How to Get and Keep Good Clients, 2nd Edition. Best-selling author Jay Foonberg gives time-proven tips and techniques that you can use for long-range and intermediate marketing success. It includes sample letters, homespun advice, and personal anecdotes. Published by the National Academy of Law, Ethics & Management, Inc.

How to Start and Build a Law Practice, 3rd Ed. Jay Foonberg's classic guide has been updated and expanded. Included are more than 10 new chapters on marketing, financing, automation, practicing from home, ethics and professional responsibility.

Last Frontier: Women Lawyers as Rainmakers. Explains why rainmaking is different for women than men and focuses on ways to improve these skills. Shares the experiences of four women who have successfully built their own practices.

Lawyer's Guide to the Internet. A no-nonsense guide to what the Internet is (and isn't), how it applies to the legal profession, and the different ways it can—and should—be used.

Leveraging with Legal Assistants. Reviews the changes that have led to increased use of legal assistants and the need to enlarge their role further. Learn specific ways in which a legal assistant can handle a substantial portion of traditional lawyer work.

Making Partner: A Guide for Law Firm Associates. Written by a managing partner, this book offers guidelines and recommendations designed to help you increase your chances of making partner.

Planning the Small Law Office Library. A step-by-step guide to planning, building, and managing a small law office library. Includes case studies, floor plans, and questionnaires.

Practical Systems: Tips for Organizing Your Law Office. It will help you get control of your in-box by outlining systems for managing daily work.

Results-Oriented Financial Management: A Guide to Successful Law Firm Financial Performance. How to manage "the numbers," from setting rates and computing billable hours to calculating net income and preparing the budget. Over 30 charts and statements to help you prepare reports.

Through the Client's Eyes: New Approaches to Get Clients to Hire You Again and Again. Includes an overview of client relations and sample letters, surveys, and self-assessment questions to gauge your client relations acumen.

The Time Trap. A classic book on time management published by the American Management Association. This guide focuses on "The Twenty Biggest Time Wasters" and how you can overcome them.

Win-Win Billing Strategies. Represents the first comprehensive analysis of what constitutes "value," and how to bill for it. You'll learn how to initiate and implement different billing methods that make sense for you and your client.

TQM in Action: One Firm's Journey Toward Quality and Excellence. A guide to implementing the principles of Total Quality Management in your law firm.

Winning with Computers, Part 1. Addresses virtually every aspect of the use of computers in litigation. You'll get an overview of products available and tips on how to put them to good use. For the beginning and advanced computer user.

Winning with Computers, Part 2. Expands on the ways you can use computers to manage the routine and not-so-routine aspects of your trial practice. Learn how to apply general purpose software and even how to have fun with your computer.

Women Rainmakers' 101+ Best Marketing Tips. A collection of over 130 marketing tips suggested by women rainmakers throughout the country. Includes tips on image, networking, public relations, and advertising.

WordPerfect® in One Hour for Lawyers. This is a crash course in the most popular word processing software package used by lawyers. In four easy lessons, you'll learn the basic steps for getting a simple job done.

WordPerfect® Shortcuts for Lawyers: Learning Merge and Macros in One Hour. A fast-track guide to two of WordPerfect's more advanced functions: merge and macros. Includes 4 lessons designed to take 15 minutes each.

Order Form

Qty	Title	LPM Price	Regular Price	Total
____	ABA Guide to Int'l Business Negotiations (511-0331)	$ 74.95	$ 84.95	$_____
____	ABA Guide to Legal Marketing (511-0341)	69.95	79.95	$_____
____	ACCESS 1994 (511-0327)	29.95	34.95	$_____
____	Becoming Computer Literate (511-0342)	32.95	39.95	$_____
____	Beyond the Billable Hour (511-0260)	69.95	79.95	$_____
____	Breaking Traditions (511-0320)	64.95	74.95	$_____
____	Changing Jobs, 2nd Ed. (511-0334)	49.95	59.95	$_____
____	Flying Solo, 2nd Ed. (511-0328)	59.95	69.95	$_____
____	How to Get and Keep Good Clients, 2nd Ed. (511-0347)	99.00	99.00	$_____
____	How to Start & Build a Law Practice, 3rd Ed. (511-0293)	32.95	39.95	$_____
____	Last Frontier (511-0314)	9.95	14.95	$_____
____	Lawyer's Guide to the Internet (511-0343)	24.95	29.95	$_____
____	Leveraging with Legal Assistants (511-0322)	59.95	69.95	$_____
____	Making Partner (511-0303)	14.95	19.95	$_____
____	Planning the Small Law Office Library (511-0325)	29.95	39.95	$_____
____	Practical Systems (511-0296)	24.95	34.95	$_____
____	Results-Oriented Financial Management (511-0319)	44.95	54.95	$_____
____	Through the Client's Eyes (511-0337)	69.95	79.95	$_____
____	The Time Trap (511-0330)	14.95	14.95	$_____
____	TQM in Action (511-0323)	59.95	69.95	$_____
____	Win-Win Billing Strategies (511-0304)	89.95	99.95	$_____
____	Winning with Computers, Part 1 (511-0294)	89.95	99.95	$_____
____	Winning with Computers, Part 2 (511-0315)	59.95	69.95	$_____
____	Winning with Computers, Parts 1 & 2 (511-0316)	124.90	144.90	$_____
____	Women Rainmakers' 101+ Best Marketing Tips (511-0336)	14.95	19.95	$_____
____	WordPerfect® in One Hour for Lawyers (511-0308)	9.95	14.95	$_____
____	WordPerfect® Shortcuts for Lawyers (511-0329)	14.95	19.95	$_____

*HANDLING	**TAX		
$ 2.00-$9.99 . . . $2.00	DC residents add 5.75%	SUBTOTAL:	$_____
10.00-24.99 . . . $3.95	IL residents add 8.75%	*HANDLING:	$_____
25.00-49.99 . . . $4.95	MD residents add 5%	**TAX:	$_____
50.00 +. $5.95		TOTAL:	$_____

PAYMENT

___Check enclosed (Payable to the ABA)   ___Bill Me

___Visa   ___ MasterCard   Account Number:_____-_____-_____-_____

Exp. Date: _____   Signature_____

Name_____

Firm_____

Address_____

City_____ State_____ ZIP_____

Phone number_____

Mail to: ABA, Publication Orders, P.O. Box 10892, Chicago, IL 60610-0892

PHONE: (312) 988-5522 **Or FAX:** (312) 988-5568

 **THE SECTION OF LAW PRACTICE MANAGEMENT**

CUSTOMER COMMENT FORM

Title of Book: _____

We've tried to make this publication as useful, accurate, and readable as possible. Please take 5 minutes to tell us if we succeeded. Your comments and suggestions will help us improve our publications. Thank you!

1. How did you acquire this publication:

☐ by mail order   ☐ at a meeting/convention   ☐ as a gift

☐ by phone order   ☐ at a bookstore   ☐ don't know

☐ other: (describe) _____

Please rate this publication as follows:

	Excellent	Good	Fair	Poor	Not Applicable
Readability: Was the book easy to read and understand?	☐	☐	☐	☐	☐
Examples/Cases: Were they helpful, practical? Were there enough?	☐	☐	☐	☐	☐
Content: Did the book meet your expectations? Did it cover the subject adequately?	☐	☐	☐	☐	☐
Organization and clarity: Was the sequence of text logical? Was it easy to find what you wanted to know?	☐	☐	☐	☐	☐
Illustrations/forms/checklists: Were they clear and useful? Were there enough?	☐	☐	☐	☐	☐
Physical attractiveness: What did you think of the appearance of the publication (typesetting, printing, etc.)?	☐	☐	☐	☐	☐

Would you recommend this book to another attorney/administrator? ☐ Yes ☐ No

How could this publication be improved? What else would you like to see in it?

_____

_____

_____

Do you have other comments or suggestions? _____

_____

_____

Name _____

Firm/Company _____

Address _____

City/State/Zip _____

Phone _____

Firm Size: _____ Area of specialization: _____

We appreciate your time and help.

Fold

BUSINESS REPLY MAIL
FIRST CLASS   PERMIT NO. 16471   CHICAGO, ILLINOIS

POSTAGE WILL BE PAID BY ADDRESSEE

AMERICAN BAR ASSOCIATION
PPM, 8th FLOOR
750 N. LAKE SHORE DRIVE
CHICAGO, ILLINOIS 60611–9851

Fold

Brand New

The *American Bar Association Family Legal Guide* explains comprehensively in easy to read language how the legal system works and how the law affects individuals at home, at work and at play. It helps consumers steer clear of legal pitfalls and helps readers understand their rights and responsibilities under the law. A straightforward question and answer format combines with numerous sidebars, charts, graphs and maps to deliver detailed information simply. This authoritative volume offers practical information on a wide variety of contracts, on buying or selling a home or auto, renting an apartment or merely using a credit card. It covers the legal facts on marriage, separation and divorce and unmarried couples who live together. It answers the most frequently asked questions about legal topics such as personal injury lawsuits, wills and estates, bankruptcy and the law of the workplace. It even explains when and how to find the right lawyer. The *Guide* lays a foundation of legal knowledge for individuals, families or organizations. 752 pp. $35.00. Order from Publication Orders, American Bar Association, PO Box 10892, Chicago, IL 60610-0892, or call (312) 988-5522. Please specify PC#235-0024 and add $4.95 for handling.